LOVE OR NOTHING

Tom Prideaux

Love or Nothing

THE LIFE AND TIMES OF ELLEN TERRY

Charles Scribner's Sons

New York

Library of Congress Cataloging in Publication Data

Prideaux, Tom.
     Love or nothing.

     Includes index.
     1. Terry, Ellen, Dame, 1848–1928.   I. Title.
PN2598.T4P7   792'.028'0924   [B]   75-19175
ISBN 0-684-14380-1

The author acknowledges with thanks permission to quote as follows:

From *The Diaries of Lewis Carroll,* reprinted with permission of the Estate of
Lewis Carroll, Cassell & Co., Ltd., and Oxford University, Inc.

From *Ellen Terry & Bernard Shaw: A Correspondence,* copyright 1931 by Bernard Shaw and Elbridge L. Adams. Illustrated edition published by
Theatre Arts Books, 1949. Reprinted with the permission of the publisher,
Theatre Arts Books, New York, and The Society of Authors, London, on
behalf of the Bernard Shaw estate.

From *Ellen Terry's Memoirs,* courtesy Walter L. D'Arcy Hart, Bischoff & Co.,
London.

1 3 5 7 9 11 13 15 17 19   V/C   20 18 16 14 12 10 8 6 4 2

To my mother and father
with increasing love
and amazement

Contents

LIST OF ILLUSTRATIONS

ix

LIST OF ILLUSTRATIONS

ACKNOWLEDGMENTS

The author wishes to thank the following sources for illustrations used in this book.

Endpapers and 21, courtesy the Mansell Collection; 1, photograph by Julia Margaret Cameron, courtesy the Gernsheim Collection, Humanities Research Center, the University of Texas at Austin; 2, 25, 37, courtesy Edward Craig; 3, 33, courtesy John R. Freeman & Co., Ltd.; 4, courtesy Kerrison Preston Esq., photograph by John Donat; 5, photograph by Julia Margaret Cameron, courtesy the John Hillelson Collection; 6, 12, 13, 16, 17, 26, 30, 32, 34, 35, 36, courtesy the Raymond Mander and Joe Mitchenson Theatre Collection; 7, courtesy the *London Times;* 8, drawing by F. L. Griggs, from *The Laurel and the Thorn* by Ronald Chapman, Faber and Faber, 1945, courtesy David Higham Associates; 9, 10, photographs by Lewis Carroll, courtesy the Gernsheim Collection, Humanities Research Center, the University of Texas at Austin; 11, photograph by Lewis Carroll, courtesy the Lunn Gallery, Washington, D.C.; 14, 20, 29, from *Gordon Craig* by Edward A. Craig. Copyright © 1968 by Edward A. Craig. Reprinted by permission of Alfred A. Knopf, Inc., and the Kurt Hellmer Agency; 15, from *The Story of My Life* by Ellen Terry, courtesy Hutchinson Publishing Group, Ltd.; 18, courtesy the Macmillan Company; 19, copyright the Savage Club, London. Reproduced by permission; 22, 23, 24, 27, 31, courtesy the Meserve Collection; 28, courtesy the Tate Gallery, London.

"I am convinced that with you a
human relation is love or nothing"

—*George Bernard Shaw to Ellen Terry, 1897*

CURTAIN-RAISER

"Whatever prompted you to write a book about Ellen Terry?"

I heard the question a dozen times, and it always sounded less like a question than an accusation. My stock reply was, "Read the book and find out," until I began to realize that a crusty answer would not win me many future readers. The question, as I came to think of it, wasn't really so unreasonable. Most of my interrogators knew that for some thirty years I had been reviewing the Broadway theater for a national magazine, keeping ahead of the times, pursuing the *avant garde*. So why was I retreating now to the Victorian theater, prying into the life and times of an English actress who died in 1928 and today is unknown to most Americans under forty?

Ellen Terry herself, for me, was the primary lure. There was no escaping that she was an exceptional creature; the vote was unanimous. Her star witness, George Bernard Shaw, testified, ". . . every famous man of the nineteenth century—provided he were a playgoer—has been in love with Ellen Terry," and many of them, he added, "found in her friendship the utmost consolation one can hope for from a wise, witty and beautiful woman." Alfred Tennyson, Lewis Carroll, Oscar Wilde, Matthew Arnold, John Singer Sargent, Edward Burne-Jones, Oliver Wendell Holmes, William Gladstone, and Winston Churchill paid homage. To Henry James she had "charm—remarkable charm," but he disliked her style of acting—she was too schoolgirlish and lovey-dovey on the stage. Still he chose to send her one of his plays in hopes (unfulfilled) that she would act in it.

1

From her early girlhood, Ellen indicated that she was going to be more than another pretty maiden. There were hints of something archetypal, allegorical—heaven knows what. When England's great champion of art and social reform, John Ruskin, first saw her as an ill-fated child bride, he called her "the absolute ideal of an English girl." When H. G. Wells, some years later, met her at a country inn on the Thames, where she was studying a role and being visited by England's foremost actor, Henry Irving, he compared her in her fluttering muslin to "one of the ladies in Botticelli's *Primavera*." Wells reported that he instantly forgot his engagement to a Miss King and was soon "permitted to punt the goddess about, show her where the white lilies were to be found, and get her a great bunch of wet forget-me-nots." This was the kind of thing that Ellen Terry did to bright young men: start them babbling about lilies and goddesses.

Ellen was equally appreciated by women. Her two most celebrated rivals on the stage, Sarah Bernhardt and Eleanora Duse, adored her as if she were an old school chum; Isadora Duncan, after a crushing tragedy, found comfort and consolation in Ellen's mothering arms. Queen Alexandra, the gracious wife of Edward VII, sent her birthday telegrams, which nobody else knew about until after Ellen's death, when her daughter found them tied up in a packet. And three of England's most distinguished women writers, Virginia Woolf, Edith Sitwell, and Vita Sackville-West, wrote loving and poetic tributes in her memory.

A phenomenon in her own times, Ellen was also a portent of the future when movie stars and other popular entertainers would attract an immense following among all classes. Long before Ellen Terry was born, stage stars were favored persons, but their position was cramped by the stigma attached to their calling. Shunned by decent society, theater folk could only be accepted in playhouses or after hours. In Ellen's time, at last, the actor's status was rising, a process wherein she figured both as contributor and beneficiary. Well-bred girls tried to wangle an introduction to Ellen and crowded around her backstage, praying she could help them become actresses. Ellen was welcomed socially in almost any lofty circles, though she once confided to Shaw: "It's odd, but so many what are called 'Society people' are very fond of me. I don't particularly hanker after them. . . ." Then she added, fair-mindedly, ". . . but I don't know them well, perhaps that's the reason why."

A century ago, in her expanding stardom, Ellen had a foretaste of the same problems that confront the superstars of today. Along with trying to safeguard her privacy, she was intensely concerned with raising her children, a problem aggravated in her case because they were illegitimate and their father had virtually abandoned them. Inevitably, her gifted son and daughter were growing up in a confusingly equivocal position, dazzled by their mother's fame, given special privileges because of it, yet feeling handicapped by their very advantages. Today it is not uncommon for the children of Hollywood celebrities to be given psychiatric guidance through these choppy waters, but Ellen had little to steer by, save her own love for them and the advice of her friends. In one way or another, Ellen was a century-spanner, with one foot in the future and the other in the past.

Behind her, Ellen Terry trailed a fabulous swatch of theatrical history. Born into a family of roving players, she made her stage debut with a leading London troupe that epitomized the old-fashioned, elegant Victorian theater. Then she acted in a string of important playhouses, made two astonishing unions with older men before she was twenty-two, and came to full flower professionally at the Lyceum Theatre with her great partner, Henry Irving, where they reigned for twenty-four years as the most distinguished acting pair of the English-speaking stage.

On a recent visit to London, I looked forward to a sentimental pilgrimage to the old Lyceum. I knew a fair

3

amount about its tumultuous history and was warned that it had fallen on inglorious days. But as I passed the Savoy Hotel and turned off the Strand into Wellington Street I was stirred to see, through the scrim of summer twilight, its stately pillared facade exactly as it appeared in old prints: six Corinthian columns, supporting a now rather battered pediment. Here in the Irving-Terry heyday nearly all of Britain's royalty, statesmen, artists, and great men of letters had clattered up in their coaches and cabs. "It was not then so much a theater," wrote one critic of the day, "as a temple to be entered with bated breath. There was a sacerdotal air about the entire building. The entrance hall was covered with somber hangings. The lighting was dim. Small boys like acolytes distributed the programs." And the box-office man, the report went on, officiated like "a high priest."

Walking closer, I saw how the temple had been defiled. A pink neon sign advertised it as the MECCA BALLROOM, and a clutter of little billboards listed a variety of good times: dancing, sing-alongs, dining, variety acts, and door prizes. The Monday special, for example, was "a box of chocolate for each girl when she leaves." A week later the Monday handout was "an after-shave sample for every boy," and finally, to top the Monday series, "a holiday for two in Majorca." I couldn't have been more shaken at seeing the Parthenon converted into a bingo parlor.

The only vestige of the Lyceum's noble past was a picture of Irving and Terry in the small lobby and a reprint of an old playbill. After paying eight shillings admission, I climbed to the dress circle and looked down on the main floor. The whole area, including the famous stage, had been leveled off, although the proscenium arch and the side boxes remained more or less as they used to be. A master of ceremonies, standing roughly where Ellen Terry as Lady Macbeth once cried, *"Out, damned spot,"* led the audience in singing *Bye, Bye Blackbird.* Most of the singers were seated at long tables fanning out like spokes of a wheel from the small podium. Far back in a corner a drummer and lady pianist banged out all the music for the evening and did a heroic job. The middle-aged customers had come largely, I learned, in tourist parties from other parts of England, and they were getting "a fabulous evening of fun" at bargain rates. At the entrance they had been given souvenirs, cardboard "straw" hats for the men, paper bonnets for their wives. A few daring men and women were wearing the hats of the opposite sex. After the sing-along, the M.C. cajoled the customers into a mammoth snake dance all over the theater. At one time he ordered everybody to stand still and hug the waist of the person in front. For a moment it seemed the sing-along might become a love-along.

The Lyceum evening swept to a climax with a tenor singing *Celeste Aida* and a young blond juggler, the Great Maxelli, doing tricks with goblets, twirling plates, and three flaming torches. He ended his act, torches in hand, by running into the audience and sitting on a woman's lap. While the flames reflected and danced in her gold-rimmed spectacles, her smile was trapped between pleasure and fright. Holding his torches higher, he was Prometheus just down from the sky with his blazing fennel-stalks crying, "Look, Ma, fire!" He kissed her on the cheek and disappeared, dancing on a big rolling ball.

By now I was convinced that the temple was not really being defiled. If Ellen's spirit were paying a visit now to her old home, she would have been a cordial ghost. She liked good times in a theater. I suspect, though, she would have begged off the snake dance and sing-along.

The next afternoon I called on the Lyceum's general manager, Mr. A. A. Hutchins, in his upstairs office, located in the same corner as the old dressing rooms of Terry and Irving. With tufts of sandy hair on his head and chin, he looked young but fatherly and spoke with a tranquilizing confidence designed to soothe and control high-strung en-

tertainers. On his wall was a lithograph of the Lyceum por-
tico in the 1870s with posh people in top hats and evening
wraps leaping from carriages, close by an earlier portrait
of a rhinoceros which had been a Lyceum star in 1790. A
printed blurb beneath the rhino made attendance seem a
moral duty. "The singularities of this prodigy have attracted the observant, the wise and the great, from time
immemorial . . . a sight of this formidable beast which
forms so conspicuous a link in Creation's chain, will please
any rational beholder. Admission: One Shilling."

Mr. Hutchins took me on a Lyceum tour that led up
beyond the dress circle to the top balcony, which today's
public never sees. Stripped of seats and carpets, all that remains is a concrete amphitheater, the basic bones of a
playhouse, bare as the ancient Greek theater in Epidaurus.
"I like to come up here and look down," said Mr. Hutchins. I liked it too. I knew I was getting hooked on the
Lyceum, and I knew I was going to spend too much time
around the old hulk, thinking about its past.

Two factors had shaped the history of London theater,
and especially the Lyceum. The first resulted from the com-
monly held notion that all theaters were hotbeds of sin,
with harlots soliciting through the aisles and corridors and
all manner of vice practiced on the premises. To dispel this
not wholly unjustified reputation, theater managers tried to
attract more genteel patrons by advertising their places of
amusement as "Museums" or veritable academies of learning. Built in 1772, the first version of the Lyceum was
called a Room for Exhibitions, Concerts, and Entertainments. Along with the rhinoceros, it presented an Irish
giant, a mechanical model of the solar system, wire-
walkers, jugglers, boxers, a hot-air balloon (inflated in-
doors), and a public debate on "whether the fashionable
infidelities of married couples are more owing to the de-
pravity of the Gentlemen or the Inconstancy of the Ladies."

The drift toward gentility had many benefits. Better-
lighted and sweeter smelling, the theaters acquired car-

peted floors, upholstered and reserved seats, and were safe for women and children. During Ellen Terry's childhood, the fashion for historical accuracy in stage decoration became a very big thing: audiences were urged to believe that the theater added to their education. A visit to *Julius Caesar*, with its authentic trimmings, was said to be as improving as a trip to Rome.

The second factor that influenced theater history was the idiotic monopoly of "patent" theaters. With the restoration of public drama after the Puritan suppression, Charles II in the 1660s granted licenses or patents to only two London playhouses, Covent Garden and Drury Lane. These houses had exclusive rights to offer straight dramas *without music*. This royal edict was intended to promote serious, high drama, by limiting the competition in the field. But it had the opposite effect.

For nearly two centuries, the rival nonpatented theaters had music thrust upon them by law, and as a result they produced a flood of musical burlesques, burlettas, and the fantastic holiday pantomimes, all relentlessly tuneful. The silly law specified that at least five songs be sprinkled throughout these entertainments, somewhere, anywhere, so that tunes were tossed into plays where they made no sense at all. Some producers, determined to put on a play without music in a nonpatented house, managed to evade the law by having a few gratuitous chords struck offstage and calling them songs.

But there was a curious and, I think, little-recognized advantage to all this musical madness. It helped produce a robust school of melodrama, sprinkled with music and sensational stage effects. Rubbish, yes. But irresistible to mass audiences. One thing they could count on: the theater was not going to be dull. What happened on the stage might be dreadful (and usually was), but there were horns and fiddles, songs and dances, to brighten it up. By 1843 the patent laws were abolished and there were no more injunctions about compulsory music, but by then a good slice of the

London public had acquired a taste for popular theater in reasonably respectable surroundings. Critics could, with justice, lament the lack of dramatic literature, yet the playhouses did business, triumphant in their trash. The achievement of the Victorian theater was not the development of drama, but the development of large, eager audiences that thought of the theater as a place for fun. To this day they are helping to make London the world's liveliest capital of entertainment.

The Lyceum has survived almost every imaginable calamity. It has burned down twice (1809, 1830) and has been periodically gutted and rebuilt. Just as Mr. Hutchins handed out free chocolate and shaving lotion to his customers, so the desperate manager in 1835 offered free ices. As a further enticement, Signor Namo, the Gnome Fly, was hired to clamber up the wall and across the ceiling.

The Terry family got its first foothold in the Lyceum in the 1860s when Ellen's famous sister Kate played there for two seasons as leading lady to the great lover Charles Albert Fechter. Also at the Lyceum, Sarah Bernhardt coughed herself to death in *Camille*, and Fyodor Chaliapin sang himself to death in *Boris Godounov*. The theater was rebuilt as a cathedral for *The Miracle* and invaded by revues and operettas, including the all-Negro American hit, *Lew Leslie's Blackbirds of 1936*, and Noël Coward's *Bitter Sweet*. In 1939 the London City Council doomed the Lyceum to demolition to make room for a block of shops and flats. Expecting to be the Lyceum's last tenant, Sir John Gielgud moved in as Hamlet, which was still another form of Terry tenancy since Gielgud's grandmother was Kate Terry and Ellen was his great-aunt. But the outbreak of World War II postponed the Lyceum's demolition, and at the war's end a snag in the real estate plans saved it again. Although all the movable contents of the theater had been sold at auction, several impresarios tried to rent and restore the great landmark as a temple of drama. The council saw fit to lease it to the highest bidder, the Mecca Ballroom Association.

Mr. Hutchins told me that his Lyceum in the last few years has housed many rock-music groups, either for public concerts, rehearsals, or recording sessions. Thus the old Lyceum, already known for its dizzy diversity of entertainment, broke the sound barrier into a new era by adding to its attractions The Beatles; The Rolling Stones; Donovan; Sly and the Family Stone; Elton John; Emerson, Lake, and Palmer; Led Zeppelin; and The Grateful Dead. In its divers incarnations, the Lyceum has surely catered to a wider variety of human tastes and needs than any tabernacle in the world.

In my last visit to London, the Lyceum was offering *Quadrophenia*, the latest rock opera by the noted rock group The Who. Over three thousand young people were lined up around the outside of the theater, some of them for thirty-six hours, hoping they would somehow be lucky enough to buy a ticket. The sight of such a queue reminded me of the queues that were said to surround the Lyceum to see Terry and Irving, some of them all-night affairs. Ellen used to stop and chat with the people, just as I'm sure she would do today. She would have found them, as I did, oddly docile and well-behaved (the cop told me he had never seen a more orderly group), and she would have joined us all sprawling on the floor of the auditorium to hear the opera. I doubt if she would have cottoned to the electrically magnified music and gloomy libretto, but I am sure she would have felt sympathetic with most of the young audience.

If one may still use the word "hippie," Ellen was a hippie sympathizer ahead of her time. In her fashion, she was a school dropout, having never gone to school at all. She had the earmarks of a "flower child" and might easily have worn a patch saying "Make love, not war." In her casual home apparel, she anticipated a sort of hippie simplicity, going in for uncorseted, vaguely Greek garments and Japanesey kimonos. She lived a century too soon for the faded-blue-denim boom, but one of her biographers,

Marguerite Steen, tells us that Ellen "liked horrid butcher blue linen, crudely stitched for cushion covers and table mats."

But Ellen stood apart from much of today's youth on two counts. She did not scorn elegance; on occasion she loved to doll up magnificently. And she possessed a consuming zeal for hard work.

Ellen was also in tune with today's Women's Lib tenets, although she was too busy earning her independence to theorize much about it. Through a painful early marriage, and later "living in sin," she gained a sexual freedom that for women was practically unheard of in mid-Victorian times, and in her last years she achieved a social acceptance that amounted to idolatry. She was too generous to be really rich. But if we add to her salary, which at times was three hundred pounds a week, the many windfalls from extra benefit performances, she was one of the highest-paid women in Britain.

"My line is comedy," she once wrote, and her critics concurred. Her natural habitat seemed to be the last act of every Shakespearean comedy where lovers' quarrels are patched up and perfidy is pardoned. For Victorian England, with its unstable mixture of gloom and optimism, Ellen was a tonic. Bringing with her a breath of earlier, bonnier times, she was an antidote for what Matthew Arnold, in 1853, called ". . . the strange disease of modern life, with its sick hurry, its divided aims."

Ellen was never at home in the new drawing-room comedies being adapted from the French or written in English by Arthur Wing Pinero. "I can't play a modern woman in society," she confessed. Shakespeare's heroines suited her best because they made use of her strengths. Commenting on her performance in a new comedy by J. M. Barrie, Max Beerbohm wrote, "The play is not big enough for her . . . one longs for Shakespeare, who alone among dramatists can stand up to her . . . and one wishes that the theater itself were bigger—better proportioned for the wildly ample sweep of her method."

On the Shakespearean stage, Ellen found elbow room. ". . . When the curtain rises, I go in and out of Athens, Venice or Messina, or along the old London ways of Wolsey's time—here, on this glowing stage, I meet the great people of the Earth: today King Leontes and his lovely queen—tomorrow the wicked King John. . . ." In Shakespeare she moved through grand halls, magic forests, streets, caves, warrior camps, heaths, and courtrooms. When she could be Beatrice in Leonato's ducal gardens, how could she be content as the second Mrs. Tanqueray cooped up in a London drawing room?

In the drama of her own life, Ellen Terry played three principal roles that merged and overlapped. First and always, she was the trouper, a pure product of the zestful, varied Victorian theater, who by sixteen had acted more than fifty roles in England's finest playhouses. Secondly, she was the domesticated Ellen, at times a demon mother, and an incurable collector of cottages, where she liked to hide out with her children and friends. The third Ellen is the hardest to find a name for, because it must describe her essential virtue, her high-spirited goodness, her independence. She exemplified, in her own style, what Ralph Waldo Emerson had to say about self-reliance, "Whoso would be a man, must be a nonconformist." At the darkest period of her youth, when she felt that society had kicked her aside for her "sins," she put into practice what Emerson put into words: "I do not wish to expiate, but to live." The third Terry might be called the "Emersonian Ellen."

Ellen's virtues were best revealed in the casual words and incidents of her daily life. When her son, later known as Gordon Craig, was planning to spend a week at the seaside resort of Ramsgate, she wrote to him, "Use your time there with the fishermen. Give some intelligent looking one a shilling and talk to him each morning. You'll learn a lot from him if *you* are intelligent and turn him out properly—of course, upon the subject of himself, his calling and his home. I do envy you down there."

The boy was seventeen. The letter was part of a barrage of advice that Ellen fired at her son while he was away at boarding school, much of it standard maternal clucking about his manners, his socks, his studies, along with promises to send him hampers of cakes, jams, and sardines, and money to buy banjo strings. But the letter about Ramsgate spoke peculiarly for Ellen herself. She knew that her son, deserted by his father and reared in a household of doting women, had a lot to learn from a rugged, sensible fisherman, and she put the boy on his mettle by suggesting shrewdly that it was the measure of his own intelligence to tap the man's store of wisdom.

Another side of Ellen emerges in a remark she made to close friends who had rented her their vacation cottage near London. When they advised her that the country neighbors might be shocked at seeing the greatest lady of the British theater dancing barefoot on her lawn, swirling her nightgown through the early-morning dew, Ellen told her friends not to worry. At that hour, the genteel neighbors were still asleep; only the farm laborers might see her. "And I don't mind amusing *them*. It's so good for the poor dears." She never thought that her rustic audience was in any way unworthy of her performance.

If it might appear that Ellen Terry had too many virtues to avoid monotony, it should be remembered that the path of virtue is a collision course.

Chapter One

LOVE IN PORTSMOUTH—AND OTHER PLACES

Ellen Terry's mother and father were both born in Portsmouth, England, where the challenge to pack up, set sail, and get out of town was carried on every breeze off the Channel. Neither parent had any forebears in the theater, though Portsmouth itself was a perpetual theater of sorts, with its backdrop of shifting sails, masts, and pennants, a huge cast of sailors and naval officers rolling in and out of port, and always a rum-dum ballad from the grog shops, extolling the joys of the bounding main and the bounding mattress. Ellen's mother was Sarah Ballard, and her intention of marrying Ellen's father in 1838 was sternly opposed by her family.

The Ballards were dedicated God-fearers. Mr. Peter Ballard, a lay preacher in the Wesleyan congregation, was also a builder and Master Sawyer in the boatyards. Peter's wife, Sarah, was a Copley and Scottish and very proud of being both. One of her ancestors was John Singleton Copley, the outstanding American portrait painter of his day, whose father had settled in Boston, where John was born in 1738 and first became renowned. Having moved to England, the painter was elected to the Royal Academy. With the Wesleyan God and the Royal Academy tied up in their combined families, the parents of young Sarah Ballard looked down on their daughter's choice of Ben Terry as husband.

Ben, after his father died, helped his mother run a perfectly respectable Portsmouth tavern called the Fortune of

War. The widow Terry was a Wesleyan, too. But a female publican could not hope to be as respectable as a male preacher. The Terrys never seemed quite securely moored. One of Ben's uncles, sentenced to five years at sea for smuggling, was drowned when he fell or was pushed off a ship's mast; and one of his aunts toppled off a chair while she was hanging a picture and died later from her fall. Ben himself used to put a chair on top of a table where he perched and played his guitar for sailors dancing with their girls in his mother's establishment. But Ben fared better. He never fell off, and for the rest of his life he kept his balance better than anybody, except Sarah, thought he would.

Beyond question Ben had a theatrical temperament, along with an Irish grin, blue eyes, and tawny hair. He was tall, handsome, and welcoming, a host as well as an entertainer. Ben was introduced to the backstage world by his older brother, George, who played the fiddle in the High Street Theatre orchestra. This little playhouse endured the precarious fortunes of most provincial theaters in the 1830s. It was either locked up for some scandalous high jinks on its premises or because it lacked enough candles or fuel to keep the place cozy; or its luck changed and it achieved favor with a show put on by the officers of the Queen's Navy or with a slapped-together stage version of *The Pickwick Papers,* based on the new novel by Portsmouth's hometown boy Charles Dickens. Ben Terry joined the orchestra as a drummer. And the more he hung around the theater, the less Papa Ballard wanted the jolly rascal to marry his daughter.

Whatever doubts Sarah had about marrying Ben—and why shouldn't she have some?—she could take heart from the example of a theatrical family, the Shalders, who came to roost at the High Street Theatre. Husband, wife, daughter, and a small son, they toiled as a team, fixing costumes and scenery, scrubbing floors, selling tickets, copying scripts, and then, as a crowning reward, acting in the plays. Day and night, as tightly bound as an aboriginal hunting tribe, they shared one another's hunger and hope, watched the weather, and prayed for audiences. This tribal solidarity was common in the show world, especially among circus and vaudeville players, demonstrating that the family that plays together stays together. The nineteenth-century English theater could virtually be called a family affair.

Since Ben Terry attached himself to the Shalders, to help and to learn the ropes of theatrical production, it was inevitable that Sarah observed the Shalder menage and, despite her own family's dismay, realized that a trouper's life with Ben might be feasible. It meant defying her religious beliefs, it meant being ostracized by many of the people she had known and giving up the simple, solid comforts of her class. But if she followed Ben into his raggle-taggle playlands, the chances were that she would always be close to him, night and morning. Ben would need her—to fetch and haul, cook and sew, redden her lips and slip on a gaudy costume to dress the stage. While her own father spent most of his waking hours apart from his wife, working at the boatyard with hammer and saw, Ben would need to keep Sarah within shouting distance and, in a pinch, put *her* to work with hammer and saw.

But what finally brought Sarah to terms with the theater was her awareness of its importance to Ben. She knew from their shared childhood how Ben used to run off to the High Street playhouse to guffaw at the comics and wink at the flouncy girls. But she also knew how impressed he was by the occasional glimpses of style, by the snatches of Shakespearean poetry and the moments of high sentiment. All these Ben had absorbed into himself, a little in his manners, a little in his clarity of speech, and more in the dandyism of his clothes. The theater was as close as Ben Terry ever came to elegant schooling. It made him shine, made him feel more a man. Sarah made up her mind.

According to her plan, she was going to slip secretly

out of the house, meet Ben at the church, and have her beloved sister Lizzie as a witness. But no. In order to keep Lizzie on the right side of her family—after all, she had to go on living with them—Sarah instead enlisted a girl friend to be the witness. Legally the bride and groom could do what they pleased. They were both twenty-one—or almost. Ben lied, swearing he was twenty-one when he was really two weeks younger. Also, when Ben signed the marriage license and was asked to give his "Rank and Profession," he committed a terrible impertinence, simply writing "Gentleman."

Right after the wedding, Sarah and Ben joined a group of players; but there is no record of their wanderings for the next five years. They simply vanished down country roads, into provincial theaters and modest rooming houses, ranging from Southampton to Winchester to Oxford and back to Southampton, or from Hopefulness to Misery to Anxiety and back to Hopefulness. They usually traveled in jolting wagons, with their pots and pans clattering beside them, besides scepters, crowns, wigs, kingly robes, and wooden thrones. Sarah never aspired to glitter on the stage; that was Ben's department. She took small roles or joined the extras, who in the English theater were billed as Walking Ladies or Walking Gentlemen, as if what they lacked in importance they made up for in refinement.

An attractive and diligent pair, Sarah and Ben gradually built up a reputation on the provincial circuits and ventured into bigger towns. At the Liverpool Theatre Royal in 1844 they acted in a stage version of Dickens's *Martin Chuzzlewit*, Ben playing merry Mark Tapley and Sarah the shrewish Charity Pecksniff. At Glasgow she was the "Fourth Singing Witch," Hecate, in *Macbeth*, causing one to wonder how lovely Sarah could possibly be turned into a sinister hag. Sarah's beauty, caught in a little pencil sketch by Sir Martin Archer Shee some years after her barnstorming days, emphasizes her graceful symmetry.

The golden hair is parted primly in the middle above a high forehead and pulled tight to each side where it gives up severity to curl and nestle over the ears. Eyes, widely separated, gaze outward with a detached composure that is at odds with the full, sweet lips. The sketch calls to mind the portrait drawings being done by Ingres in Paris at the time, drawings of calm, unrumpled ladies for whom classic simplicity was a religion.

Once married, Sarah had changed her stage name to Miss Yerret—Terry spelled more or less backwards. But a year or so later she changed back to Mrs. Terry for the simple reason that she was patently pregnant. Within the next twenty-five years Sarah was to give birth to eleven children, three of whom died in infancy. The first was Ben, Jr., born in 1839. The next four included two who died in infancy (the dates of their births and deaths are not known) and two daughters who became noted actresses at an early age, Kate and Ellen. Kate Terry, born on April 24, 1844, struck her father right off as a potential actress. Who knows what baby smile or histrionic gurgle gave him hope, or whether it was only wishful thinking, since his own career was hardly spectacular and young Ben, Jr., showed no signs of carrying on the torch? At the age of three, Kate was on the stage dancing a hornpipe, wearing white ducks, a sailor's blouse, and cap. Her father also taught her to play the piano a bit and dressed her up in an old crone's shawl and bonnet to croak a preposterous ditty, *I'm Ninety-five.*

Ellen was born in a theatrical rooming house of uncertain address on Market Street in Coventry. Her correct birth date, February 27, 1847, was confirmed by her excellent chronicler, Roger Manvell, from the Coventry registry of births. Until then, Ellen's biographers, members of her family, and Ellen herself always assumed she was one year younger. In all other books and documents they reported her natal day as February 27, 1848. In Ellen's case, it seems unlikely that she was resorting to the actress's prerogative of falsifying her age to gain one year's grace. The confusion remains a mystery.

In Ellen's earliest years, Kate loomed imposingly. Older, bigger, a singing and dancing menace, Kate, moreover, was receiving special attention from Ellen's own dear father, stealing his love while he coached and rehearsed her at home, wherever home happened to be. Since Kate was being groomed to be a family breadwinner, she was treated with an implied respect that Ellen could not understand but sensed nontheless. Ellen's critics and admirers alike have agreed that as long as they knew her, she appeared immune to jealousy, not as if jealousy were something she had overcome, but as if, like another language, it were something she had never known. However that may be, Kate's example taught Ellen that growing up in the theater was a fact of life, simply what good little girls were supposed to do.

Sometime during her first eight years, Ellen later claimed, she had a searing experience with a mustard pot. Kate put in a counterclaim, insisting that it happened not to Ellen, but to her. Whatever the truth, it is less important than Ellen's desire to hug the story to herself. During the rehearsals of a pantomime, possibly in Glasgow, a child was needed for the Spirit of the Mustard Pot. Ellen's father offered her for the role, and the stage manager tried to stuff the child into the pot to see if she would fit. Ellen let out such a shriek at being squeezed into a dark, probably evil-smelling hole, that her father took mercy and pulled her out, yelling at the stage manager, "Damn you *and* your mustard pot!" Ellen loved the story because it presented her father as a powerful friend and defender. Taking her home, he sighed, "You'll never make an actress."

Ellen's position as second fiddle was altered in 1852 when Kate, whose fame had begun to spread, was invited to London to join the troupe of Charles Kean and his wife at the Princess's Theatre. This was a remarkable honor for an eight-year-old and could brighten the future for all the Terrys. But how was the family to be deployed? Finally it was agreed that Sarah must head for London with Kate, brother Ben, and the new baby, George; while father Ben, tied by contract to the Theatre Royal, would have to remain in Liverpool. And, wonder of wonders, Ellen would be left "to look after him." To Sarah, this seemed almost as desirable as it did to Ellen, for Ben's roving eye for pretty women might be somewhat stabilized by the need to watch over his little chaperone. In the end it was a nice question of who was looking after whom.

Before Sarah left, Ellen was taught to cook porridge for her father and do a few other household chores. Considering that she grew up to be an absentminded cook and a sketchy housekeeper, her ministrations for Ben were probably even more casual than one would expect from a child of five, and meals were often eaten picnic-style with fun and games. Ben taught all his children reading, writing, and sums, and he took pains to coach Ellen in speeches from Shakespeare as part of her day's schooling, exacting a good performance from her at mealtime. So unless she recited flawlessly Puck's farewell speech from *A Midsummer Night's Dream*, no apple. Ben always adored Ellen, but he was not overpermissive. As Ellen recalled in her *Memoirs*, "Sometimes he hastened my perceptive powers with a slipper, and always he corrected me if I pronounced any word in a slipshod fashion."

Sarah's entry into London at Euston Station, standing among her boxes and bundles with baby in arms and Kate and young Ben at her side, would have been an ideal subject for such popular genre painters as Frith or Nicol, whose works *The Railway Station* and *Waiting for the Train* caught the excitement and poignance of people on the move. An artist would have pounced on Kate in her best dress and bravest bonnet, trying to look like a grown-up actress, and he would have relished little Ben with his carefully combed hair, aware that he was now the man of the family, and Sarah, peering about her, wary and protective. As for the baby, George, the artist would have had to choose whether to paint him asleep amid the tumult at the station or to show his alarm at the shouting porters and the snorting locomotives. Already the new railroads were hastening the growth of the English theater and the migration of actors.

After the Terrys had taken a cab to their lodgings, the next major event was Kate's audition for Mr. and Mrs. Kean in their little temple of drama on Oxford Street. The Princess's was less imposing than the Lyceum, or Drury Lane, or Covent Garden, but it was an honored playhouse because it was favored by Queen Victoria. Charles Kean, owner and resident impresario, was not as fine an actor as his celebrated father, Edmund Kean; but he had other advantages. His father, raised in poverty, vowed that if fortune ever smiled upon him, he would send his son to England's great prep school, Eton. And so he did. Who can doubt that the touch of Eton helped make Charles more worthy of special patronage?

Nobody has reported what Kate performed in her audition, but it is a safe bet that she did passages from Shakespeare, a dance, and a song or two. She was rushed into rehearsals for a Christmas pantomime, *Harlequin Billy Taylor*.

Back in Liverpool, devouring Sarah's letters over the breakfast porridge, Ellen and Ben were thrilled by the accounts of Kate's first splash. According to the program Sarah sent, Kate was billed as "Miss Kate Terry" in the role of "Britannia, Tutelary Genius of Old Albion, continually ruling the waves." She made "an unexpected appearance . . . enthroned on one of her 'wooden walls,' and attended by her trusty guard of Blue Jackets." ("Wooden walls" was a metaphor for ships.) At the end, Kate descended from her throne amid bursts of colored fire and waved her fairy wand to produce the standard climax of every pantomime, the "Grand Transformation Scene." History is too mean-minded to tell us how the battleship was transformed, although there is a reference to a "Magical Metamorphosis" and "a Regal and Floral Ovation to Britannia."

Ellen and Ben could hardly take it all in: little Kate representing the whole British Empire! A trusty guard! And a Floral Ovation!

The next letters brought even grander news. On February 6, 1852, Kate journeyed with the Princess's company to Windsor Castle to play before the queen. In Shakespeare's *King John* she had the juicy role of the wicked king's little nephew, who is threatened with torture. And although she was never invited to meet Her Majesty, she could always say she had been a guest at the castle. The next year, in fact, Kate made two more calls at the castle to play juvenile roles in *King Henry IV* and *King Henry V*.

The custom of performing at the castle began when, for Christmas, 1848, Prince Albert arranged for the first Royal Command performance at Windsor: Charles Kean and his troupe in *The Merchant of Venice*. This was a significant boost for show business. To quench Queen Victoria's growing interest in the theater her enterprising consort provided many more such treats. In the next thirteen years, thirteen other Shakespeare plays were presented at Windsor, along with nineteen frothier works, including *The School for Scandal*, *The Rivals*, and *Box and Cox*.

Ben Terry seems to have joined his wife briefly in 1852, when he played a minor role at the Princess's, then resumed his engagements in and around Liverpool. Ellen's memory was hazy. It is possible that she spent part of this period with Sarah's sister Lizzie at Portsmouth. "I can't recall much about those two years," she wrote, "except sunsets and a great mass of shipping looming up against the sky. The sunsets followed me everywhere; the shipping was in Liverpool, where father was engaged for a considerable time." Separated—or should one say liberated?—from her mother's more conventional ideas of behavior, Ellen developed in her father's company the exuberant side of her nature and the playful imagination that led her to picture herself being chased around by sunsets.

In 1853 Ben joined the Keans in London on a long-term basis, and the whole family of six was reunited in what might be called their first home, crowded into the top floor of a house in Gower Street. This meant a steep climb for Sarah, who was pregnant with her daughter Marion, but Sarah was dauntless. Kate and Ben continued as breadwinners, yet salaries were small and expenses were increasing. As London performers in a reputable theater they had to dress well, and young Ben had to look suitably smart in school. So Sarah, along with cooking, tending children, and sewing for her own brood, took on a job as wardrobe mistress at the Princess's, which, in view of the heaps of costumes that had to be mended and refurbished for dozens of fancy productions, meant a formidable amount of extra work. Since Sarah's first youthful beauty had dimmed, she could no longer be hired as a Walking Lady. But her family desperately needed extra shillings, so Sarah knuckled down.

The Princess's troupe, under the Keans, was a progressive institution. Though at that time Britain boasted no drama schools, the Keans created something akin to an academic atmosphere. Taking young actors as well as old-timers under their wings, the Keans conducted a sort of tutorial system, training their charges for "exams," which were the periodic premieres when everyone, including the Keans themselves, was judged by the public and press. The Kean "faculty" comprised a ballet master, a director of music, and a head designer, along with crews of carpenters, gas men to handle the lighting, and a staff to keep the theater spruce. Ellen recalled that it was hard, though, to get rid of the rats that roamed the back courtyard to nibble the paint off the stacked-up scenery.

During their nine-year reign at the Princess's, the Keans averaged ten major productions a year. Almost half were Shakespeare plays, often garbled and rearranged to please the sentimental taste of the era and also to afford the set designers a chance to go hog-wild with spectacular effects. The craze for historical accuracy, mentioned earlier, was starting, but it still had a way to go. Mrs. Kean, as the noble matron Hermione in *The Winter's Tale,* prided herself on her authentic Roman draperies; but under them, as a rebuke to paganism, she wore a multitude of Christian petticoats.

Ellen's first role, won in competition against several other child actors in the Kean academy, was Prince Mamillius in *The Winter's Tale,* partly set in Sicily during the ancient Greek conquest. Ellen recalled her outfit in horrific detail: a red and silver dress that ended just above her knees, "very pink" baggy tights, and sausage curls that her mother had banked on each side of her head. The costume was hardly Greek, but the toy cart that she was obliged to drag around by a long wooden handle was absolutely authentic, having been copied by the Princess's head prop man from a painting on an ancient Greek vase in the British Museum.

The show opened on April 28, 1856, and in it Ellen Terry made her stage debut. The evening was virtually a family affair, Ben playing an officer of the Court of Judicature and Kate, a servant to an old shepherd. The Keans, of course, played the chief roles of Hermione and Leontes. The premiere was attended by Queen Victoria. So Ellen, in effect, had caught up with Kate.

Onstage early in the first act, Ellen was intensely princely with her authentic go-cart. King Leontes gazes lovingly at the little prince and muses upon his own boyhood. "How like I then was to this kernel, this squash, this gentleman." It was odd to be called "a squash," but Ellen knew the king meant it in a nice way. He addresses her directly: "Mine honest friend, will you take eggs for money?" By this he meant "Would you allow yourself to be imposed upon?" Ellen answered fiercely, "No, my Lord, I'll fight." The audience approved this show of mettle. Then the king, well pleased, urges his boy to run off: "Go play, Mamillius, thou'rt an honest man." Ellen strode off proudly, but just as she was about to leave the stage, she tripped over the long handle of the go-cart and landed in unprincely fashion flat on her back. The audience tittered. Ellen got up and ran into the wings and burst into tears. She received a token pat of sympathy from Mrs. Kean, but no more. She had another scene coming up; no time for hurt pride.

The *London Times*, reviewing the play on May 1, called Ellen "vivacious and precocious . . . a worthy relative of her sister Kate." Without further mishap, Ellen played Mamillius for 101 more performances, one of the longest runs in the Princess's history.

The tale of Ellen's spill has been gratefully seized on by her biographers, for it adds the right tone to her legend, suggesting that she was a normal little girl, capable of losing her balance like any other child and spunky enough to triumph over her downfall. But, more interesting, the episode may lie at the root of Ellen's unshakable aplomb which she exhibited on stage throughout her career. The aplomb did not save her from fits of opening-night nerves, but it kept her calm during embarrassing emergencies. Whenever she forgot a line—fairly often in her later years— Ellen would turn to another actor with a sweet, forgiving smile as though *he* had lost the line and would wait for him to rescue her. On other occasions, she would simply call to the prompter, "Line, please." Ellen carried off these upsets with such serenity that audiences never felt sorry for her, and the plays flowed on without a ripple. Having taken a pratfall before Queen Victoria and recovered, what more was there to fear?

Another legend-supporting mishap occurred when she was Puck in *A Midsummer Night's Dream*, her second role at the Princess's. At the end, Ellen rose from the basement through a trapdoor preparatory to reciting the epilogue, "If we shadows have offended, think but this and all is mended." Ellen had barely reached stage level when the stagehand below shut the trapdoor a second too soon and crushed her toe. Caught like a little animal in a trap, Ellen shrieked with agony and cried out to Kate who was on-stage acting Queen Titania. But Kate was powerless to help, except to pound on the floor with her foot, which only made the man below try even harder to shut the jammed trapdoor. Finally, Mrs. Kean ran on, shouted instructions down to the stagehand, and Ellen was released.

"Finish the play, dear," she whispered to Ellen, who was faint with pain, "and I'll double your salary."

Mustering all the courage she possessed as a nine-year-old actress, Ellen spoke out through her sobs, begging the spectators' indulgence in Shakespeare's words; "Gentles, do not reprehend: If you pardon we will mend." The mending of Ellen's toe was mercifully expedited by the presence in the audience of a Mr. Skey, president of St. Bartholomew's Hospital, who rushed backstage and, as Ellen wrote later, "put my toe right. He remained my friend for life." Mrs. Kean, for her part, kept her word, and Ellen's salary was doubled to thirty shillings a week.

With this addition to the family funds, the Terrys were able to move from their top-floor flat to a house at 92 Stanhope Street, a tidy red brick box with a modest balcony in front and French windows in the back parlor that led to a small walled garden. The new house was a factory for living. At sunup babies crowed. Tom or Fred, or whoever was too young to jump out of bed alone, howled to be fed and cleaned. Then the going-to-school shift steamed up, needing to be fueled and packed off. Then, later, came reveille for actresses who worked at night and deserved to sleep late. Whenever Ben or the girls were not running off to rehearsals, they pitched in to help Sarah. They bathed babies, went marketing, and shopped for secondhand furniture to fill the new house. Ben bought a piano, and a number of hands tackled it, especially Kate who became relentless about the *Moonlight Sonata*.

Sarah, to be sure, was foreman of the factory, supervising meals and plying her needle that was always flashing up and down like a tiny piston. Keeping her daughters stylish in the Victorian mode required a mastery of ribbons and braids. With tireless fingers, Sarah produced the trimmings of respectability: a ruffle for elegance, a fringe for refinement, a jabot for modesty, and a spangle for good luck. Ellen told of coming home late at night and finding her mother sewing by lamplight on dresses for her two oldest daughters to wear at a Christmas party given by a duke on fashionable Half Moon Street. Ellen danced with the duke in the dress her mother made.

Deprived of orthodox family life and schooling, Ellen's upbringing offers a provocative case history. How much was she handicapped? How much did she gain? According to a recent scholarly report on the alienation of modern youth, "Our children are not entrusted with any real responsibilities. Little that they do really matters. . . . If a child is to be a responsible person, he must not only be exposed to adults engaged in demanding tasks but also must himself participate in such tasks."

With these views in mind, it would seem that Ellen's rearing had much in its favor. In the theater she participated, side by side with her parents, in the tasks they performed; she was a breadwinner along with the rest of them. From the night she broke her toe and doubled her salary, Ellen became doubly useful to her family. They not only loved her, they needed her, just as they needed Kate. Every week Ellen was allowed to receive her salary in her own hands, but she gave it all to her father, who, in turn gave her back sixpence to save or squander.

Was Ellen being cheated out of childhood's freedom, her sacred right to wander lonely as a cloud and indulge her imagination? Free of responsibility she seldom was. Yet the stage itself was a cloud world where children were expected to dress up and make believe. To be sure, make-believe in the theater has its own strict set of rules; but so does most make-believe, and that does not necessarily spoil the fun. Ellen's case obviously cannot be compared to other forms of child labor in England, which were abominable. Her position, and Kate's also, was exceptional. It certainly had its liabilities, including the lack of a systematic education; yet, all considered, the upbringing of Ellen and Kate Terry was likely to make them happy and responsible people.

Mrs. Charles Kean ruled her young actors like a schoolmarm. Whenever a new role had to be cast, she held tryouts so no child would take his or her priority for granted. Once Ellen was outraged because Mrs. Kean bestowed the role of Dragonetta, a horrid fairy, on a ravenhaired little girl and cast blond Ellen as the heroine, namby-pamby Goldenstar. Later in the pantomime's run, Ellen got a chance to play nasty Dragonetta, but not before learning that she could not always have her own way.

During rehearsals, child actors as well as adults stayed in the theater for fourteen hours at a stretch, sometimes until four or five in the morning. Like exhausted soldiers in a bivouac, they curled up and napped in odd corners, backstage or in the greenroom, having bribed somebody to shake them awake when their scenes were due. But Ellen usually chose to observe rehearsals from a seat in the dress circle. She kept close watch on Mrs. Kean, who always sat at one side of the stage, looking like a plump Turkish bandit with her head turbaned in a white kerchief. When her husband was not acting, he sat in the empty stalls, holding a large dinner bell. Whenever he was displeased by anything in the rehearsal, he clanged. Then he and Mrs. Kean conferred, and she set it to rights. By following rehearsals day after day, and watching how actors responded to their coaching, Ellen absorbed an immense amount of stage learning. She claimed that by the time a play opened, she had memorized all the women's roles. As if she did not see and hear enough of Mrs. Kean in any long day's work, she once stole a dagger from the property room and cut a slit in a canvas wing so she could hide backstage and watch the great lady play Hermione.

Suddenly, for obscure reasons, storm clouds boiled up

over the Terrys, and Mrs. Kean spoke her mind in a letter to Kate, who was fourteen at the time. There were rumors that headstrong Ben Terry behaved disrespectfully to Charles Kean and perhaps had egged Kate on to complain or threaten to leave the company unless certain demands were met. Kean was regarded by some of his troupers as a pompous, humorless popinjay, so maybe Ben's dereliction, whatever it was, was not unjustified. At any rate, Ben thought best in the end to write an apology, withdrawing his "uncourteous observation." Though Mrs. Kean's letter sheds no light on the actual ruckus, it presents the sender as an articulate and forceful matriarch of the theater.

March 23, Monday, 1857

My dear Kate Terry,

I am really very sorry for you, and look with extreme regret upon the short-sighted policy and ungrateful conduct which have so broken up your fair prospects. If this had been the first circumstance of the kind that had angered Mr. Kean, I might have been able to do something for you in softening his displeasure; but repeated displays of unwarrantable discontent and vague threats of withdrawal have at length so disgusted me also that I feel little inclination to enter protestations or to use my time and knowledge for a family whose heart appears to be utterly insensible to the benefits already received.

I have taken a very true and motherly interest in you, Kate, an interest which at your tender age you can neither appreciate nor understand—but when years have passed over and your memory turns to when and why I have often severely reproved you, the worldly knowledge you have acquired will then show you how sincere a friend I have been. I wish you very well, my dear Kate, and take this last opportunity of reminding you to avoid affectations, to be true and natural, and my very last warning to you is to not allow people to turn your head with flattery.

Yours sincerely

Ellen Kean

By the time the theater closed for its annual summer recess, the troubles were patched up, and the Terrys were assured of being back at the Princess's in the autumn. For vacation, Ben took his family to the seaside village of Ryde on the Isle of Wight, only five miles from Portsmouth where Sarah and Ben had grown up and courted. The little tribe crowded into Rose Cottage, rented from Sarah's sister Lizzie, a few steps from the beach; and Ben found a small pavilion which he rigged up as a playhouse and started to rehearse an all-Terry show, light and comic for the summer trade, featuring three fun-makers, Kate, Ellen, and Ben. Ellen recollected that it was called *To Parents and Guardians;* she played a mischievous fat boy named Waddilove making her first entrance with her hands covered with jam. The annals of British theater do not mention *To Parents and Guardians,* but the little farce gave the Terry girls a useful fling at the ancient clown arts of sight gags and funny faces.

Another summer benefit was getting the younger Terrys acquainted with their family background. Sarah did not cross over to Portsmouth often; both her parents were dead, and Lizzie was married and living in the north. But Ben took the boys across, showed them off at the family tavern, Fortune of War, and introduced them to his mother who wept with joy. Both Ben and his hometown had changed notably in twenty years. Now he was a smart Londoner, attached to England's most illustrious house of high drama and, along with his two daughters, he had performed Shakespeare before the queen. Portsmouth, too, was putting on airs. Everything had nearly doubled: its population, its rail and sea traffic. Chess players in Portsmouth and London had conducted a game with each other over the new electric telegraph.

Back at the Princess's, refreshed by the sea air at Ryde, Ellen marched on in a succession of bit roles. She carried a basket of live doves in *The Merchant of Venice,* climbed a pole to watch a procession in *Richard II.* Then she played an imp in *Faust and Marguerite* and was an angel in the vision scene in *Henry VIII.* During a dress rehearsal in this

29

latter production, Ellen on her high perch got sick from the intense heat of the gas jets overhead. The stages of Victorian theaters often looked and felt like ovens, with rows of fires on all sides.

The most demanding role in her three years at the Princess's was Prince Arthur in *King John,* a part that Kate had already played. Just as younger sisters are used to getting hand-me-down clothes from their older sisters, Ellen was starting to wear Kate's old roles.

In the play, the young prince is in fearsome trouble. Because Arthur is King John's nephew and a claimant to his uncle's throne, John is trying to disable the child for ruling by having his eyes burned out.

At early rehearsals, Ellen did poorly. Perhaps she was flummoxed by the magnitude of her role, or maybe she had a swelled head from her former successes. At any rate, Mrs. Kean rose up in wrath and slapped her face. Ellen burst into tears, and while she was still weeping, Mrs. Kean commanded her to go on rehearsing Arthur. Ellen obeyed, gasping out her lines between her sobs and snuffles. "That's it, that's it!" cried Mrs. Kean. "You've got it! Now remember what you did with your voice . . . AND DO IT." Ellen was always a good mimic; now all she had to do was mimic herself. At the rehearsal's end, Mrs. Kean sent her home to bed with a hearty hug and a kiss.

At the actual premiere, Ellen was keyed up to do or die. The first act was easy; she could simply stand around and look lordly because Richard the Lion-Hearted is one of her uncles; the Duke of Austria kisses her on the cheek; and King Philip of France, played by Ellen's father, calls her a noble boy. But in the fourth act, villainy breaks loose. She is in the hands of King John's henchman, Hubert, who has been ordered to supervise her torture. The executioners discuss the hot irons. Prince Arthur is summoned into the chamber, where Hubert blinks back his own tears as he shows the lad the king's written orders.

"Must you with hot irons burn out both mine eyes?" cries the prince.

"Young boy, I must," confesses Hubert.

"And will you?"

"And I will."

The boy pleads for mercy. Hubert weakens, then steels himself again and calls back the tormentors with their hot irons and ropes to tie the boy down. The scene is skillfully and shamelessly prolonged, as Shakespeare wrings out all its pathos and horror. Ellen and John Ryder, the crusty old actor who played Hubert, kept the audience in silent agony except when some spectator let out a sob or a moan. The prince finally agrees to the ordeal, if only Hubert will dismiss the terrifying executioners and perform the hideous deed himself. But when left alone with the little lad, Hubert finally relents and promises the boy never to harm him; the audience heaves a mighty sigh, followed by a roar of approval.

In Scene 3, Ellen had still another swig of glory. High on the castle wall, the little prince steals on alone, disguised as a ship's cabin boy, trying to flee forever from black John.

"The wall is high," says the little refugee. "And yet will I leap down. Good ground, be pitiful and hurt me not."

He leaps. His little frame "lies shattered" on the rocks below.

Exactly how Ellen managed this jump is not reported. Was the stage floor padded? Were some of the rocks pillows?

A group of nobles come on, and Ellen freezes every muscle, praying that neither sneeze or hiccough will mar her heroic demise. This is her first Shakespearean death, to be followed by a lifetime of fearful endings, by drowning in *Hamlet*, suffocation in *Othello*, poisoning in *Romeo and Juliet*, hanging in *King Lear*, and madness in *Macbeth*. Right now Ellen hears the nobles gasp as they discover her corpse.

"This is the bloodiest shame, the wildest savagery . . ." speaks one.

"Heinous spectacle . . . damned and a bloody work," cries another.

Once again Ellen feels the shocked silence in the audience, broken only by a sound of weeping in the dress circle.

Her friend Hubert comes on the stage and is blamed for the prince's death. "Thou art more deep damn'd than Prince Lucifer," cry his accusers. And Ellen hears herself being called "this ruin of sweet life . . . too precious-princely for a grave. . . ." She loves being a "ruin of sweet life."

After Hubert clears himself of the prince's death, he kneels down and lifts Ellen's body in his strong arms. Ellen adored this venerable actor, "in appearance like an old tree that has been struck by lightning, or a greenless, barren rock."

One of the nobles speaks to Hubert: "How easy dost thou take all England up! From forth this morsel of dead royalty, the life, the right and the truth of all this realm is fled to heaven. . . ."

And for a sharp, sweet moment, Ellen felt that *she* was all England, she, Nelly Terry, the truth of all the realm.

After the show, Ellen walked home to Stanhope Street with her father and Kate, who was the queen of Spain in the play, but did not get a chance to die. On chilly nights after the show, Ben used to make the long walk back to Stanhope Street with a daughter on each arm, and his heavy cape buttoned around all three of them. The girls' heads were hidden inside for warmth, so that anyone who saw the trio walking along in unison might suppose it was a six-legged beast with the single head of a man. More surprising, the beast sang in several voices, for Ben and the girls shortened the trip with songs from Shakespeare and music-hall ballads. Between songs, Ben would shout out what shops they were passing, so the girls inside their cocoon could know where they were.

When they got home, Sarah was waiting up for them, and while they were getting a bite to eat, they might talk about the next rehearsal schedule—for *Macbeth*. It had been decided that Ellen would play Fleance, son of Banquo. Another death scene for Ellen? Not quite. Fleance is *supposed* to be assassinated along with his father, but he escapes.

After Kate and Ellen had gone to bed, Ben and Sarah discussed the strong possibility that the Keans would terminate their operation at the Princess's. It had been a popular success but a financial loss, owing to the high cost of production, and now the Keans were contemplating a tour of America. The Terrys were stunned and saddened. Although Ben never liked Charles Kean, he recognized that the Keans were a blessing to his family. They had enabled the Terrys to work and live together, to keep Kate and Ellen under close supervision. Normally, in the English theater, if an actor fell sick, he was instantly off the payroll. But if Kate or Ellen were indisposed, the Keans, with almost unprecedented generosity, paid them anyway. Through the Keans, the Terrys had made many influential friends; Tom Taylor and Charles Reade were both playwrights and journalists who invited the Terrys to their pleasant homes and heaped the girls with encouragement and affection. Now, with the Keans pulling up stakes, the Terrys must start to look for jobs; a new era was ahead.

Upstairs, falling asleep, Ellen was still under the timeless spell of the theater, hearing herself applauded and loved, "This ruin of sweet life . . . this morsel of . . . royalty!"

Chapter Two

MARRIAGE: THEME AND VARIATIONS

None of the Terrys were invited to the Keans' farewell banquet, nor, for that matter, were any of the Princess's performers or staff. The affair, sponsored by Charles's class-
mates at Eton, was held on July 20, 1859, in St. James's
Hall, where 550 male guests gathered to toast and cheer
good old Charles and make sentimental references to the
Eton rowing crew. The guests included many men of noble
birth and at least one noted man of letters, William Make-
peace Thackeray. No women were fed on the premises, but
nearly 400 of them, including Mrs. Kean, were seated in a
gallery where their presence caused "excitement and animation." No actor-manager had ever been granted such a
social honor. The Duke of Newcastle presided. Kean sat on
his right, and at the Duke's left sat the Chancellor of the
Exchequer, William Gladstone.

A few nights later, after a performance of *Henry VIII*,
Kean gave a farewell address to his audience. This time the
Terrys and the whole Princess's company were on hand to
hear their master. Kean reminded them all of his contribution to learning, his lavish productions (he had helped pay
for them out of his wife's inheritance), and the army of people he kept on his payroll. In *The Winter's Tale*, for example, he had presented "Dionysian orgies staged with
three hundred people at one time." Kean's recital of his
own considerable achievements could hardly fail to
impress Ellen and Kate and fill them with something of the
pride that other girls might feel upon graduating from a

respected ladies' seminary. It gave them confidence to face the future.

Now, how was Ben Terry going to keep the family together and keep the girls working? To rely on hit-and-miss jobs would be difficult—Ellen was only twelve. He decided to continue his summer-style diversions and rehearsed the girls in two farcical playlets, which he called *A Drawing-Room Entertainment,* figuring that thousands of people who still disapproved of the theater would be enticed by the genteel title. Ben heightened the propriety by billing the girls as "the original representatives of Ariel, Cordelia, Arthur, Puck, etc. (which characters were acted by them upwards of one hundred consecutive nights, and also before Her Most Gracious Majesty the Queen). . . ." The little show opened in the Royal Coliseum, a recreation center in Regent's Park that included exhibition halls, a concert room, and a fake ghostly grotto that ranked as one of the "Sights of London." In her spare time, Ellen used to retire to this musty cavern and work herself into a terror while studying the tomb scene in *Romeo and Juliet.*

Playing for thirty nights to more than thirty thousand people, *Drawing-Room* provided the Terrys with a welcome flow of cash to help keep the boys in school, equip the new house, and lighten Sarah's burdens. Loath to let a good thing go, Ben proposed to take the show on tour, leaving young Ben and the smaller children in London. Would Sarah come too to chaperone the girls and help backstage with their costume changes? After weighing the yeses and noes, she came.

The exact route of the four itinerant Terrys, who were augmented by a young piano player named Sidney Naylor, is long forgotten. Ellen says they stayed out almost two years, visiting such places, near and far, as Croydon, Belfast, and Plymouth and going back for a summer booking at Ryde. She recalled one occasion when, being either out of funds or out of vehicles, they walked from Bristol to Exeter and for once justified the term "strolling players." For

Ellen, "When they asked me what I was thinking as we drove along, I remember answering, 'Only that I should like to run wild in a wood forever!' At night we stayed in beautiful little inns . . . more cheap and comfortable than the hotels of today. In some places we were asked out to tea and dinner and very much feted."

Ben was the big boss, unpacking and setting up the props, fixing lights, selling tickets, greeting the public; Sarah looked after costumes, made sure the girls ate sensibly and napped enough to look fresh for each performance, and cast a sharp eye to see that nothing was left behind when they packed up. The plays could be set up almost anywhere: in a school room, guildhall, or a proper theater.

The opener, *Distant Relations*, showed the two girls in a parade of different roles and lightning costume changes. In the prezipper age this was a notable feat. "I was all things by turns, and nothing long!" wrote Ellen. "First I was the page boy who admitted the relations (Kate in many guises). Then I was a relation myself—Giles, a rustic." Giles performed a drum solo, which Ellen had learned from a drummer in the Princess's orchestra. In another gratuitous interlude, Kate did a serious imitation of Mrs. Kean playing Constance in *King John*.

In the main playlet, *Home for the Holidays,* Kate was a young lady named Letty awaiting the homecoming of her shy brother, played by Ellen. Remembering how he hated to be sent off to school, she plans to welcome him with kisses and sympathy. But when Harry struts in, puffing a cigar, she sees that bad companions have corrupted him. When Letty chides him, he jeers at her and she runs off. Backstage, Kate claps on a wig and dashes back as another person, Mrs. Terrorbody, a virago who boots Harry from the room. Next we overhear Harry in a street fight, with offstage sound effects of yelps and whacks created by Sarah and Ben. When Harry returns after his battle, he explains that he was fighting a bully because he struck a little girl.

Letty sees that her Harry still has a noble side, and they are happily reconciled.

If it seems shocking that such arrant hokum should beguile large audiences, it should be considered that most Englishmen are born laughter-prone. They will laugh, as Shakespeare proved, at almost any shameless clowning or punning, and in the democracy of their merriment they will roar alike at a Christmas pantomime or a duel of wits between Sheridan's dandies. When Thackeray wearied of Shakespeare, he described that raffish treasure *The Beggar's Opera* as "the pleasantest play in our language" and beamed as he shouted, "In a few more days the pantomimes! Huzzah!" Though the Terry sisters were ambitious young actresses, they did not consider it beneath their dignity to have a crack at farce and slapstick in the provincial theaters.

After their tour ended, Kate—clearly the family star so far—was invited to join the company at the St. James Theatre under Mr. and Mrs. Alfred Wigan, who were also respected alumni of the Princess's company. Since Mrs. Wigan took the leading feminine roles as her due, Kate played secondary leads. Ellen received no offers from London, so Ben listed her with a theatrical agent. As a result she was summoned by a little French actress-dancer, Madame de Rhona, who had been a success in Paris, St. Petersburg, and briefly at Drury Lane. Now Madame was hell-bent to be an actress-manager. At fourteen, Ellen felt lank and ungainly, so for her audition she borrowed Kate's pink bonnet trimmed with black lace, possibly in the hope that it made her look French. Her father went along for the interview, and just as he once rescued her from the mustard pot, so he rescued her from nervousness by assuring her that she looked lovely and that pink was her color.

Madame de Rhona hired her at once for several roles and buzzed around her at rehearsals, calling her stupid, telling her to stop hiding her big hands up under her arms because it made her look like an ugly chicken, and, finally, after molding her closer to her liking, giving her a pretty pin—Ellen's first gift of jewelry.

In *Attar Gull*, the opening gun of Madame's season, Ellen played opposite a python. Portraying the daughter of a Jamaican planter, Ellen is locked in a summerhouse and attacked by the enormous serpent. As she tries to climb out a window, the monster coils around her neck, and Ellen produced a cadenza of shrieks carefully graded to express horror, panic, and mortal agony. In four months Ellen did ten plays for Madame de Rhona.

Over at the St. James Kate had a small part in a play adapted from Victorien Sardou and also understudied Miss Herbert in the star role. As often happens in the mythology of the stage, the star fell sick, and Kate took over the next evening. Faithful to the legend, Kate was a sensation, and two of London's best critics turned up to witness and report it. A cynic might write off Tom Taylor's rave as homage from a family friend; but Clement Scott, who had no such connection, wrote, "No one knew that we had amongst us a young actress of so much beauty, talent . . . and dramatic power."

Ever the wise guide of his daughters' careers, Ben pulled Kate out of the London theaters immediately. True, her position in the Wigan company, after having outshone the star, would not be comfortable. But Ben thought further than that. Although Kate could have had other London jobs, Ben knew that she needed more basic training in a variety of roles. With this in mind, he had her accept an offer from the Bristol stock company, under the sound direction of James H. Chute.

Once again the family separated, Kate and her father moving to Bristol while Sarah stayed with Ellen until she finished with Madame de Rhona. In the fall of 1862, Ellen was invited to join the Bristol troupe, so most of the family was back together again. Ellen's first role, as Cupid in a burlesque called *Endymion*, obliged her to wear miniwings and a tunic that almost exposed her knees, shocking some members of the audience but enabling her to leap like a gazelle with her bow and arrow. Kate, as usual, upheld the family dignity: she played the goddess Diana in an ankle-length dark robe with a discreet crescent moon in her turban.

Bristol was more open and airy than teeming London, and Ben found pleasant rooms in Queen Square not far from the Theatre Royal in King Street. Ellen and Kate attracted an army of young admirers who saw them on the stage and hung around the stage door for a closer glimpse. Sarah and Ben were fiercely protective of their daughters, forbidding them to talk to their pursuers, as the girls, with capes and hoods pulled over their heads, scurried to and from the theater like little duchesses incognito. Any gifts were promptly returned to the senders, with polite but firm no-thank-you notes from Sarah or Ben. The girls were allowed, however, to keep floral tributes.

Another favorite at the Theatre Royal was Henrietta Hodson, a singing and dancing soubrette, who, in burlesques, played the "principal boy." As Ellen wrote, there were two factions among the town's young blades, the Terryites and Hodsonites, each defending their respective goddesses and raising the Royal roof with competitive cheers and applause. Since all three girls were friends, this was a source of common amusement and giggles. Ellen and Kate were catching up on some of their missed girlhood.

During her first weeks at the Theatre Royal, Ellen read and cut out a newspaper column called "Jottings," simply signed "G." It covered all aspects of theater production but with emphasis on settings and costumes. Whoever "G" was, he had the eye of an educated and discerning artist.

The question of "G's" identity was answered when the Chutes introduced the Terry family to Edward William Godwin, who was to have an incalculable influence on Ellen and who became the man she most loved. At twenty-nine, Godwin was an outstanding architect and amateur archaeologist, living with his cultured, beautiful wife—a few years his senior—in a five-story house in fashionable Portland Square. Godwin's father, a successful dealer in leather, had collected stone carvings from Gothic churches, which he displayed in a garden on his small estate. To his son, these remnants were more than romantic souvenirs of the past; they were concrete evidence of the builder's skill. He studied them with scholarly zeal and resolved to become an architect himself. By the time Ellen Terry met Edward Godwin, he was a self-assured, many-faceted gentleman whose designs for public buildings had won prizes. Along with advancing his own career, he was concerned with bettering the educational opportunities for other young architects. Ellen, always drawn to people who could enrich her own knowledge, gravitated at once to Godwin. He was tall and handsome in a fine-grained arrogant way and as strongly attracted to women as they were to him.

Godwin enjoyed recruiting his friends to read Shakespeare in his Portland Square home. Both Ellen and Kate were invited to a *Midsummer Night's Dream* session, which they attended with the permission of their parents. Kate was charming and ladylike, but Ellen was too excited to think about her charm or manners. The house entranced her. Its elegant simplicity defied the taste of the times. The walls were painted in pale, airy colors and hung with a few Japanese prints. Instead of being carpeted, the polished floors were covered here and there with Persian rugs. The furniture consisted of a few carefully chosen antiques of varying styles, each a masterwork. In its classic spareness, the Godwin house harked back to the eighteenth century; but its array of objects, chosen for their beauty rather than as emblems of wealth and current fashion, suggested a timeless connoisseurship.

The guests, sitting around the uncluttered drawing room, read aloud, each from his own copy of the play. The girls felt they were being valued not as curiosities, but for their professional skill. This was different from being applauded in a theater; it was being accepted in private life.

One of the guests, Godwin's business partner, Henry Crisp, invited Godwin and the girls for a Sunday afternoon at his cottage at nearby Coombe Dingle, Westbury-on-Trym. On this outing, Ellen stood at the top of a flight of stairs, leaned forward and gripped the side rails with both hands, swung her legs forward, and leaped to the floor with one jump. This sort of thing always made Kate nervous. In fact, according to Kate's future grandson, Sir John Gielgud, Ellen made Kate nervous for the rest of her life.

During her Bristol stay, Ellen performed for the inauguration of a new theater a few miles away at Bath. After a short opening ceremony, in which Ellen was the Spirit of the Future, she wound up the evening as Titania in *A Midsummer Night's Dream*. "Mr. Godwin designed my dress, and we made it in his house in Bristol," she recalled. He showed her how the wet cloth was pulled into a long "rope," then wrapped tightly with cotton thread. "When it was dry and untied," she went on, "it was all crinkled and clinging. This was the first lovely dress I ever wore, and I learned a great deal from it." What she learned, in all probability, was that women feel happier in dresses that are especially designed for them.

Ellen became a frequent visitor at the Godwins' home. "I now felt that I had never really lived before. For the first time I began to appreciate beauty, to observe, to feel the splendor of things, to *aspire*." She was enjoying the kind of stimulation that some students get from a particularly inspiring teacher, and she was having her first whiff of England's new bohemian world of artists, a world that included the Pre-Raphaelite painters and poets and that would supply her with many future friends. Having spent most of her sixteen years rushing from place to place and from stage set to stage set, now she could take root in her newfound environment. Ellen overestimated this new world, imagining it to be loftier, kinder, and more liberated than it was. Yet she yearned to become part of it.

Directly after her Bath venture in the clinging Titania dress, Ellen was called back to London to appear in *The Little Treasure*, a farce adapted from the French, which she had already done successfully in Bristol. Playing the title role, Ellen made her debut at the famous Haymarket Theatre. "It presents Miss Terry in an entirely new light," wrote the *Times*'s critic. ". . . she is matured into one of the happiest specimens of what the French call the *ingenue* that has been seen on any stage."

Ellen had no special penchant for *ingenue* roles; she was simply becoming an all-purpose actress. Within two months in London she had played a minor role in *Much Ado about Nothing*, and then, on two days' notice, she jumped into Desdemona in a fly-by-night *Othello*. Such an eleventh-hour scramble would be unthinkable to a modern actress. But Ellen tossed it off easily enough, having already memorized most of the major Shakespearean roles for women.

For almost a year Ellen scattered her talents in all directions. Kate, on the other hand, conquered London as the leading lady of Charles Fechter, whose fencing and lovemaking made his audiences gasp. According to Ellen, Kate was soaring in "a blaze of triumph" while poor Ellen zigzagged: another few weeks back at Bristol, then to the Haymarket again.

At sixteen, Ellen was becoming dissatisfied and self-critical. While longing for muted refinement, she found herself in a whirl of comic actors who carried on the flamboyant mannerisms of Sheridan's time, especially in a revival of *The Rivals*. As for her own role in the play, she admitted, "I played Julie very ill," while the others around her were going at it with high-style gusto, italicizing every curtsy, underlining every bow. Reminiscing in later years, she kicked herself for having been priggish and uppity when she might have profited by studying the jackanapes at the Haymarket. But it was no use. She was in no mood for garrulous Mrs. Malaprop and her "allegories on the banks of the Nile," and offstage she scorned the lewd gossip and Rabelaisian jokes that she overheard from the actors in the greenroom.

Her particular bane was Edward Askew Sothern, a notorious practical joker who had become a national institution playing the foppish Lord Dundreary in Tom Taylor's *Our American Cousin* (the play that Abraham Lincoln was watching in Ford's Theater when he was assassinated). For a few years the Dundreary craze swept England, and half the nation's dandies copied his bushy sideburns, his twirling cane, and the cut of his dapper waistcoats. In Taylor's original play, the caricatured Britisher was balanced by uncouth Asa Trencher, a cartooned Yankee from Vermont. But the English audiences, with their addiction to self-criticism, had far more fun laughing at their own fool than at his American cousin.

In *Our American Cousin,* Ellen played successively two roles during its run: the prissy Georgina and the heroine, Mary Meredith. Whatever she did, Sothern tormented her. Onstage he pulled her hair and tried to make her forget lines or break up with laughter. It was customary for some of Sothern's coplayers to collapse with giggles, or at least pretend to, during his ad-lib horseplay—an old actor's trick that makes audiences think they are seeing an impromptu bit of fun. It is entirely possible that Ellen turned up her nose at all this teasing and fakery and thereby got on Sothern's wrong side.

Ellen was still dreaming of realms far beyond the Haymarket zanies, and her dream, as it must to all Goldenstar girls in the pantomimes, would soon come true in a Transformation Scene dissolving from a grubby backstage greenroom to a glorious artist's studio. The magical change was probably set in motion by Tom Taylor, who was a friend of the artist George Frederick Watts. An accomplished portrait painter, Watts preferred to spend his undeniable talent on blurry, high-minded allegories that, in the history of art, fall in and out of fashion and are currently on the upswing again. Remarking on Watts's misty people, the English painter Walter Sickert wrote, "The sexes are distinguished solely by the fact that the male is painted mahogany and the female the color of a candle."

Kindly Tom Taylor kept an eye out for models that might be useful to Watts. To Taylor, in fact, picking models for Watts's allegorical works was not unlike casting actors for his own plays. Taylor was convinced that Miss Kate Terry, now the most important young actress in London, would be a perfect subject for Watts. Accordingly, Taylor persuaded Sarah Terry to take her eldest daughter to the studio in Little Holland House. The only hitch was that Mrs. Terry was too busy tending her smaller children to accompany Kate herself, so she sent Ellen instead to chaperone her older sister and uphold the proprieties.

After taking a horse-drawn bus to Hyde Park Corner, Kate and Ellen set out to walk the two miles to Watts's studio. Little Holland House was part of the magnificent estate of Lord Holland, surrounded by lawns, open fields, haystacks, and a splendid chaos of shrubs, vines, and trees. With Ellen it was love at first sight. The girls were welcomed by a cordial, portly lady who led them inside to a red baize door—clearly a sacred portal—through which they were ushered into the presence of a small, delicate, bearded man who somehow seemed both a captive and a monarch in his two-story-high studio.

While Ellen tried to fade into the background, Watts began his sketches of Kate. But the chances of Ellen fading into any background were slim. Her eyes explored everything in the room—plaster casts, tapestries, brocades, and the Italian-style murals painted by Watts himself. Ellen was an unwitting scene-stealer, which is the worst kind. Watts could not keep his eyes off her. Finally, making the only possible decision, he asked her to pose side by side with Kate and proceeded to paint a double portrait. By the time she and Kate left the studio to walk back home, Ellen felt that at Little Holland House she had found an extension of the ideal world she had discovered at Godwin's house, "a world full of pictures and music and gentle, artistic people with quiet voices and elegant manners." And she wanted to embrace all of it.

Watts at forty-six and Ellen at sixteen were extravagantly ill-suited to each other, although they had some circumstances in common. They were both born on the edge of the established Victorian world, not outcasts or misfits, but outsiders looking in. Both had exceptional talent and the magnetism to attract admirers. Neither had any orthodox schooling, though Ellen had a far more normal and affectionate family life.

London-born and raised in pinched gentility, Watts was so weakened by asthma and headaches that he could not attend school. He was the idol of his widowed father, an ineffective inventor of musical instruments who counted on his son's success to console him for his own failures. At the age of ten, Watts was befriended by the sculptor William Behnes, and lived with him and his two younger brothers in their Soho home. Watts got on so well that he sometimes sang for joy, thus manifesting his lifelong predilection for feeling at home only in other people's houses.

Watts's early career was spectacular. At eighteen, after a few weeks at the Royal Academy school, he loftily walked out because he found the teaching mediocre and later went on to win three hundred pounds in a mural contest for decorating the new Houses of Parliament. With his prize money he headed for Italy, and through a chance encounter on a boat he gained an introduction to the British ambassador in Florence, Lord Holland. The ambassador and his pretty wife opened their hearts and home to Watts and helped him obtain portrait commissions from their friends. Once again he had found another household in which to feel at home.

When the Hollands returned to England, they turned over their Florentine villa to their friend, Lady Duff-

Gordon, and her two daughters, Georgina and Alicia; and Watts stayed on with the villa. In the evenings he played the guitar and composed a serenade to Georgina, who responded with sufficient ardor that her mother decided to hurry the girl off to Rome before any foolish alliance was formed. After all, there were class differences that could not be serenaded away. On April 15, 1846, he started back to London. Having intended to visit Italy for a few weeks, he had stayed nearly four years.

In England Watts found, thanks to Lord Holland's influence, that his stock had risen among art experts. Now his ambitions vaulted, and he dreamed of creating a huge allegorical project to be installed in a special hall and to be called *The House of Life*. He envisioned it as the Sistine Chapel of the nineteenth century. Living alone in his own studio, he fell prey to his old headaches; his project foundered, and in desperation he wrote to Georgina Duff-Gordon for help: "If possible, find me a wife." Apparently, Watts felt incapable of wooing one for himself, and doubtless he was right.

Georgina ignored his request, but help did arrive in the plump, squat shape of a remarkable woman called Mrs. Thoby Prinsep. She came to his studio as a chaperone to her beautiful sister, Virginia, later Lady Somers, who was sitting for her portrait. For Mrs. Prinsep, interference was an art form. In no time at all she added the willing Watts to her domicile on Chesterfield Street; but finding it too cramped now for her dream of a cultural salon, she persuaded her husband to rent Little Holland House from Lord Holland. Thoby Prinsep had his own art form, which was taking-things-easy. Retired from distinguished civil service in India, he was content to sit back and watch his wife busy herself with the care and feeding of celebrities. He submitted affably to her orders, including her injunction that both he and Watts should have a good lie-down in the same room after lunch. To stimulate their digestive and intellectual juices at the same time, she had provided a young lady to read aloud to them.

Once ensconced in the new studio wing at Little Holland House, Watts was waited on by Mrs. Prinsep, frequently assisted by two of her six sisters, Lady Somers and Julia Cameron, a gifted and tireless photographer. Each of the ladies had a sobriquet: Lady Somers was Beauty; Julia, Talent; Mrs. Prinsep, Dash. And Watts, who had always disliked the name Watts—so blunt and vulgar—was gratified now to be called "Signor." It was Dash who had admitted Kate and Ellen Terry, through the red baize door, to Signor's studio.

As the Terry girls returned for several more sittings for their joint portrait, which Watts called *The Sisters,* Ellen grew more enthralled. She would have laughed at the idea that the studio itself was making love to her, but she could not have denied that the room made her feel euphoric. As she examined it more thoroughly, it reminded her oddly of backstage in a theater. The larger canvases leaned against the walls, like flats of stage scenery. Draperies were flung here and there, and beautiful objects—a goblet, an urn, a brocade pillow—were set on shelves like props for *Romeo and Juliet* or *Othello.* But whereas theatrical props looked crude and flimsy when she scrutinized them, here the solid craftsmanship was a promise of permanence, as if the drama being enacted in this setting were more real, more enduring. There was no curtain to ring down.

Both girls had been photographed many times, a dull business of taking their costumes to a photographer's studio and being told exactly how to freeze their expressions and stand like statues in front of a box. But being painted by a noted artist, whose sitters had numbered lords, ladies, statesmen, and great men of letters such as Tennyson and Carlyle, was an awesome event. In *The Sisters* Ellen had an easy pose. She snuggled her head against Kate's shoulder, and Kate rested her cheek lightly on Ellen's shining hair. It pleased Ellen to realize that every time Watts dipped his brush into color and transferred it to canvas, he was creating a new Ellen Terry—his own interpretation of her—that might live for centuries. At times, he would peer searchingly at her mouth, her eyes, and then carry his impression through the muscles and nerves of his own hands to his easel. He was dismantling her bit by bit and putting her back together on canvas.

In the finished work, Ellen steals the show. While Kate is poetically anonymous, Ellen is firmly Ellen. Her eyelids and nostrils are tenderly molded, as if Watts had caressed them into shape. And with loving accuracy he calibrated the precise tilt of the Terry nose, the long, clean curve from chin to earlobe.

Kate never appeared again in a Watts picture, possibly because of her stage commitments; and Ellen became his favorite model. Watts was best at painting people of genuine mettle and stature. He failed at glamorous Lillie Langtry and fumbled the "fat superficial face" of the Prince of Wales. But give him a Gladstone, a Florence Nightingale, or Cardinal Manning, and he caught some essential dignity in his subject. Speaking of the cardinal, G. K. Chesterton said that Watts's portrait of him looked too much like a church and too little like a man. Yet Watts, at least, had caught Manning's institutional grandeur. Ellen so far had no status, no national fame; but her inner authority was becoming evident. Her face harmonized with his allegorical visions. Far more than Kate, she fitted into his circle of nymphs and nixes, Daphnes and Floras and Loves Triumphant. Once, painting her as Knightly Purity, he kept her posing in heavy armor until she fainted. Watts saw her in so many guises that he may have felt relieved of the responsibility of seeing and treating her as a single human being.

Mrs. Prinsep could hardly fail to notice that Ellen's presence had a tonic effect on Signor. He acquired a brighter gaze, a springier gait. Dedicated as she was to his welfare—provided that she could manipulate it herself—she agreed with Watts that Ellen should become his wife. In this daring enterprise she was abetted by Tom Taylor, who felt it would be a splendid marriage, getting little Nell settled for life. While Mrs. Prinsep reinforced Watts's inclinations, Taylor went to work on Ellen's parents. He encouraged them to imagine their Ellen assured of social prestige, security, and refinement, living in that aristocratic old farm on the edge of London. For Sarah, who had struggled so long to wrap her children in respectability, Ellen's leap to permanent grace was the answer to her prayers. Ben, too, saw the advantages, but he may have wondered whether Watts, with his lofty ideals and limited vigor, would make an appealing mate to his high-spirited daughter.

Watts had cause to view the marriage with confused emotions. On one hand, he was beguiled by Ellen and found her a valuable adjunct to his studio. On the other, he must consider that she came from a commonplace family, though hardly more so than his own, and had been raised in a profession still regarded, in many quarters, as disreputable. Watts may have doubted that he could satisfy Ellen sexually—some people believed he was incapable of normal sexual relations—yet he could reason that by rescuing her from the iniquities of the stage and making her Mrs. George Frederick Watts he was doing her a favor that more than compensated for his shortcomings.

Would the world condemn him as a silly fool, marrying a girl thirty years younger than himself? Yes, he risked that verdict. But he took care to emphasize, to himself and others, that he was wedding Ellen as a moral duty, to improve her mind and manners, and that far from being condemned he should be admired for his pains and sacrifice. Watts fancied himself as a man of noble aims, who, as he once wrote to Georgina Gordon, "will gladly devote the rest of my time principally to the object of being useful and doing good." On the subject of his impending marriage he wrote to his friend Lady Constance Leslie, "To make the poor child what I wish her to be will take a long time, and most likely cost a great deal of trouble, and I shall want the sympathy of all my friends."

The implied complacency of these words, making himself a hero and begging for sympathy, is repellent. Yet, in defense of Watts, it must be borne in mind that in Victorian times the pressure to adopt noble attitudes and be a do-gooder could be overwhelming. Self-deception was often essential to self-esteem; the man who dared to examine his true motives and admit their unflattering ambiguity could feel himself an outcast in the eyes of society and of God.

What might have frightened Watts most legitimately was Ellen's obvious lack of experience as a social hostess. On that score, Mrs. Prinsep reassured him from the start. Dash had no intention of deserting him. Everything would go on just as it had before. Little Ellen would be an ornament to the establishment, nothing more.

Ellen's first hint of a marriage seems to have come one day after a posing session when Watts kissed her. Recalling the episode years later in a letter to G. B. Shaw, Ellen wrote that she had told her mother that she had to marry because she was carrying Watts's baby. "Oh, I tell you I thought I knew everything . . . and I was sure that kiss meant giving me a baby!" Ellen soon learned that marriage was not mandatory for the reason she supposed, but marriage was in the air anyway; and after Watts made a formal offer and her parents gave formal consent, Ellen embraced the idea with dazed wonderment.

Her theatrical experience gave her confidence in her adaptability. She was used to being uprooted, used to making her home in new places. Trusting herself and trusting others, she expected people to love her if she worked hard. It is probable that Mrs. Prinsep gave her stern lectures on decorum, impressing upon her how privileged she was to have a celebrated husband, and Ellen probably took them with good grace. After all, she had been slapped by Mrs. Kean and bawled out by Madame de Rhona, and afterward they hugged each other and everything worked out happily. She was accustomed to mastering new roles.

The wedding was ominously gloomy. On February 20, 1864, Ellen began the morning gaily enough at Stanhope Street by giving a bath to four of the littlest children, Floss, Charlie, Tom, and the baby. But scrubbed and shampooed as they were, they did not attend the wedding. The most likely explanation is that Signor was feeling too nervous to face "a crowd." Ellen's father accompanied her to the ceremony at St. Barnabas Church, Kensington.

Ellen had the honor of wearing a wedding dress designed by Watts's friend William Holman Hunt, a leading Pre-Raphaelite painter, whom Burne-Jones described as "a splendour of a man with a great wiry golden beard and faithful violet eyes." Somewhat less colorful than its creator, Ellen's dress was brown silk. She wore a shawl from India and a white quilted bonnet bearing a sprig of orange blossoms. As she left the church, she put on a sealskin jacket adorned with coral buttons and a sealskin cap. (She posed later in this dress for her husband's portrait of her, *Choosing*.)

The only eyewitness account of the wedding is attributed to Watts's friend Lady Leslie, who was distressed by the contrast of the "atrabilious" bridegroom walking slowly and heavily up the aisle with the radiant child bride dancing up it on winged feet. Despite Watts's letter bidding for her sympathy—or maybe because of it—the lady's heart went to the bride. When Ellen broke into tears after the ceremony, Watts voiced his own form of distress: "Don't cry. It makes your nose swell." As a painter, was he fearful lest the red nose would clash with the coral buttons?

There was no honeymoon, but simply a return to Little Holland House with Mrs. Prinsep. The particulars of the alliance caused conjecture among London's elite bohemians. George du Maurier tells that at the weekly dinners of the

Punch staff, "Ruskin's impotence, Swinburne's relationship with Adah Isaacs Menken, G. F. Watts's marriage to Ellen Terry, were all the subject of obscene jokes." According to Marguerite Steen, a close friend of Ellen's in her late years and a lively biographer of the whole Terry dynasty, "On her marriage night Nelly was discovered crying bitterly on the staircase outside the nuptial chamber. Her initiation at the hands of a fumbling and neurotic lover was a sad one." This account seems plausible enough. But one wonders who "discovered" Ellen on the stairs. Mrs. Prinsep?

The first months of marriage were occupied chiefly with posing, which brought the newlyweds together without the obligation to talk or touch—and with the continued education of Ellen. It is not likely that Mrs. Prinsep ever entrusted her with preparing food, nor is it likely that Ellen would have been much good at it. Ellen was repeatedly enjoined to curb her exuberance and to emulate those well-behaved children who are seen but not heard. When the usual galaxy of notables called at Little Holland House— Browning, Thackeray, Tennyson, Gladstone, Disraeli, and Julia Cameron with her camera—Ellen was often ignored, with the tacit understanding that it was for her own good. Before the marriage, Watts had let it be known that he was "determined to remove the youngest Miss Terry from the temptations and abominations of the stage, give her an education and if she continues to have the affection she now feels for me, marry her." So now that Signor was keeping his side of the bargain, his friends did not want to see all his noble work go for nothing. Ellen must be kept on a leash until she had been tamed.

To George du Maurier, with his caricaturist's hard eye, the ambience of Little Holland House was vaguely distasteful. Noting the three Pattle sisters, Dash, Beauty, and Talent, in action, he described how the visiting luminaries "receive dinners and incense, the cups of tea handed to them by these women almost kneeling," and he observed in the whole setup "a slight element of looseness." At times du Maurier was inclined to be a bit prim, so it is probable that he meant nothing very sinister by "looseness." Still, one cannot help wondering what the child bride being rescued from "the abominations of the theater" thought of the peccadillos of fashionable Bohemia.

A few months after her wedding, Ellen spent a summer at Freshwater on the Isle of Wight, with Watts and his retinue, in Mrs. Cameron's house, Dimbola. Their close neighbor was Lord Tennyson in his imposing home, Farringford. Julia Cameron, one of England's finest photographers and the first woman to excel in her field, was a dauntless eccentric. Short and stout, she darted about in crimson and violet draperies, stained by the chemicals she used to develop her pictures. Her specialty was dressing up people to represent figures out of legend or scripture, grabbing a grizzled old farmer to represent Father Time with a scythe, or waylaying a passing servant girl to represent Fair Rosamund. Equally relentless with her eminent sitters, she bullied the astronomer Sir John Herschel into washing his white hair so it would stand out like a halo, and she once had to be restrained from barging into Thomas Carlyle's bedroom to confer with him about a suitable pose while he was changing his trousers. At Dimbola, Mrs. Cameron's eye inevitably fell on Ellen. But rather than put her in a stagey costume, she posed her with the utmost simplicity in Tennyson's bathroom, probably because the light was good and she liked the wallpaper. This superb portrait, as lovely as anything Mrs. Cameron ever did, captured Ellen in a languid mood, her head lowered, her hair tossed backward over her shoulders, and her hand lifted to show her ring.

For Ellen, perhaps the pleasantest thing about being at Dimbola was its proximity to the Tennyson family. "I was still young enough," she wrote, "that I preferred playing Indians and Knights of the Round-table with Hallam and Lionel. . . ." Tennyson's sons, aged ten and twelve, must have been bowled over by "a wife" who at one moment climbed trees and swung on gates with them and then, when they switched to make-believe, waxed dramatic as Guinevere and Morgan le Fay—not that Ellen would have stuck to women's roles, she who was soon to pose for her husband as a knight in armor. Enjoying the father as much as the sons, she used to take sunset strolls with England's poet laureate. "He would point out to me differences in the flight of the different birds. . . . He taught me to recognize the barks of trees and to call wild flowers by their names. He picked me the first bit of pimpernel I ever noticed. I was always quite at ease with him."

Tennyson's grandson Charles fills in a detail of young Ellen's good times with the poet, based on Tennyson's recollection: "In the evening she would run up to Farringford to hear him read, and she delighted in preparing his clay pipe, dipping the mouthpiece in *sal volatile* to prevent it from sticking to his lips." Ellen remembered best his vocal effects for Robert Browning's "Ride from Ghent to Aix." It was a little comic, until one got used to it. "He used to preserve the monotonous rhythm of the galloping horses . . . and made the sounds ring out sharply like hoofs upon a road."

After the painful tensions of her marriage, Ellen was comforted by Tennyson's theatrical voice and appearance, by what Thomas Carlyle described as the poet's "loud laughter and piercing wail, his great shock of dusty-dark hair, his clothes cynically loose, free and easy, and his infinite tobacco." He was as openhearted in his way as she was in hers.

Back in London, the taming and humbling of Mrs. Watts progressed. A minor incident assumed symbolic importance. A lady visitor reported that one day after lunch she and Mrs. Prinsep and Ellen sat together in the drawing room. Ellen was strikingly lovely, the lady said, with brilliant eyes and very beautiful hair. Then in a sudden imperious gesture, Ellen leaned over the arm of her chair and pulled the pins from her hair, "which tumbled about her shoulders like a cloak of shining gold."

The visitor gazed in delight as Ellen swayed her head gently from side to side, and the mass of shimmering hair shrouded her face and swept the floor. Mrs. Prinsep was outraged. The golden hair waved like an unfurled banner of defiance. "Ellen, Ellen," her oppressor cried, "put up your hair instantly."

Ellen obeyed, coiling her hair on her head and stabbing it with pins. But the rebellion was successful. She had asserted her beauty and youth.

Another uprising took place at one of Mrs. Prinsep's dinner parties, at which Ellen was expected to be demure. After a short absence from the company, she danced back into the room as Cupid in pink tights. It was probably the same outfit she wore in the Bristol *Endymion*, and as she threw back her cape she could have shouted her old lines, "And so to throw off all disguise and sham, let me at once inform you who I am! I'm Cupid!"

Again, Mrs. Prinsep was furious. Not that such an impromptu frolic was uncommon in her circles, where guests loved dressing up for charades or recitations and song exhibits. But Mrs. Prinsep interpreted Ellen's caper as a rank act of insubordination—which it probably was—and a calculated insult to the dignity of Watts and his guests, whoever they were. This, added to her other mutinous acts, sealed Ellen's doom. The situation was intolerable. The girl had to go. She must be expelled as quietly and discreetly as possible, so as not to upset Signor. In fact, all he had to do was sign the separation paper, and Mrs. Prinsep would handle all the rest.

This wretched document, doubtless prepared by Watts's legal-minded friends, stated: "That although considerably older than his intended wife, he admired her very much and hoped to influence, guide and cultivate a very artistic and peculiar nature and to remove an impulsive young girl from the dangers and temptations of the stage."

As the spokesman for Watts continued in the self-righteous verbosity that injured parties have adopted in courts of law for centuries, he returned with an almost audible licking of chops to the evils of the theater. "That very soon after his marriage, he found how great an error he had made. Linked to a most *restless* and *impetuous* nature accustomed from the very earliest childhood to the stage, and forming her ideas of life from the exaggerated romance of sensational plays, from whose acquired habits a quiet life was intolerable and even impossible, demands were made upon him that he could not meet without giving up all the professional aims his life had been devoted to.

"That he did not impute any immorality at that time, but there was an insane excitability indulging in the wildest suspicions, accusations and denunciations driving him to the verge of desperation and—"

Here the dirty innuendos were planted; no immorality *at that time,* but presumably just around the corner, an *insane* excitability, sowing the suspicion that Ellen might be losing her mind.

When Ellen was informed of her dismissal, she did not oblige with any sensational theatrics. She was stunned and proceeded in numb obedience to pack up her belongings and return, after ten months of marriage, to dingy Stanhope Street. Her mother had been warned in enough time to prepare a little bedroom on the top floor. The smaller children could not understand why Ellen, who had departed in such glory, was being sent home. Had she misbehaved?

Older people asked the same question. One story had it that Ellen had spent the night with her friend Edward Godwin while he was visiting London; another tale, more suited to the jokesters at the *Punch* dinners, proclaimed that at a dinner given by Mrs. Prinsep for a conclave of bishops, Ellen had burst into the room and danced on the table, naked.

At seventeen Ellen had collided with a circle that could not accommodate her individuality. What could she do now? Not once during her marriage had she regretted leaving the stage, and she still had no desire whatsoever to resume her career. Financially she was not pressed, because Watts had promised her an annual payment of three hundred pounds "as long as she shall lead a chaste life." But who would report on her chastity? Her private life now could become a matter for public examination.

Chapter Three

"I HATED MY LIFE"

"It has never been in my power to *sustain*," Ellen Terry wrote. "In private life, I cannot sustain a hatred or a resentment. On the stage, I can pass quickly from one effect to another, but I cannot fix *one*." In view of her fluid nature and obstinate goodwill, it is all the more remarkable that for the rest of her life Ellen looked back on the period that followed her breakup with Watts as a time of utter misery. Here was a fixed landmark, a sustained effect. "I hated my life, hated everyone and everything," she admitted in her *Memoirs*. In public, Ellen kept a decorous silence about the husband who had rejected her, but, writing to her young artist friend Mary Ann Hall, Ellen cried out, obviously in reference to Mrs. Prinsep, "God forgive her for I *can not* do so—I suppose I'm very, very wicked to feel so but indeed, Mary Ann, I think . . . what I have done that she should use me so." As a rule, Ellen had a forgiving nature, but her sustained anger at Mrs. Prinsep was an exception. Eventually, she turned it to good use in the theater, for it added to her vocabulary of emotions and deepened her feeling for characters who experience bitterness and injustice.

Her banishment made her feel she had been pushed into a blind alley. Besides losing an exalted husband, she had been expelled from the Watts paradise of art and beauty, where she had been so trustingly at home. She knew she was being gossiped about, in high and low places. Poor little Nelly Terry. Tried to fly too soon. Crashed ignominiously. What could she do but pick herself up and go back to the family roost in Stanhope Street, with its "hideous" furnishings, its tiny backyard that could only remind her, by contrast, of the aristocratic meadows and woods of Holland Park?

Sarah and Ben tried to be kind, as if nothing had happened. But Sarah couldn't always conceal the shame, even the recrimination, in her eyes. And Ellen saw that worldly Ben was blaming himself for allowing the marriage, fearful that his "little duchess" had permanently cooked her goose.

Sensible Kate might be sympathetic, but Kate was terribly busy. At this time, her life seemed almost diabolically designed to show up Ellen's failures, as if anything Ellen could do, Kate could do better. In the theater, Kate was soaring. She was leading lady to the celebrated Charles Fechter, who had taken over the refurbished Lyceum and made it an imposing temple of drama. Her biggest hit there was as Ophelia, with Fechter as a flaxen-wigged Hamlet, sporting a slight French accent. Some people could not stomach him, but they all loved Kate. Charles Dickens called her "perfectly charming . . . the very best piece of womanly tenderness ever seen on the stage." In 1864, Kate joined a younger, comelier star, Henry Nevelle, at the Olympic Theatre and acted a half-dozen melodramas by the Terrys' loyal friend and the most popular dramatist of the day, Tom Taylor. Still keeping her grip on Shakespeare, Kate in *Twelfth Night* rather monopolized the evening by playing both Viola and her brother, Sebastian.

Off the stage, Kate also began to eclipse Ellen. She became engaged briefly to a handsome actor named Montagu. "If the course of that love had run smooth," reflected Ellen, assuming that Kate might have stayed in the theater with her husband, "where should I have been? Kate would have been the Terry of the age." But if the breakup of Kate's romance cleared the stage for Ellen's future reign, it also cleared the way for Kate, in due time, to marry the most perfect young man in London—at least for Kate Terry.

Meanwhile, Ellen settled into a state of retirement. Her family urged her to forget her distress by returning to the stage; but that was unthinkable. Just before marrying Watts she had soured on the theater. Now, crawling back to a profession she felt she had outgrown seemed like an admission of defeat. She would have to be billed on posters and programs not as "Miss Ellen Terry," but, according to the custom for married actresses, as "Mrs. Watts." It was sad enough to lose the popular family name; it was worse to be linked to Watts, which was as good as advertising her humiliation.

Ellen's life in this gray period went largely unrecorded, save for some scant but helpful mention in the diaries of the Reverend Charles Dodgson. This young Oxford don, better known as Lewis Carroll, whose *Alice in Wonderland* was published in 1865 while Ellen was back at Stanhope Street, became her lifelong, though somewhat guarded, admirer. Along with his enthusiasm for mathematics, which he taught at Oxford, his interests turned toward the theater, photography, and enchanting little girls. "He was as fond of me," Ellen wrote, "as he could be of anyone over the age of ten."

Dodgson had seen Ellen in her first role, as Mamillius in *The Winter's Tale*, pulling her toy wagon. His diary testifies that he "especially admired the acting of little Mamillius, Ellen Terry, a beautiful little creature who played with remarkable ease and spirit," as if he already foresaw that the little wagon was hitched to a star. Eight years later, through his friend Tom Taylor, Dodgson obtained a note of introduction to the Terry family; he visited them on December 20, 1864, to discuss taking some pictures. Happy to meet the famous Kate, he confided to his diary, "I thought her very ladylike and natural in manner," as if he had expected actresses to be unnatural and unladylike. He regretted, though, not seeing "Mrs. Watts," who he learned was staying with her family "on a visit of two or three days," but just happened to be out when Dodgson called.

This casual clue probably indicates that, eleven months after her marriage with Watts, things were awry with Ellen at Little Holland House, and she was taking temporary refuge with her family. Despite Ellen's absence, however, Dodgson wrote, "I mark this day with a white stone," a translation of a Latin phrase tantamount to "a red-letter day."

Dodgson came back the next day with samples of his photography, still hoping to meet Ellen. "Polly and Benjamin met me in the hall," he wrote, "and in the drawing room I found Miss Kate Terry, Florence, and to my delight, the one I have always most wished to meet of the family, Mrs. Watts. Mr. Tom Taylor called in later to read Miss Terry some of her part in a MS. play [Settling Day], and I remained to listen. I was very much pleased with what I saw of Mrs. Watts—lively, and pleasant, almost childish in her fun, but perfectly ladylike."

He was delighted that another denizen of the stage had turned out to be ladylike, for it gave him hope that God might forgive him his actresses. To his diary he added, "I mark this day also with a white stone."

By agreement, Dodgson was to return someday with his camera. But for several reasons, including a spell of fog and the difficulty of rounding up the various Terrys, Dodgson's camera session was put off seven months. At last, on Thursday, July 13, 1865, he wrote, "Drove to the Terrys with the camera, etc." There he left all his equipment. Thus well prepared, on the next day he wrote, "Spent the day at the Terrys, and took: Miss Kate Terry, Mr. and Mrs. Terry, Mrs. Watts, a large one of Polly, Polly and Flo, Flo, Charlie, etc."

Again on the next day he was back on the job, though delayed because he had to stop off at Macmillan, his publisher, and autograph twenty copies of *Alice,* fresh from the press, to be given to friends. "This took so long that I did not get to the Terrys till 12:30, where I photographed till about 4:30. Then I had a game of Castle Croquet with Miss

Terry, Mrs. Watts and Polly. I made a sort of dinner of their tea, and ended by escorting Polly to the Olympic to see *The Serf*. We had Miss Terry's season ticket, and got good places in the dress circle. After *The Serf* I took Polly around to the stage-door to join her sister, and went back to see *Glaucus,* a very pretty burlesque. I mark these last *three* days with a white stone." Here is the only instance of three white-stone days in a row, all of them Terry days.

Small wonder that the Terrys enthralled Dodgson. They represented the theater, which he adored; Ellen herself was perennially childlike; and three of the younger children were on the right side of ten: under. A typical entry in Dodgson's diary read, "Went to the Terry's about five, and spent the evening with them, in croquet, card tricks, and finally story-telling."

Dodgson's photographs of the family turned out to be beautifully grave and impressive, though Ellen and Kate betray traces of grins and banked chuckles.

Generally, it has been supposed that the stiff camera portraiture of the nineteenth century revealed less of human character than the unposed shots of modern cameramen, who snap their subjects with pants down and psyches in disarray. But often the exact opposite is true. While candid-camera portraiture has undeniable values, the older photographic style has its own tremendous magic. In the solemn sense of occasion engendered by a picture session, and in the earnest effort to cooperate with the black-hooded magician, sitters often revealed some deep, still essence of their being. The concentrated act of composure often brought the inner self to the surface.

Before she was twenty, Ellen Terry was well recorded. She had been painted repeatedly by George Frederick Watts and had posed for two of England's finest amateur photographers, Charles Dodgson and Julia Cameron.

Ellen's limbo year of 1865 drifted to a close. In the following February she made a brief foray into the theater,

unchronicled and brought to light only by a letter un-
earthed by the Terrys' biographer, Marguerite Steen. Ellen
and her father were acting together in an unspecified play
in an unknown town, accompanied by Polly, aged thirteen,
who came along for the fun and to chaperone Ellen. In all
probability, Ben had set up this minor engagement to help
Ellen get back her nerve. The letter was written by both
girls, in installments. Polly began: "My dear Mama, we
have all arrived safe and sound. The first thing we did was
to take a cab to the theater and enquire about lodgings, but
we did not succeed. Then Papa thought we would go to the
George an hotel. We slept there one night. The next morning Papa looked for lodgings and did succeed that time
luckily."

Polly chattered on about seeing a provincial revival of
The Hidden Hand, a play that Kate had recently done in
London, and rated it "something awful." Writing under
Ellen's stern eye, Polly wound up in a flurry of affection,
especially for her new baby brother, Tops (Fred). "Nelly
says I can't have any more paper . . . so give my love and
kisses and thousands to Tops." And then, allying herself
with the forces of law and order like a grown-up, she
closed: "Tell George Flo Charlie Tom and Tops that I will
not forget them if they are good. Believe me, my dear
Mama, ever your affectionate daughter Polly."

Now Ellen took up the pen and told her mother how
Polly had busied herself backstage and fretted over a scene
in which Ellen had to take a risky tumble. "Poor old Polly
was as nervous as either of us I believe. She helped me
with my change (for which there was plenty of time!) and
'felt so relieved when you had *done* your fall, Nell!' Pa
played the Major *very well indeed.* He was very nervous,
and will, I feel sure, act better tonight than last night. He
lacked what I possessed and I lacked what he possessed. I
was too *fast*—he was too *slow.*"

By her next words Ellen kills the rumors that mother

63

and daughter were on bad terms at this period. Ellen seemed to be drawing Sarah aside and whispering in her ear when she wrote, "Read this to yr self!!!"

"I went to bed and dreamed not of the Theater (isn't that strange?) but of Mr. Watts! I dreamed he was dying, and I woke up in the greatest grief—crying. This is the 20th of the month. my Wedding day! Married 2 years ago today! and it is such a day. *Pouring* with rain! and altogether wretched! Oh! . . . with all thy faults I love thee still!"

Voicing her sense of loss and the tender feelings she still held for Watts, this final passage also establishes that she could turn to her mother for understanding.

Soon afterward, Ellen took her first trip to Paris. Though her *Memoirs* do not say who accompanied her, it was probably her old friends, the Casella family; a photograph taken in Paris shows Ellen standing by little Marie Casella. The father and his daughters, all involved in the arts, were her lifelong friends.

It was springtime 1866, the height of the empire under Napoleon III. Offenbach melodies poured from the cafes. Empress Eugénie, driving in the Bois de Boulogne, reminded Ellen of "an exquisite waxwork." At a Salon exhibit, Ellen joined the crowd around Rosa Bonheur's *Horse Fair,* and in the long galleries of the Louvre she suffered the art lover's complaint: tired feet. She visited the studio of Ernest Meissonier, the master of battle scenes, and met the engaging young painter Joseph-Jacques Tissot. With "the friend who took me everywhere in Paris," she saw the exotic Sarah Bernhardt who was in her early twenties and, Ellen said, "thin as a harrow." She got useful tips on makeup from the reigning goddess of the French stage, Marie Favart, who told her not to use black paint under her eyes; it was necessary when the stage was illumined from below but looked ugly with the new overhead gas lighting. Ellen enjoyed the ritualistic high-style acting at a Comédie Française production of one of Molière's plays, so different from the sloppier, more spontaneous English style. Comparing them, she said, perhaps more wisely than she knew: "Old School—new School? What does it matter which, so long as it is good enough."

She made the obligatory visits to the fashionable cafe Tortoni's, where she might easily have seen the younger Dumas or the Goncourt brothers, and, in her own words, "often went to three parties a night."

Once back in London, her family persuaded her to act with her sister Kate in *The Hunchback* for a single benefit performance given on Kate's behalf. "Benefits" were a standard practice in the British theater. They could be instigated by almost any actor or his friends, for the purpose of securing extra profits. Actors agreed to perform on behalf of a colleague on the assumption that some day the favor might be reciprocated. As in the case of Kate Terry, the benefit did not necessarily imply that the beneficiary was flat broke. A benefit could be an act of homage as well as an act of charity. At a time when there were no theatrical guilds, unions, or funds for the needy, the benefits were a godsend, contributing to both the comradeship and welfare of actors.

In her first London comeback, Ellen said she "was feeling wretchedly ill, and angry too, because they insisted on putting my married name on the bills," but nonetheless she performed well. According to the Reverend Charles Dodgson, who predictably was in attendance on the night of June 20, 1866, "Miss Terry and Mrs. Watts took the (only) two female characters—their acting was a treat, about the best I have ever seen."

Halfheartedly, Ellen accepted a few more engagements: at Bristol for two weeks and in several trashy London items with Kate. But while Ellen was still marking time, Kate was taking notice of that perfect young man who might alter her future. He and she saw a fair amount of each other while rehearsing a semi-amateur production of an operetta.

Arthur Lewis was a product of the merchant classes,

which were enriching Victorian social life. He belonged to the same breed as the shipping magnate Frederick Leyland and the Greek merchant Alexander Ionides, men who were opening their houses and cash boxes to Rossetti, Whistler, Burne-Jones, and other stars in the sky of art. Arthur Lewis was not quite as rich, nor as powerful, but he had the same cordial attitude toward the arts—mainly the lively arts— and he was rich enough to entertain delightfully. Arthur needed a wife who was perfectly proper but worldly and who, to run his fairly elaborate household, possessed a practicality in harmony with his own background.

Arthur's Welsh father, together with a partner, created the noted firm of Lewis and Allenby in Regent Street, which served as silk mercers to the queen. At age eleven, Arthur was packed off to study French in Geneva, so he could eventually help his father as an interpreter on business trips abroad. He learned about fine velvets and brocades, but on his trips he also soaked up culture in the museums and concert halls. Perhaps due to his Welsh heritage, Arthur Lewis was devoted to music.

In his bachelor quarters in Jermyn Street, he formed his own instrumental group named, punningly, the Jermyn Band. Invitations to Jermyn Street usually read, "Music at 8:30. Oysters at 11." The guests included journalists, explorers, or anyone else with musical leanings. When Arthur moved in 1863 to a more rural residence called Moray Lodge, only a short stroll from the great Holland House, the band changed its name to the Moray Minstrels and was called "the finest glee club in London."

Arthur's Saturday evenings were widely appreciated. George du Maurier wrote, "You can't imagine anything jollier than Lewises. . . . the artists made a noble appearance there." In *Trilby*, his best-selling novel, du Maurier used Arthur as a model for a popular host whose guests "were not packed together sardine-wise . . . [but] could get up and walk around and talk to their friends between pieces . . . and stroll in the lovely grounds by moon or star or Chinese lantern light." Perhaps the most thoughtful observer was Holman Hunt, the Pre-Raphaelite painter. Watching "the merry crew that greeted each other as they drove up to the Lewis domain," Hunt went on, "It was a strange mixture of company . . . for the entertainment became famous, and men of all classes were pleased to go into Bohemia for a night."

On a spring evening when the wind was right, it was more than likely that Ellen Terry in the first months of her marriage at Little Holland House could hear the Moray Minstrels in full jubilation and wish to heaven that she were right there singing with them. Her wish was answered after a three-year delay.

In 1867, the Minstrels put on a short operetta, *Cox and Box*, by the editor of *Punch*, F. C. Burnand and Arthur Sullivan (before he joined W. S. Gilbert). To expand the evening's entertainment, both Terry sisters were recruited. The program was given at Moray Lodge, then repeated at a matinee at the Adelphi Theatre for the benefit of the widow of a *Punch* artist. As an added fling, the Minstrels took the show to Manchester for another benefit performance.

During the five-hour Sunday train ride, all the cast sang. One member wrote later, "Of the row made . . . no idea can be given." After a Monday morning rehearsal, the cast was invited to dine on the estate of Tom Agnew, where lawn games were played and "Ellen charmed the whole group by capering about." After the evening show, du Maurier, who acted Box, bet a fellow actor named Blunt that he, not Blunt, would win the honor of taking Ellen Terry to her carriage. To gain his goal, tricky du Maurier left a tempting piece of pastry on the floor outside Blunt's dressing room, which the hungry Blunt stopped to gobble and thus lost the bet.

All this skylarking was—and always remained—the breath of life to Ellen. But when the party was over it was Kate who was well on her way to becoming Mrs. Arthur Lewis; Ellen was well on her way to nowhere.

Three months later Kate Terry, after playing Juliet, bade farewell to her London admirers. Mountains of flowers were thrown at her feet, she wept, threw good-bye kisses, wept, dashed offstage, and put on her street clothes; then, because the audience was still yelling, she dashed back onstage, wept, and finally sneaked outside the theater on the Strand where Arthur Lewis awaited in a brougham and clop-clopped her away from the theater forever—well, almost forever.

In Manchester five weeks later, Kate obliged her fans with a three-act trifle, *Plot and Passion*, which was Kate's final benefit for herself. Ellen came, too, acting on the same bill in a playlet, *Little Savage*. In the interval, the orchestra rendered *The Kate Terry Valse*, composed especially for the bride-to-be, and after her final bow, Arthur Lewis in her dressing room floored her with an extraordinary gift. It was a wide gold bracelet, engraved on the outside, "To Kate Terry on her retirement from the stage, from him for whom she leaves it." Engraved on the inside in tiny letters were the titles of one hundred plays that Kate had acted, with the name of her role in each play. To assemble this compendium of her career, Arthur doubtless had the help of Kate's family. Yet the idea itself was a stroke of genius, for it testified that Arthur appreciated the extent of his wife's achievement and, far from wanting her to forget it, took pains that she should remember it proudly. If in later years Kate were tempted to complain to her husband, "You don't realize what success I gave up for you," he could reply, "Oh, yes, I do, dear—every single play that you ever acted in."

To Ellen, the contrast between Kate's entry into marriage and her own must have been painful to consider. Kate left the theater in triumph; Ellen had left unsung. Kate's husband respected the theater; Watts called it "an abomination." Kate was entering a household over which she had full authority; Ellen had been granted no authority. Arthur Lewis planned to, and did, curtail his flamboy-

ant entertaining in favor of a more intimate domestic life
with Kate; Watts never appeared to alter his conduct in any
way for Ellen. Arthur welcomed all the Terrys to Moray
Lodge and jollied the youngsters with picnics, running
games, and impromptu theatricals; Watts had been too
aloof, too near invalidism to enjoy the Terrys. By coincidence, both Kate and Ellen had faced wedlock in the same
territory, both under the shadow of the great Holland
House, almost as if Kate had moved into the same theater
and now on the same stage were enacting her marital
drama where Ellen's marriage had failed dismally.

On Friday morning, October 18, 1867, Kate and Arthur
were married in St. John's Church, Kentish Town. Of the
quintet of bridesmaids, Ellen was the first. A crowd overflowed the church to see the illustrious bride in white
moiré trimmed with white lace and the bridesmaids in
white trimmed with green. With everybody peering and
jostling, Kate could hardly make her way to the altar. When
the service was finished, the Reverend Mr. Colvert spoke
his mind; he reminded the congregation that they had
come to see "a religious ceremony, not a spectacle."

Six days after Kate's marriage, Ellen opened with a
new troupe at "the singularly elegant" New Queen's Theatre, which enhanced its refinement with a frieze of draped
Greek figures, painted over the proscenium by Albert
Moore and loosely inspired by the Elgin Marbles. The company was run by the Alfred Wigan, who had once employed Kate. Mrs. Wigan, a deft comedienne, went after
Ellen mercilessly about her tendency to fidget and actually
shouted and terrified her into calming down. Her first two
plays, by her friends Charles Reade and Tom Taylor, were
soon-forgotten flops; the third, included on the Christmas
bill, is remembered only as a landmark. It was David Garrick's one-act mutilation of *The Taming of the Shrew*, retitled *Katharine and Petruchio*. Ellen was Katharine, of
course, and her tamer was an odd, ambitious fellow, aged
twenty-nine, who had changed his name from John Henry

Brodribb to Henry Irving. Irving and Terry were to become the most celebrated acting team in English history; but in their first joint effort there was no hint of things to come. Irving thought Ellen was "charming as a woman, but hoydenish as an actress"; she said he "played badly" and was "stiff with self-consciousness."

Equally harsh on herself, she added, "I was just then acting very badly: caring scarcely for my work or the theater, or anybody belonging to the theater." She did notice, though, that Irving, besides acting, worked overtime as stage manager at the Queen's and was more diligent than all the other actors put together. This she admired. And she was pleased when on payday, as she dashed in late and hurried to pick up her weekly salary at "The Treasury," Irving gave her his place in the long queue. It registered, perhaps subconsciously, that he was an expediter and a protector. Their work together lasted only a few days; they had no more to do with each other for ten years.

For the role of protector, Ellen found a far more congenial candidate in the person of her old friend Edward Godwin, the Bristol architect, whose business led him occasionally to London. The details of their reunion have been kept vague, as often happens in Victorian life histories whenever there are hints of a sexual liaison, with the result, ironically, that innocent encounters are allowed to be misunderstood. It has been said that Godwin often visited Ellen and her husband at Little Holland House, after which Ellen nursed Godwin through a night of illness in his own quarters. All this seems unlikely, not only because there is no solid evidence to back it up, but also because Godwin was too acerb, too independent, to feel at ease in the Watts hothouse; and, moreover, he occupied no London quarters until after Ellen and Watts had finally separated. The reunion was probably quite simple. Being greatly interested in theater architecture, Godwin visited the New Queen's, saw Ellen perform, and naturally resumed his old friendship. Since Ellen had last seen Godwin, his wife had died. Now, at thirty-five, he was a vital, self-sufficient spirit, respected in his field and very attractive. That his friends called him "the wicked Earl" implies his romantic appeal.

On Saturday night, October 10, 1868, Ellen turned her back forever on the Queen's Theatre, where she had been playing for nearly a year. The next day, Ellen Terry and Edward Godwin took up residence in a small cottage near the village of Wheathampstead in Hertfordshire, about thirty-five miles, or an hour by train, from London.

Leaving without warning to her friends, Ellen had vanished from the earth. It was an unbelievable cruelty to inflict on her loving family, who had no clue to her fate except a two-word note, "Found Drowned," that she had attached to a photograph of Watts. "Found Drowned" was the title of a Watts painting of a girl's corpse taken presumably from the Thames. He had painted the work eight years before he married Ellen. It was natural that Ellen's parents would infer from this lugubrious clue that she meant to drown herself, and their fears seemed confirmed when Ben Terry visited a morgue and identified the corpse of a blond girl recently drowned as his daughter.

The image of a "fallen girl" coming to a dismal end by the Thames, paying the wages of sin, held a horrid fascination. It attracted the illustrators of penny dreadfuls and fine artists alike. In Rossetti's painting *Found,* a beautiful derelict crouches by the river while her former rustic lover views her with alarm. Another fair outcast, painted by Augustus Egg, huddles under a murky archway by the Thames to nurse her baby. Then, in addition to Watts's *Found Drowned,* there were pictures of drowned Ophelia, portrayed on canvas most sumptuously in 1852 by John Millais. That Ellen should meet such a theatrical death must have seemed not at all unlikely to her father.

Ellen's young sisters, Marion and Floss, were already dressed in mourning when their mother decided to visit the morgue and inspect the body. Describing this visit,

Ellen wrote later, "She kept her head under the shock of the likeness, and bethought her of 'a strawberry mark on my left arm.' . . . That settled it, for there was no such mark to be found on the poor corpse."

Sarah's discovery proved that Ellen was not necessarily dead, but her whereabouts were still a great mystery. In a further attempt to solve it, Ben Terry joined forces with Kate's husband, Arthur J. Lewis, who sent an urgent telegram to the Terrys' friend Tom Taylor, begging him to help them in the search. Taylor's involvement in the case was recently made known through the discovery of two letters from his loving wife, Laura, who was doubly upset, first by the disappearance of "Nell," then by having her husband summoned just as the family was enjoying a brief vacation in the country. Neither letter is dated but they were doubtless sent in mid-October 1868. The first letter was probably mailed the day after her husband had hurried off to join Lewis. Lewis's letter to Taylor, which Mrs. Taylor felt she should open, was probably a follow-up after Lewis's wire.

Tuesday
(Rainy melancholy day)

My own dearest,

We have all been full of anxiety for you ever since you left and I long to hear from you of your safe arrival and that the great anxiety for poor dear N. is partly relieved. I opened A.J.L.'s letter this morning as I felt sure you would wish me to do so, but the contents, though kind, have not conduced in *any way* to set our minds at ease. The whole thing still remains a mystery and a most painful one. It is still so difficult to conjecture why *your* immediate presence was necessary? I live in hopes of your letter tomorrow which will cheer and comfort me and tell me of your future intentions. I hardly dare hope for your coming back here. . . .

After some random comments about cold pigeon pie, a chimney sweep, fog, and rent due on The Castle, she adds, "Give my love and sympathy to Kate and also to the family, especially the poor mother who is doubtless in great distress."

The next day Mrs. Taylor received a letter from Tom that cleared up most of the mystery. Although she was relieved enough that Ellen was alive and well with Godwin, she was angry that her husband had been roped into the affair.

Wednesday

My own dearest,

Many thanks for your letter just received which I had so anxiously expected. The solution to the mystery is *most uninteresting,* and I must think in no way justified the telegram. . . . I think it wrong of them to put your name in any way in connection with this unworthy affair, in which the father and brother-in-law were surely the proper and sufficient agents. . . . I feel truly sorry that you ended in making so unnecessary a sacrifice of all our plans and pleasures.

As to Nelly, I feel more sorry than surprised, though I should not have expected that she would have shown her vice in so hard and uninteresting a way. Her foolish talk of drowning herself etc. I can well understand but I can scarcely forgive the melodramatic act of sticking the "found drowned" in the corner of Watts' photograph. She has been left sadly too much to herself latterly and has doubtless felt reckless and forlorn. . . . I cannot help feeling angry that instead of enjoying yourself on the Cheviots you should be sent about the country making disagreeable enquiries with a detective! The episode of the dead body is most curious and we must feel much for poor Mr. Terry on the occasion. *Surely that was the proper duty of* Mr. Lewis. Before quitting this painful and disagreeable subject let me ask why *you* were supposed to be able to let any light upon it? Why we never once thought of Mr. Godwin! Certainly I did not— . . .

Mrs. Taylor's surprise that Ellen was involved with Godwin is noteworthy. It seems to invalidate the old rumor that Ellen was seriously involved with him at the period of her separation from Watts, for if there had been such a liaison at that time, or since, it is likely that her friends would have sought out Godwin at least on the chance that he knew something about her disappearance. It is possible, of course, that she had been seeing Godwin in the months before they decamped. But if so, it was not common knowledge.

Ellen never recounted the efforts of her father, Arthur Lewis, and Tom Taylor, not to mention the detective, to track her down. But she did write that when news "came to her" that she had been found dead, "I flew up to London to give ocular proof that I was still alive."

There is no denying that Ellen managed her disappearance heartlessly, probably, as Mrs. Taylor suggested, because she felt "reckless and forlorn." But in justice to Ellen, it should be remembered that what she was trying to do was extremely difficult. She wanted to live a new life, illicitly and illegally, as Mrs. Godwin. Had they known about it, her family, from her sisters in school to Kate and Arthur Lewis starting their respectable married life at Moray Lodge, would have felt disgraced. Ellen hoped to live decently as Mrs. Godwin in the hamlet where she settled. But if her family and friends saw fit to visit her there, they might inadvertently spill the beans and brand her "as living in sin." Then there was the problem of Watts's payments to Ellen "as long as she shall remain chaste." Did she imagine he might continue to send the money to Stanhope Street? Would he give her a divorce? The complexity of the whole situation was more than she could cope with. Her strongest impulse was to bolt. If she had stopped to argue and justify herself she might have lost her nerve. And nerve was what she most needed. The essential fact is that Ellen Terry at twenty-one had the courage to take her life in her own hands and shift its course daringly.

Years later, to her favorite grandson, Edward Craig, Ellen told of the first cottage where she lived with Godwin. Rented from a local family, the Gibsons, "it was called the Red House, though some called it The Firs because of a couple of trees in the garden. It had a hall and two rooms with bay windows downstairs, a kitchen and a bakehouse in the back, and two rooms and a hall upstairs."

She described how Edward Godwin put his individual stamp on the tiny dwelling, protesting against the usual Victorian somberness by making the interior as light and airy as a Japanese print. "The walls were painted pale yellow and the woodwork white; the furniture, designed by Edward, was slender and black."

Behind the garden over the field was a hamlet named Mackery End. Behind that, a mile or so, was Wheathampstead, where cows and geese grazed on the village common, tended by youngsters in white overalls.

Since Godwin was often away for several days at a time, surveying sites and talking to clients, Ellen managed the household. She hired a little maid-of-all-work for five pounds a year, but she kept tabs on everything, or tried to. She and Godwin got up at six. He either worked at home or took the morning train to London. Ellen scrubbed and fed the pony that drew Edward's trap to the station, tended the garden, and went to market. The household included a bulldog for protection, a parrot for repartee, an unruly goat, a lazy monkey who liked to snooze on Ellen's foot by the fire, and, at one time, more than two hundred chickens and ducks.

At night, the little cottage looked like an atelier. Ellen learned to help Edward with his drawings. She was a neat copyist and could skillfully brush in watercolors over his ink or pencil renderings. They made a big project of reading each of Shakespeare's plays aloud together, and jotted down their ideas about settings, costumes, and other production matters, all of which benefited Godwin when he came to write his articles, *Architecture and Costume of Shakespeare Plays*. The play reading carried Ellen back five years to Bristol, when she had first read *A Midsummer Night's Dream* with Godwin in his house. They had simply picked up where they left off. Ellen saw almost nobody ex-

75

cept Godwin. Sometimes he brought his associate, William Burges, to the cottage to help him work. Burges was a humorous, open fellow, and Ellen enjoyed having him visit. She helped both men with their drawings.

It is hard to imagine how two people could be more useful to each other than Ellen and Godwin were at this stage of their lives. Godwin enabled her to rusticate under the only circumstances that would have been acceptable to her. She would never have been content with a common-or-garden country gentleman any more than a common-or-garden country gentleman would have been content with her. Godwin, steeped in the arts and theater, eased her exile from London, and, from his trips to the city, he kept her posted on news and gossip of the world she knew best. Thanks again to Godwin, Ellen could enjoy her long rural entr'acte on her own terms.

In summing up her life, Ellen left no doubt that Edward Godwin was her greatest love. Without him, she might never have known a prolonged physical love or become a mother. After marriage with Watts, Godwin was a welcome change, a confident and practiced lover. He had no wish to save her soul or keep her on display as an entrancing child model. He needed her to be a woman, a hardworking woman. He bruised her at times with his lack of consideration, but he never blighted her with gentle condescension. Being himself a rebel, he approved of Ellen's innate nonconformity. This was heady medicine for Ellen. For the first time she was being approved wholly for herself, not for the other women she impersonated.

Godwin reassured her on still another score. He represented the world of art from which Ellen had been ousted by Watts. If anything, Godwin was the more deeply cultured man. He not only specialized in Shakespeare but was also an authority on Chaucer and Dryden. His researches into architecture and archaeology gave him a formidable store of learning. Ellen's lover was her academy.

Godwin kept many irons in the fire. Primarily an architect, he also designed furniture, wallpaper, textiles, and tiles and wrote extensively for various learned journals. He urged better schools for young architects and better opportunities for them in business. Women, he held, should be employed by architectural firms; and actors should not be subjected to filthy dressing rooms and backstage squalor. In his range of talents and interests, Godwin invites comparison with the painter-craftsman William Morris, who was a year younger. Both men were enemies of machine-made gimcrackery, both were admirers of the Middle Ages, and both believed that an architect should have control over all elements in designing a building, including furniture and carpets and textiles. Godwin's furniture was less bulky than Morris's. "I don't like to eat dinner," said Godwin, "in a chair suited to Edward the Confessor." Morris had an independent income to subsidize his ventures. Godwin had to scramble for cash.

One of Godwin's closest friends was James McNeill Whistler, whom he met in London galleries and clubs, whose paintings he defended, and whose love of Japanese art he shared. He also seemed to share Whistler's lordly, cavalier attitude about debts and business contracts. When Godwin's seven-year partnership with Henry Crisp ran its course and was dissolved, there were puzzling questions about financial obligations and about two leaky Irish castles that the firm had built. Not that Godwin could be blamed for the leaks; but he appeared to say, "Let 'em leak and be damned." In Godwin's behavior there was a growing indifference to leaving people in the lurch.

At the end of the day, when Godwin had been away on business, Ellen looked forward, like any modern commuter's wife, to picking him up at the station. She squinted to see the little locomotive's approaching lantern. As it grew bigger and brighter, she welcomed the crescendo of wheel music. But when the train stopped, and no Godwin got off— Of course, he must have missed the last train, or been detained. It had happened before. After all, how could he let her know? No phones. No nearby telegraph office.

On the lonely ride home, she drove beside a dark woods. Suddenly, out of the gloom an oafish man lunged toward the pony cart. With one leap he was in the cart, squeezing beside her. From his foul breath she knew he was drunk. Gripping her whip, she walloped him on the head. He toppled from the cart, and her pony dashed ahead. She never saw the intruder again, yet she could not forget the lonely fright, and the irrational feeling that Godwin had deserted her at a time of danger.

Ellen seldom left her country retreat to visit her family on Stanhope Street. But on April 6, 1869, the Reverend Mr. Dodgson wrote in his diary, "I also visited the Terrys and had a long chat with Mrs. Terry; Mrs. Watts is still staying in lodgings, but had called at the house that day." Presumably, "lodgings" was Sarah's way of covering up Ellen's residency with Godwin. Had Ellen come home for a short visit to announce the possibility that she was pregnant? Her first child was born eight months later, on a snowy December 9.

Godwin was away. When the pains began, Ellen and her servant girl pulled a mattress downstairs in front of the living room fire. Then the girl ran off to bring the neighbors, Dr. Rumball and his wife. It was unfortunate that Godwin could not help. Perhaps the baby arrived a bit off schedule. And Godwin did know that Ellen had good help close at hand. As if to console his first child for her illegitimacy, he named her Edith after Eadgyth, daughter of Godwin, Earl of the West Saxons.

Two years later, Ellen had another child, later known as Edward Gordon Craig. Like his sister the boy was never baptized, though when his father registered the birth locally—January 16, 1872—he made a teasing reference to Ellen's legal husband by writing her name as "Eleanor Alice Godwin, formerly Watkins."

Having enlarged his family, Godwin designed a larger

house, which he built on a twenty-acre plot at nearby Harpenden. The house sat on a hill only a few steps from the little railway station, making commuting much easier for everybody. Even before the house was built, Godwin sketched a diagram of the garden, and Ellen planted it. Potatoes dominated, supplemented by carrots, beans, parsnips, celery, rhubarb, greens, cabbages, and beets, along with four clumps of sunflowers. The house, with its high pitched roofs, gables, and tall chimneys, had a sturdy medieval look. Godwin put in an organ, which he loved to play. Bach became Ellen's favorite composer.

The new house helped to reassure Ellen that the liaison was permanent, and now she asked for little else. "If it is the mark of the artist," she tells us in her *Memoirs*, "to love art before everything, to renounce everything for its sake, to think all the sweet human things of life well lost if only he may attain something, do some good, great work—then I never was an artist. I admire those impersonal people who care for nothing outside their own ambition, yet I detest them at the same time, and I have the simplest faith that absolute devotion to another human being means the greatest *happiness*. . . .''

After the death of Dr. Rumball, his widow became an invaluable member of Ellen's household. Young Teddy named her "Boo." Boo had helped her husband run an asylum in the neighborhood. But when she had to take full charge of the lunatics, according to Ellen, "they kept escaping, and people didn't like it. This was my gain, for Boo came to look after me instead, and for the next thirty years, I was her only lunatic and she was my most constant companion and dear and loyal friend."

Ellen's offspring had few playmates. By the time Teddy was born, Kate had already had three of her four children, all girls. But, however broad-minded Kate and her husband felt in private, they could not jeopardize the social status of their own brood by inviting their little bastard cousins to their games and parties. Growing up in comparative isolation, Ellen's two children could hardly be run-of-the-mill. Edy was cool and bossy. She loved her baby brother, a pudgy sybarite addicted to puddings. But when Edy saw him misbehaving, she banged him on the head with a wooden spoon. When he confessed one day that he was afraid of the dark, Edy told him to buck up and "be a *woman*." Edy had need to be a tyrant. She was born to compete with two of the most all-conquering charmers in the British Empire, her mother and her brother; so, unable to hold her own with blandishments, what could she do but use a wooden spoon?

Determined that his children should grow up with sound artistic values, Godwin let them play only with simple wooden toys. When Edy was given a mechanical, windup toy that ravished her, Godwin snatched it away. Later, when she received an ordinary girl doll dressed in gaudy pink, she flung it aside with "How vulgar." Both the children honored the new aestheticism by wearing little Japanese kimonos given to them by Whistler.

At her first circus, Edy saw a clown walk a tightrope and, after pretending to lose his balance, tumble to the ground with a bang of a drum. Horrified, Edy rebuked her mother: "Take me away! You ought never to have brought me here." But when the children were taken to see a Japanese juggler, no complaints were voiced. Anything Japanese was permissible.

After settling in the new house, Ellen and Godwin took a trip to Normandy. For Ellen, freed of domestic worries, it was a blissful vacation, a honeymoon. The baby stayed home with Boo, but Edy came along. As they traveled and explored together, bound by common interests and by being strangers in a foreign land, there was nothing to remind Ellen that she was not really Mrs. Edward Godwin. To satisfy Godwin's craving for Gothic architecture, they visited Lisieux, Mantes, and Bayeux. Godwin sketched in little pocket notebooks, capturing details that he could incorporate later in buildings, textiles, and furnishings. These exquisitely precise little drawings, as much as anything he ever did, reveal his immaculate artistry. Watching over his shoulder and seeing through his eyes, Ellen followed him up into belfries and down into crypts. Edy followed, too, when she felt like it. Once, Edy preferred to sit alone in a church pew, listening to a choir practice. When they came to pick her up, she greeted them like a small saint, "Shhh, Miss Edy has seen the angels."

Years later, Ellen said that whenever she was playing a role and felt "hard as sandpaper," she could make herself feel "soft and melted" by recalling the sublime music that she heard with Godwin in the French cathedrals. One of her strengths as an actress was that she did not waste her memories, but kept them ready to be called forth and put to work for her.

Upon returning home, the travelers were confronted by piles of bills for the new house and, worse, by the bailiff who camped on the premises until Godwin arranged to pay up.

Ellen took the first decisive step to meet this crisis after a trifling accident that may have determined her whole future. One morning while she was driving her pony cart in a narrow lane, a wheel fell off. Just as she got out to survey the damage, a hunter on horseback bounded over a nearby hedge like a rescuing angel in a pink coat. "Good God," the angel cried, "it's Nelly. Where have you been all these years?" It was her old friend Charles Reade, who, the story goes, just happened to be hunting in the neighborhood at this crucial time.

"I've been having a very happy time," Ellen replied.

"Well, you've had it long enough," Reade answered in a bit of dialogue breezy enough for one of his own plays. "Come back to the stage!"

"Never," cried the heroine.

"You're a fool," parried Reade.

Then Ellen remembered the bailiff and the bills and the chance she now had to help Godwin. Recklessly, she agreed to come back to the theater for forty pounds a week, a higher salary than she had ever earned. She half-believed, and half-hoped, that her demand would be turned down.

Reade thought quickly. He had a new play running, *The Wandering Heir,* based on the notorious Tichborne claimant's case, involving the lost heir to a vast family fortune. Its London run was endangered because the star, Mrs. John Woods, had to leave for another engagement, so Reade needed a replacement who would excite public interest. Ellen filled the bill perfectly. He agreed to her salary demand.

One cannot help suspecting, without a shred of evidence, that Reade might have sought out Ellen deliberately. Perhaps they arranged for the meeting, and invented the cart tale to use later as picturesque publicity or to allay any rumor that Ellen was so worried about Godwin's finances that she was looking for a way to help him out. In any case, Reade issued a teasing report that "an eminent actress" was coming out of retirement to grace his play, which was fair enough, although Ellen's real eminence was still ahead.

Sensibly, Godwin seemed to support Ellen's decision. It would mean a new, more complicated mode of family life, but the advantages were obvious. After signing up with Reade, Ellen was no longer the lonely stay-at-home, waiting for her man on the evening train. The sudden change was reflected instantly in the few random notes written by Godwin in his "Rough Diary and Scribbling Journal," which he always carried in his pocket. Hardly more than shorthand, they suggest glimpses of Ellen and Godwin going to London together, Godwin visiting the manufacturer (Collenson and Lock) who commissioned his furniture designs, and, at the end of a day, Godwin jotting down what bills he paid and how he spent every shilling. On the day of the first entry, little Teddy was two. Ellen, of course, was "mother."

Jan 16, Fri.   Ted's birthday . . . paid Williams coal 6.16
Jan 20, Tues. To town with mother
Jan 27, Tues. To London very early from St. Alban. Left trap at Station Hotel. At office most of day.
Jan 28, Wed.   To London with mother by 4:6 train. To office, then to Simpson and then to C. Reades, left there with mother at 10:30.
Jan 31, Sat.   To London with mother, dinner at office.
Feb 2, Mon.   Housekeeper, 3.96. Valentine and ink, 5.9.
Feb 4, Wed.   To London. Took mother to Mott's Hotel. gave her cab 5/ Refresh at Temple Club /4. Opera comique. Bad night.
Feb 11, Wed.   To Japanese warehouse. Evening to Queens [theater] with mother.
Feb 12, Thur. Office to Japanese warehouse, dinner at office with mother and Floss. Bought 2 chests of drawers & center table & cream. 2 side tables and 1 sideboard, 25, 10, 0.

With Ellen returning to the stage, a home in London was needed. While keeping the country place, mainly for the children, Godwin rented a house in Taviton Street. Probably his purchases at the Japanese warehouse helped furnish it. The cryptic "bad night" on February 4 might have referred to a poor performance at the Opéra Comique or to Godwin's poor health or to almost anything else. The mention of Ellen's sister Flossie, who was nineteen at the time, suggests that Ellen was on friendly terms with her family.

Feb 21, Sat.   Edy and Mrs. Rumball came to town.
Feb 22, Sun.   Dull day, stayed at home, C. Reade called.
Feb 23, Mon.   Saw Edy and Mrs. R. off by train. Ill.
Feb 28, Sat.   (W.H. opens) Mrs. Rumball came up.
Mar 9, Mon.   Stayed late to see *Rachel the Reaper*.
Mar 24, Tue.   Office in evening—very ill.
Mar 25, Wed.   To office. Gave mother for pocket money 1 pound. Design for cottage, Easy chair, C. & L [Collenson and Lock]
Mar 29, Sun.   Called on Reade, left card, not in.

Mar 30, Mon.　To office morning, C & L called gave me accept. at 3 months retainer, and paid for designs to this date, 37, 10, 7; a check paid into bank, and home. Ill with cold.

Several entries raise tantalizing questions. Was Ellen handing over her salary to Godwin, who doled it out to her as "pocket money"? Was there any special reason that Godwin was calling on Reade, who was Ellen's manager and patron? Was Godwin trying to arrange for advance payments on her salary? It is known that Godwin and Reade disliked each other.

That Godwin made no comment on Ellen's opening in "W.H." (*The Wandering Heir*) is not significant. His diary was merely a record of facts and figures. But in Ellen's own words, the play was "a tremendous success . . . and the newspapers were more than flattering." Her friends welcomed her, she said, "as if it were six minutes not six years" since she had disappeared from their world.

Outside the theater, Ellen was still very much a social outcast. The Reverend Charles Dodgson, who saw the play a little later, did not go back to the stage door to express his good wishes in person. Only to the safety of his diary did he dare confide that her performance was "simply wonderful."

Ellen Terry,
shortly after her marriage,
was photographed by Julia Cameron
in Tennyson's bathroom. *Left: at nine, she
acted with Charles Kean in* The Winter's
Tale. *Below: While acting Puck, Ellen rose on
a stage lift such as this and broke her toe.*

In Choosing, one of George Frederick Watts's many paintings of his wife, Ellen whiffs a camellia. Of all the portraits ever done of her, this one was Ellen's favorite.

Fanciful photography abounded in Victorian times. Below left: Watts posed with unidentified children for Julia Cameron's Whisper of the Muse. Right: In a faked picture, Kate Terry sits by a mirror, which "reflects" sister, Ellen.

Both Terry sisters married into delightful houses. Above: Kate in the 1860s sits beside her new husband at Moray Lodge, with servants in attendance. Below: Nearby was Little Holland House where Ellen lived less happily with G. F. Watts.

This unusual candid picture taken by Lewis Carroll in 1865 catches Ellen's sadness after her marriage fiasco. Now she signs herself "Ellen Alice Watts."

Left: Tom Taylor, also photographed by Carroll, was a busy dramatist, critic, and eventually editor of Punch. A friend of the Terrys, he helped arrange Ellen's marriage to Watts.

Lewis Carroll recruited eight Terrys, after much fussing, for this family portrait taken in 1865 on a balcony outside their London house on Stanhope Street. At left, Father Ben is snuggled by little Tom and Flossie. Ellen (in black) stands in the doorway by Kate, who is resting her hand on Charlie's shoulder. Polly stands next to her mother, who is privileged to sit. Three other Terry offspring are absent: the baby, Fred; George; and Ben, Jr.

The Queen's Theatre, with typical benches on the lower floor, was a landmark in Ellen's life. She was playing here when she decamped with Edward Godwin in 1868, and five years later she resumed her career here.

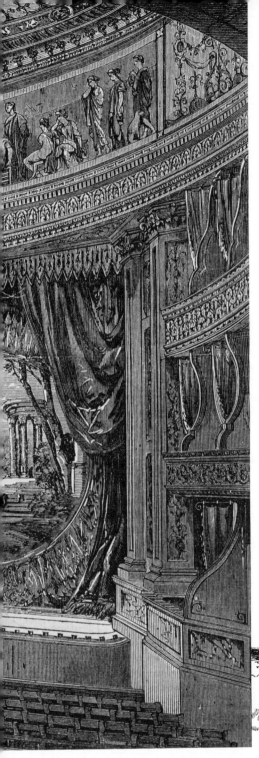

Edward William Godwin, an esteemed architect and a widower, became Ellen's lover and was the father of her two children. She lived a quiet country life with him in a village near London, certain she had left the stage forever.

As Portia in The Merchant of Venice in 1875 (inset above), Ellen had her first serious triumph.

Godwin built this romantic house for Ellen, and they lived there until she returned to the stage.

In Olivia (1878), her first big hit, Ellen sits on the floor for a cast picture while managing her children, pouting Teddy, and Edy with buttons and bangs. They were in the play briefly.

Chapter Four

"THE MIGHTY WING OF GLORY"

Once he had enticed Ellen back to the theater, Charles Reade was not about to let her escape soon. After *The Wandering Heir* had run its course at the Queen's, Reade, who was willing to try almost anything, installed it at Astley's across the Thames, where the pit was often converted into a circus ring and the smell of horses lingered. Then he patched together a road tour, adding two more of his own plays to *The Wandering Heir,* thus making an all-Reade repertory, with Ellen acting in all three. Included in the lot was *Our Seamen,* a warmed-over melodrama once called *The Scuttled Ship,* in which Reade himself took an active part in the stage effects, standing in the wings flapping a piece of dusty blue canvas over the floor to simulate billowing waves. Ellen thought it was "rather pathetic to see a man of his intellectual power and originality working the stage sea at nights." She was wrong. With Reade it was dignity be damned. While conducting a rehearsal, he stopped actors to show them how to fight, make love, or dance a hornpipe, and it probably pleased him hugely, being a mover and shaker himself, to agitate the ocean.

Reade was a dominant figure in every sense. Over six feet tall, athletic and tireless, he wore strikingly wide-brimmed hats, a great blue jacket with brass buttons, and his trouser legs were reportedly a yard wide. He was a giant, with a fussbudget streak. Since he was thirty-three years older than Ellen, it was natural for her to call him "Daddy." Among her private papers, found after her death, was a little list of "best friends." George Bernard Shaw came second. At the top was Charles Reade.

Reade's work today has fallen into oblivion, although a few people know his once-famous novel *The Cloister and the Hearth*. Yet he was a gloriously helter-skelter Victorian who wrote a dozen novels and some thirty plays (often with help from his friends). Continually revamping his old works, he turned his books into shows, or vice versa, like a woman remodeling her old hats. Also an impassioned reformer, he published tracts and pamphlets on prison abuses, evil factory conditions, coffin ships, the mistreatment of lunatics, or anything else that roused his ire. He wrote for a dozen periodicals, his outlets in America being mainly *Harper's Weekly* and *The Atlantic Monthly*. His admirers have included the young Henry James, Algernon Swinburne, and, more recently, George Orwell. Besides his fervor for the theater, Reade had a taste for music. He played the fiddle ably and wrote several scholarly articles on Cremona violins. At Tom Taylor's Sunday afternoon parties he loved to sing *The Girl I Left Behind Me*, bursting into sobs at his own pathos.

Well born and duly educated at Oxford, Reade in his twenties entered into a sort of marriage bond (an oath before witnesses) with a Scots fishwife, had by her a son, and saw her intermittently until, when he was thirty-four, the woman died. That was his closest brush with wedlock, although for the rest of his life Reade was actress-prone. He wrote two plays in praise of celebrated actresses, Peg Woffington and Nance Oldfield, and was so beguiled by the talented Mrs. Stirling—years later she played the nurse to Ellen Terry's Juliet—that he invited her to visit him for a week at Oxford where he found time to officiate, fitfully, as vice president of Magdalen College. When his mother heard what was going on, she called for her carriage, stormed over to Oxford, and surprised the couple at lunch in Reade's quarters. Mrs. Stirling made a prompt and good-humored exit.

Reade's major actress liaison was with a widow, Laura Seymour. For twenty-five years she presided over his house, sometimes served as manager of his plays, and acted in them. Even the most worldly observers believed that this devoted couple had no sexual relations. Many respectable souls came to their home, including Ellen's mother, who would have shied away had they gotten a whiff of any sin.

It was said that Reade favored actresses who were useful to him, and that he resurrected Ellen Terry as a smart investment. Reade would have admitted it happily. Both he and Ellen were firm believers in usefulness. But it is likely that Ellen had a further appeal to her "Daddy." Each in his or her own way was a rebel against conformity. Each was a maverick who struck out for his or her own idea of freedom. So in helping advance Ellen's career, along with his own, Reade was loyal to his own credo. They were birds of similar plumage.

Reade joined the long string of tutors devoted to Bringing Up Ellen. In the practice of her art, she had been coached or cuffed first by her father, then by Mrs. Charles Kean, Mr. Chute in Bristol, Madame de Rhona with her python, Mrs. Wigan, and still others. But of them all, Reade benefited—and probably maddened—her the most. Like a judge, he sat in a box during her performances, jotting notes on her mistakes and facing her with them after the show. Painful as the notes sometimes were, she saved them for years and quoted them amply in her *Memoirs*.

First he praised whatever he thought was praiseworthy: "her womanly grace, delicacy, subtlety, the variety yet invariable truthfulness of the facial expression. . . ." Then he let the ax fall, berating her, say, for her laziness: "You have limp, limp, limp business, and, in Act III, limp exits—instead of ardent exits. . . . The swift rush of words, the personal rush, should carry you off the stage. It is, in reality, as easy as shelling peas."

Reade hammered at her about tempo. "You don't seem

to realize that uniformity of pace leads to languor." He warned her not to "blur" the impact of a line by speaking during a certain bit of stage business. "Do the business, then speak the line *afterwards*." Nothing was too small to escape Reade's nagging. He even told her where to pause in a six-word line: "Now, James (PAUSE), for England and Liberty!"

Thanks to Reade's faultfinding, Ellen paid increasing attention to the details of her acting, even though it still gave the impression of being undisciplined. The stock complaint against Ellen Terry, made even by her son, was that she could only act herself, which unfairly suggested that she was not acting at all. But in truth the image she projected to her audience was a result of arduous practice and carefully controlled technique. It looked natural precisely because it was not.

To be sure, like most other actresses, Ellen could not play an unlimited range of roles. Heaven forbid that she should have tackled, for example, the murderous Medea. But still she could spread her talents over a wide territory, from Ophelia to Portia to the hoydenish French laundress Madame Sans-Gêne. In her later years, when Bernard Shaw undertook to advise her on playing certain roles, he took for granted that she was an actress of exceptional resources and could create any effect she wanted to. The notion that Ellen owed her fame merely to her charm, to not acting at all, is preposterous.

Some of Charles Reade's advice, Ellen felt, was old-fashioned, reflecting a style of acting that was growing outmoded. Ahead of her time, by instinct she acted with less pomp and flourish than tradition dictated. Yet even when she differed with Reade, she prized his criticism because it jolted her into thinking for herself.

At times, Reade disliked his protégée. "Soft and yielding on the surface," he wrote in his notebook, "egotistical below . . . always wanting something 'dreadful bad' today, which she does not want tomorrow. . . . Hysterical, sentimental, hard as a nail in money matters. . . ."

In a later footnote to this comment, he dipped his pen in a different color of ink and changed his tune. "This was written when she was under the influence of—[probably Godwin]. Since then, greatly improved: the hardness below is melting away. In good hands a very amiable creature but dangerous to the young. Downright fascinating. Even I, who could look coldly on from the senile heights, am delighted by her. . . ."

Reade, like many of Ellen's admirers, puzzled over her beauty which seemed mysteriously greater than the sum of its parts. "Ellen Terry is an enigma. Her eyes are pale, her nose rather long, her mouth nothing in particular. Complexion a delicate brickdust, her hair rather like tow. . . . Her figure is lean and boney, her hand masculine in size and form." Then he labeled her "intelligent, weak . . . abominable and charming . . . " and ended up like a doting father by calling her "Little Duck." At other times she was "artful toad" and "nincompoop."

In turn, Ellen had her innings: "Dear, kind, unjust, generous, cautious, impulsive, passionate, gentle Charles Reade . . . a stupid old dear, and as wise as Solomon! He seemed guileless, and yet had moments of suspicion and craftiness worthy of the wisdom of the serpent." Between them, this sort of affectionate raillery went on for years, as if they were a music hall team peppering each other with insults.

During Reade's three-play tour, which was doing badly, Ellen suggested that since he could ill afford her salary, now reduced to twenty-five pounds a week, he might better hire a cheaper actress. Reade exploded with mock wrath: "Madam, you are a rat. You are deserting the sinking ship!"

This was too much for Ellen's protector, Boo. "How dare you say such things to my Nelly?"

"Your Nelly," snorted Reade. "I love her a thousand times more than you do, or any puling woman." Ellen stuck out the tour.

Ellen's success as an actress—in the London run of *The Wandering Heir* she earned five hundred pounds—inevitably overshadowed her home life with Godwin. Although they kept the country house at Harpenden, where the children spent most of the time with Boo, the flat at Taviton Street was the main base, and the family shuttled between the two households. At best it was an unsettling arrangement for them all, certainly not what Godwin had anticipated when he rescued Ellen from despair and carried her into retirement. Now their roles were almost reversed. Ellen was the rescuer, helping to pay off debts, contributing largely to family expenses, and also dutifully handing over her money to Godwin as a Victorian wife was expected to do. It was an uncomfortable situation, and they both felt trapped by it.

Now, at twenty-seven, Ellen was blooming. Motherhood and country living with the man she loved had endowed her with new assurance and beauty. Her cordial reception in the theater had helped, too. As an unwed mother, to be sure, she was still beyond the pale in a certain society, but that worried her only insofar as it troubled her family and jeopardized her children. Within herself, she had started the transition from person to personage.

A new recruit to Reade's tour, Johnston Forbes-Robertson, gives a glimpse of Ellen in her home. Reade had arranged for this handsome youth of twenty-one, who became one of London's greatest romantic actors and Ellen's lifelong friend, to call at Taviton Street before the tour and introduce himself to his leading lady. Besides being an actor, he was an art student at the Royal Academy, so when a servant let him into the drawing room, he took in the Godwin-style decor with a painter's eye. "The floor was covered with straw-colored matting, and there was a dado of the same material," he observed. "Above the dado were white walls, and the hangings were of cretonne, with a fine Japanese pattern in delicate grey-blue. The chairs were of wicker with cushions like the hangings, and in the center of the room was a cast of the Venus of Milo, before which was a small pedestal holding a little censer from which rose, curling around the Venus, ribbons of blue smoke. The whole effect was what art students of my time would have called 'awfully jolly.'

"Presently the door opened, and in floated a vision of loveliness! In the blue kimono and that wonderful golden hair, she seemed to melt into the surroundings and appeared almost intangible. This was my first sight of Miss Terry. I was undergoing a sort of inspection, but her manner was so gracious that it soon cleared away my embarrassment. I was afterwards shown Master Gordon Craig in his cradle and Miss Craig, a lively little girl, black-haired, with great enquiring eyes."

While Ellen was on tour, Godwin's work in London was absorbing but not remunerative. He was appointed an adviser to a group of architects and continued to write articles for specialized periodicals, while adding to his ambitious series on the *Architecture and Costume of Shakespeare Plays.* For a new progressive magazine called *Women and Work,* Godwin wrote on new jobs for women in architects' offices and backed it up by hiring a plump, jovial art student, Beatrice Phillips, as his own office apprentice. Her father being a noted London sculptor, John Beirnie Phillips, the girl fitted cozily into the bohemian art world and at twenty-one had a pleasing gift for hero worship.

Also in this year of 1874, Godwin was hobnobbing with his American painter friend, James McNeill Whistler, who had recently exhibited his *Arrangement in Black and Gray,* eventually to be known all over America as *Whistler's Mother.* The two friends shared not only similar tastes in art, but similar character traits as well. Each had an insolent tilt to his head, a dash of the dandy, and each flaunted his self-sufficiency like a banner, although within them both was probably a chilly area where arrogance bordered on loneliness. Both of them, moreover, had illegitimate offspring to whom they paid scant attention, and both of them, successively, married the same woman.

During Ellen's absence, Godwin was beset by another wave of bailiffs at Taviton Street. But unlike Whistler, who was a genius at flicking them aside, Godwin could not prevent their carrying off most of the furniture. Back to a nearly bare house after a hard tour, Ellen found Godwin so nervous and dyspeptic that he promptly set off to visit a friend on the Isle of Wight, instructing Ellen to open all his letters and not to forward anything that might disturb him.

The currents that were sweeping Ellen and Godwin apart gained strength with the arrival one day of a pretty little woman at Taviton Street, expressly to see Ellen. Mrs. Bancroft had come by carriage from her home in Berkeley Square. Once known to playgoers as Marie Wilton, she and her husband now managed the fashionable little Prince of Wales' Theatre and had introduced a new style of entertainment, called "cup-and-saucer" drama: civilized plays for civilized people to see, set in real rooms with real doors with real doorknobs. (The advent of the doorknob, as a symbol of solid realism, did much to domesticate but not to improve European theater.)

Ellen was awed by Mrs. Bancroft, standing in the doorway in her chic black dress—Ellen called it "Parisian black." In ludicrous contrast, she herself was wearing a loose "aesthetic" garment, mottled with brown spots, which Edy, with no intent to flatter, called "the frog lady's dress."

"May I come in?" asked the caller, gazing around the room which had been stripped almost empty. Her eyes rested on the bare-breasted Venus, whom the bailiffs had evidently rejected, and she lifted her hands in stagey horror and cried, "Dear me." Then both women laughed and felt at home together.

Mrs. Bancroft hurried to the point. She and her husband had decided to deviate from their "cup-and-saucer" dramas and present *The Merchant of Venice,* with Ellen as Portia and a popular actor, Charles Coghlan, as Shylock. Would Ellen agree to—?

After receiving the quickest yes in the history of human assent, Mrs. Bancroft went on to ask if she thought Godwin might like to supervise the scenery and costume. Ellen knew he would; she could hardly wait to ask him.

When he returned from the Isle of Wight, Godwin accepted the job and began a glorious rummage through the paintings of Titian and Veronese, picking up ideas for costumes and decorative details, even down to the carving on knife handles. Seven solid settings were designed and built to promote the flow of pageantry through courtroom, palace, and narrow Venetian streets.

Ellen had reason to hope that working with Godwin on a joint enterprise might salvage their partnership. They had been drawn closer together, she recalled, when she had helped with his architectural drawings or explored Shakespearean texts, and she would never forget their happy trip to France when, side by side, they absorbed the wonders of medieval art.

But now the magic of shared enthusiasm no longer worked. During the preparation of *The Merchant of Venice,* the couple seemed to be swept still farther apart. Was Godwin jealous of Ellen's growing stature in her profession? Feeling unsure of himself, was he irritated by the obsessive shop talk of the theater, the fuss and rush of rehearsals, sulky because Ellen, even more than during her months with Reade, was neglecting wifely duties? He approved of women's emancipation, but was he ready for so much emancipation around the house? Two powerful egos were in conflict, and Ellen's was cresting. Quarrels were inevitable, and one day, according to rumor, Godwin left the house "in a towering rage," never to return.

Friends surmised that each one might have accused

the other of seeking outside companionship. But it is unlikely that they limited themselves to any single accusation. Ellen, writing later about the breakup, simply said: "He loved me, and I loved him, and that, I suppose, is the reason we so cruelly hurt each other. He went away and shut the door after him. . . ." They had been living together for nearly seven years.

A few weeks later Ellen packed up her few belongings and moved with Boo and the two children to rooms at 221 Camden Road. To support her little ménage, she had to pinch pennies. She took the horse-drawn omnibus to rehearse in the theater.

That Godwin had afterthoughts about his departure is indicated in a recently discovered letter that Ellen wrote from Camden Road to a mutual friend, Mr. Wilson, dated "before March 6th."

Dear Mr. Wilson. In all gentleness and kindness of feeling, I must beg you not to act as a mediator between Mr. Godwin and myself. Our separation was a thing agreed upon by both of us many weeks before it actually took place. The first steps were taken by him and I am certainly much astonished to hear that he professes any strong feelings in the matter. Part of our compact was that we should always maintain a kindly, friendly relation to one another. He has since last Tuesday made this an *IMPOSSIBILITY*. He tried by unfair means to get my little girl away from me (I had offered to let him have the boy) and I now distinctly refuse to hold any communication with him whatsoever.

I do feel sorry that he is ill—Glad that he has some good friends—may he CONTINUE to appreciate them through his lifetime. I thank you for many kindnesses you have shown me and my children, but I thank you still more for the fact that you are Mr. Godwin's friend now. . . .

If Mr. Godwin's friends knew his temperament as I do and the effects of change upon him, they would advise his leaving London and staying with *friends,* for a time at least. He should not go alone as he is apt to brood and imagine all kinds of things that do not exist. You say in your letter, I really fear for his reason. When I knew him in his home life 13 years ago I had the same idea, and at that time he had an *utterly sorrowless* life—a devoted helpmate—success—friends—*everything*. He never was happy—he never will be. If you choose to show him this letter I will find no objection. At the risk of being called utterly heartless I again say I will hold no further communication with Mr. Godwin, and I also say that this hard behavior on my part has been brought about entirely by his own rash conduct since the last time we were together at Taviton Street.

I apologize for taking up your time with this lengthy letter and remain sorrowfully yours in spirit tho' stronger in health and purpose.

Yours sincerely
Ellen Terry

Both children have colds, but are otherwise well.

Little Edy had been terrified during her mother's absence by her father's attempt to abduct her, a shocking episode which may have contributed to her future aversion to marriage. It is also hard to condone Godwin's refusal to take charge of his son, but it should be remembered that this kind of paternal neglect was perhaps more common in the nineteenth century than today, as both Reade and Whistler bear witness.

Ellen's debut as Portia in April 1875 was witnessed by her friend Mrs. J. Comyns Carr: "As the curtain rose upon Nell's tall and slender figure in a china blue and white brocade dress, with one crimson rose at her breast, the whole house burst forth in rapturous applause." This was Ellen's first major Shakespearean role, save for one fling as Desdemona twelve years earlier, and it lifted her overnight to the top rank of English actresses.

Her peculiar gift for Shakespeare was evident both in her husky but consummately clear diction and in what appeared to be a temperamental affinity with the poet himself, something akin to his lyric verve and humanity, which made his lines seem to originate in her own mind. The audience had the heady sensation that they were not only hearing the words, but also witnessing the thought process that produced them. Her childhood drills with her father, the memorizing, the secret playacting by herself, were bearing fruit. Shakespeare was her second language, and she spoke it fluently.

One critic called her "the mistress of her art"; another extolled her "sublime compassion"; another "the bold innocence, the lively wit and quick intelligence, the grace and elegance of manner, and all the youth and freshness of this exquisite creation." The judges had begun their long hallelujah chorus.

On that stage, for the first time, she felt she had completely conquered an audience. It began with her speech, "You see me, Lord Bassanio, where I stand." Suddenly the silence was electrically charged, and, as she said, "I knew that I had got them." It never happened quite that way again, but the memory stayed with her. "Elation, triumph, being lifted on high by a single stroke of the mighty wing of glory."

The news of her success spread quickly. "Everyone seemed to be in love with me!" she wrote. "I had sweethearts by the dozen, known and unknown." Letters of adulation began to pour in, and they kept pouring for the rest of her life. Ellen was in at the birth of a new phenomenon, stardom: fan mail, being noticed in public, feeling adopted by other people, both for the roles she played and for something within herself that made her fans worshipful and possessive.

But for all of Ellen's luster and the beauty of Godwin's production, *The Merchant of Venice* was not a popular hit. It failed mainly, people said, because Charles Coghlan appeared too feeble and subdued as Shylock. One suspects that this worthy old-school actor was so bemused by the artistic decorations and by Ellen's naturalistic acting that he repressed his normal bombast and let the play go down the drain.

Whatever the case, this *Merchant* was a milestone that, according to Sir Herbert Beerbohm Tree, "marked the ren-

aissance of theatrical art in England." Godwin had promoted the revolutionary idea that scenery could be more
than an exercise in historical accuracy, more than clever
replicas of nature. Although based on Venetian originals,
his designs and sumptuous colors bore the stamp of an independent artist and commanded the respect of his colleagues—or most of them. One fellow architect, W. I.
White, was horrified that "the most accomplished living
architect in England is spending his tried powers over the
trappings of a play." Over the years, Godwin's total output
for the theater was scanty indeed. But he opened the way
for the soaring flights of imagination that made his son,
the future Gordon Craig, a giant in his field.

When it was announced that *The Merchant* must close
after three weeks, a group including Sir Frederick and Lady
Pollock and the painter Sir Frederick Leighton proposed to
subsidize it by subscription. The project fell through, but
progress had been made. For the first time in theatrical history, a production was deemed to have sufficient artistic
value that a group of connoisseurs considered it worthy of
private support.

Ellen was proud of so much—and such—attention. The
poets Algernon Swinburne and Arthur O'Shaughnessy
turned up among the meager audience, and Ellen thought
they were "wonderful. . . . A poetic atmosphere pervaded
the front of the house as well as the stage itself." On the
opening night a young Irish undergraduate had come
down from Oxford and was so bedazzled by Ellen that in a
sonnet he wrote,

> For in that gorgeous dress of beaten gold,
> Which is more golden than the golden sun,
> No woman Veronese looked upon
> Was half so fair as thou whom I behold.

This was from the first of two sonnets to Ellen Terry written by Oscar Wilde.

Another member of the audience, perhaps more intent

than anyone else, was the actor Henry Irving, who in the same season was performing a much-admired *Hamlet* at the Lyceum under the Bateman management. It is doubtful that Irving fully appreciated the Veronese influence. But he responded inescapably to Portia, and he was astute enough to note that her charms drew a new segment of the public into the theater—artists and men of letters who were more at home in the Arts Club or the Grosvenor Gallery inspecting the latest works of Rossetti, Burne-Jones, or Jimmy Whistler. Ellen had class, she attracted class, and class meant prestige. For Irving's future plans, prestige was important.

It was sad that Ellen and Godwin could not savor their joint triumph together, for they had benefited each other greatly. Without Ellen, Godwin might have had no production at all, and Ellen, in turn, gained by being with Godwin all through the designing and studying of the play. "I knew not only every word of the part," she wrote, "but every detail of that period of Venetian splendor. . . ." So the minute she stepped on the stage she was perfectly at home in Godwin's settings and costumes, as if she had been a Venetian heiress all her life.

After the play closed, Ellen stayed with the Bancroft management for more than a year, giving herself the steady employment she needed to support a household with two small children.

At times, some of the fans she had acquired as Portia turned up at the theater again and greeted her entrances with a noisy gusto that seemed a slur on Mrs. Bancroft, who, after all, was the leading lady. Then, to add injury to insult, one night during a dagger scene Ellen by accident stabbed Mrs. Bancroft in the arm, so that the victim had to perform with her arm in a sling. Relations between the two actresses grew a bit strained, but considering everything, they remained on reasonably good terms.

In March 1876, Godwin abruptly announced his marriage to his student Beatrice Phillips, who was later to become James Whistler's wife. On the marriage day, it was said that Godwin dined with Whistler at the Arts Club, as if giving notice to the world that he did not intend to let wedlock deprive him of conviviality. For all that Ellen had ousted Godwin conclusively from her life, his marriage to a younger woman must have shocked and hurt her. It suggested that Godwin had no aversion to marriage itself, if and when the right woman came along.

Nobody knows exactly how Ellen and Godwin felt about marriage during the years they lived together, though it is most likely that Ellen desired it, especially after her children were born; and it is also likely that Watts would have granted the divorce, once he was convinced that the pair earnestly desired to to be legally joined. One can only surmise that Godwin, through the years, was stalling. A year later, as we shall see, when Ellen did indicate her desire to marry, her divorce from Watts on the grounds of "adultery with Godwin" was soon expedited. Tom Taylor no doubt applied the persuasion. The decree was made final in September 1877.

In the autumn Ellen found a new theatrical base at the Royal Court in Sloane Square, run by a gingery actor-manager named John Hare who demanded obedience from his actors and bawled them out during rehearsals if they stole an extra minute from the quarter-hour lunch break. Ellen submitted happily to Hare's tyranny because she admired the ensemble playing of his well-polished actors.

Profitably installed at the Royal Court, Ellen moved her brood to a house on 33 Longridge Road. From there both children went to a nearby "progressive" school, along with the painter Walter Sickert. For weekends, Ellen rented the first of her small cottages. (She collected cottages the way some women collect baskets.) This one was in Hampton Court, where Edy and Teddy frolicked in the forests with the deer and recited scenes from *As You Like It* to any astonished palace guards or gamekeepers they could corner.

As a further plug for the theater, they named trees after roles their mother had played: Lady Teazle, Portia, Kate Hardcastle, and so on. Teddy, at five, asserted himself by helping a vendor sell ice cream and by mounting the tower overlooking the famous Hampton Court maze, where he took pity on visitors lost below him in the hedged-in labyrinth and shouted helpful directions, "Turn left, now turn right."

Ellen's greatest worry remained the illegal status of her children. In the seclusion of Harpenden it had not greatly mattered. But now, with her own increasing prominence, and with their education ahead, it was becoming a major concern. The obvious solution was for her to marry again, whereupon the children could be legally adopted by her husband.

Ellen's choice was a sturdy widower, Charles Wardell, whose stage name was Charles Kelly. She had acted with him in Reade's plays and had tried to persuade the Bancrofts to hire him for *The Merchant of Venice*. Wardell came from solid, respectable stock, his father being a Northumberland clergyman and a close friend of Sir Walter Scott's. After fighting in the Crimean War, Wardell had taken to the theater, it seemed, for further adventure. He was the rugged type of male that often appealed to Ellen, or, as she described him, "a manly bulldog sort of man, possessed as an actor of great tenderness and humor."

Although she was making a calculated choice for a calculated purpose, it must not be supposed that her emotions were cold. Her father had warned her, as she knew already, that Wardell was inclined to drink too much. But while she was arranging things, she planned to reform him and to be a helpful wife: she would see to it that they made a good acting team.

Teddy said that his mother was married on November 1, 1877; she said a little later. They were both hazy on dates. The important fact is that Ellen brought Charles Wardell to live at Longridge Road, and the children were excited at having a hefty man stomping around the house.

Ellen's family was pleased, too, for now Ellen was an accredited "good woman." Lewis Carroll wrote immediately to ask if she would care to resume their friendship. Graciously, she said yes, and he paid her a visit. Teddy was bored by one of Carroll's puzzles, which had to do with getting five sheep across a river in a boat: he preferred the efforts of Charles Wardell to teach him to tell time by the clock.

Both Edy and Teddy were mystified, though pleased, by the sudden influx of cousins and aunts and uncles trooping into the house like the grand finale of a Christmas pantomime; they wondered where on earth all these jolly people had been hiding until now. Teddy was especially awed when Sarah, a stately, white-haired dowager, paid her first call. He politely held a chair for his grandmother to sit on but moved it a bit too far to one side, and she collapsed on the floor. "That was fun," said the old lady gamely, and considering the joyousness of the occasion, she may even have meant it.

With her new husband as her leading man, Ellen had a huge success at the Court in *New Men and Old Acres,* coauthored by her friend Tom Taylor. It brought the Court a profit of thirty thousand pounds and captured the critical heart of young George Bernard Shaw, who pronounced the play "piffle" but was impressed by Ellen's portrayal of Lilian Vavasour. Oddly, for Shaw, he noted with approval her "crying like mad in it." Ellen's popularity moved her employer, John Hare, to hire a noted Victorian dramatist, W. G. Wills, to build a play around Ellen, based on Oliver Goldsmith's novel *The Vicar of Wakefield.* This rambling little masterpice had been dramatized at least twice before without success. But Wills, with guidance from Hare, pared it down to a compact, sentimental comedy and called it *Olivia.*

Just as her Portia had endeared her to an aesthetic audience, Olivia made her a popular darling. The play, like

Goldsmith's original idyll, was set in the mid-eighteenth century, so a Victorian audience, possibly a little weary of industrial progress, could have a good nostalgic evening looking back at gentler times. Olivia is the daughter of the vicar, Dr. Primrose, who faced financial ruin and was being forced to move his dear family out of their vicarage. To prevent this calamity, Olivia plans to sell herself as a wife to a rich young rakehell, Squire Thornton, acted by dashing young William Terriss, who for many years figured in Ellen's plays. On the night of her secret elopement, the family believes she is leaving home to serve as companion to an infirm old aunt. But the audience knows of Olivia's noble sacrifice and is touched to tears at the leave-taking, the exchange of little mementos, the locks of hair, and Olivia's farewell words to her younger sister, Sophy.

"Promise me one thing . . . when they say hard things of me, say it's not true."

"What's not true?" asks innocent Sophy.

"They might say I was thoughtless; perhaps they might say I was bad. . . . Remember this, Sophy, whatever betide, you'll not be ashamed of your sister at the last."

Ellen might have spoken these same words to her own sisters at the time she eloped with Godwin. On the surface the circumstances in the play were quite different, but doubtless some of the audience, knowing Ellen's past, may well have noted the similarity and been thrilled by it, while Ellen herself could have felt she was pleading her own cause. Her daughter, writing later about Ellen's peculiar sympathy with Olivia, observed that the role "seemed to slip from her with strange ease and to reveal her individuality with strange power."

Both Edy and Teddy appeared on stage as "village children" for at least one performance and took a curtain call. Edy remembered that she handed her mother a red bouquet, making the audience aware that Ellen was not only Olivia but Ellen Terry with her own children, the little threesome standing as it were before a public tribunal, to be judged, forgiven, and adored. As always with a star, the star's impersonations and the star's personality were becoming fused.

Shop windows blossomed with Olivia's ruffled caps, and the girls who wore them tried to put on a Terry-like expression, at once demure and saucy. Olivia scarves fluttered around pretty necks like banners of a new country, and a rash of Olivia postcards spread across Britain. Picture postcards of popular actresses and fashionable beauties were becoming wildly popular in both England and America. Collected by men, women, and children, they were easy to keep in memory books, easy to tack to walls, and easy to slip under bed pillows so they could be secretly hugged and kissed. Ellen's son told how he went backstage to the dressing room of Buffalo Bill who was on tour in England and was shown a postcard of Ellen. "You see," said the Wild West hero, "I carry your mother with me wherever I go."

Bernard Shaw, recalling Ellen at the Royal Court, wrote, "Miss Terry had hidden about her at that time a certain perverse devil . . . which gave the most curious naughty-child charm to Lilian and Olivia." And a few lines later he warned his readers not to pay too much attention to his comments on Miss Terry because they were "grossly partial."

Ellen's husband was not as enchanted. He had been offered a secondary role in *Olivia* and spurned it because he thought he deserved the major role of Ellen's father, Dr. Primrose. Ellen felt his refusal had jeopardized his reputation within the profession, probably because it sounded pettish. But, she admitted sadly, "many actors are just as blind to their true self-interests!"

Just as *Olivia* was about to close, Ellen received a letter dated July 20, 1878, from 15-A Grafton Street. It read, "Dear

Miss Terry,—I look forward to the pleasure of calling upon you on Tuesday next at two o'clock. With every good wish, believe me, Yours sincerely, Henry Irving."

Irving had been prodigiously busy since Ellen complained of his stiffness eleven years before as Petruchio in the truncated *Taming of the Shrew*. He had played six hundred (?) roles all over Britain, and in recent years had become the mainstay at the Lyceum Theatre under the American impresario H. L. Bateman. Ellen had been especially moved by his *Hamlet* and by his King Philip of Spain in Tennyson's ponderous verse drama *Queen Mary*. Irving had a gift for making the ponderous popular. By a fateful series of circumstances, as we shall see later, Irving in 1878 became the sole lessee of the famous playhouse. Now he was forty, facing a momentous challenge, and he needed an actress with talent, beauty, and a following to fortify him in his new enterprise.

His interview with Ellen in her drawing room at Longridge Road was rather stiff and formal until Irving's dog, Charlie, sympathetically ill at ease, misbehaved on the carpet. By the time Ellen and Irving, with fire tongs, brush, and pan, had remedied the damage, they had laughed themselves into a relaxed state, and the greatest partnership in the history of the British stage had begun—or at least Irving and Ellen assumed it had.

A few days later, as had been planned, Ellen and her husband went on a provincial tour with a dramatized version of Tennyson's little narrative poem "Dora," which Charles Reade had expanded for the stage. It was while they were in Liverpool that Ellen realized, possibly as a result of her husband's questioning, that she was not exactly sure of what arrangements she had made with Irving, and so she wrote to him for confirmation that the deal was really on. It was. And of course she would play Ophelia to his Hamlet, which Irving was reviving for his gala opening. It was entirely typical of Irving not to fuss about business details. When he trusted somebody, he sealed the deal only with a handshake. Irving, incidentally, had also asked William Terriss from the Royal Court company to come to the Lyceum. But he had ignored Ellen's husband.

Meanwhile, Ellen apparently feared that she and Charles Kelly were not giving their best to *Dora*. Reade dropped her a cheering note: "Nincompoop! What have you to fear from me for such a masterly performance! Be assured that nobody can appreciate your value and Mr. Kelly's as I do. It is well played all around."

Ellen and little Edy, during the summer tour, visited Kelly's father in his village rectory in Winlaton, County Durham. Sitting in his sun-bathed garden amid thickets of honeysuckle, Ellen busied herself writing to a young admirer, Stephen Coleridge, whose father was the chief justice and whose great great-uncle was the poet Samuel Taylor Coleridge. Seven years younger than Ellen, Stephen was almost too good-looking for any man but a fairy-tale prince. Ellen luxuriated in his adoration, and they remained friends for half a century. After her death he published a sampling of her letters, called *The Heart of Ellen Terry;* the full batch, he said, filled fourteen bound volumes.

Ellen shaped the friendship exactly to her needs. In its early romantic phase, she seemed to enjoy playacting the tender "older woman" with a worshipful swain at her feet. Later, when Coleridge married, she made him her son's guardian and her own business adviser. Stephen grew increasingly self-important, but Ellen reduced him to human size and saw the best that was in him.

In the sweet-smelling garden, she wrote dreamily to young Stephen who was on a trip to Egypt and Morocco. "The sun is shining to make all golden, and my heart shines too . . . a letter's in my lap from my little boy Edward (6) telling me he's well and happy. . . . How much I wish you could be with me . . . how much I wish you were with me . . . we'd read together, . . . sitting in the ferns hand in hand in cool shadow. . . . Pretty boy, I'm very happy, even without you. Still you see, you are in my thoughts, or how should I be talking to you in pencil at this moment."

When he returned, she rejoiced, "Praised be blest you're safe," and she fancied the amber beads he brought her. "They look so delicious by daylight—fit to eat—you can't eat your beads and have 'em or I'd try! Did you expect to hear from me before. . . ? I've nothing to tell you, and I thought only *lovers* wrote when they'd nothing to tell and we are not lovers—though I am very loving. I could find it in my heart to love every pretty thing I meet." She was indulging in flirtatious double talk, like a Shakespearean heroine.

In 1884, Stephen called on G. F. Watts at Little Holland House, where twenty years earlier Ellen had been the painter's wife. Through Stephen, who began a long friendship with Watts, she learned that he now felt for her "no shade of ill will but rather a deep and abiding kindness. . . ." Watts approved, moreover, Stephen's relations with Ellen and wrote to him, "Nothing has weakened my deep interest. Please let me have a line to tell me that your most important friendship is unbroken."

Ellen's rise to glory was making Watts feel more kindly toward her, and it cannot be denied that it made Ellen more kindly too. In later years, they met once or twice by accident, but they were content to remain affably aloof.

Chapter Five

FIRST LADY OF THE BRITISH STAGE

Between Ellen Terry and Henry Irving there was a useful division of aptitudes. One day, back in Harpenden, Ellen saw the family goat chasing little Edy. Running to the rescue she grabbed the beast by the horns and was about to whack him when their heads almost touched; she gave him a close, hard look. "I saw that his eyes were exactly like mine," she said, and the likeness struck her as so funny that she laughed, and the goat went unpunished. There is no record that he ever chased Edy again. By coincidence, Irving had a similar encounter while walking in a lane in Cornwall and saw a young lamb peering at him over a hedge. Beaming with goodwill, Irving stuck his face close to the lamb, who took alarm and bit him. Irving, for all his kindness, had trouble feeling *en rapport* with living beings. He was too tied up in his own urgencies. Ellen related easily, almost too easily, to everything—and could look even a critic in the eye without being bitten.

At the first *Hamlet* rehearsal, Irving followed his usual custom of reading the whole play aloud to his cast, indicating how he wanted each part acted. The only role he skipped was Ophelia, by which he probably meant to show his company that he trusted Miss Terry and would not presume to boss her. This became his permanent policy with Ellen.

Ellen was grateful but uneasy. In the first days of rehearsal Irving worried over technicalities—music, duels, crowd scenes, gas lighting cues—and worked mostly with the male members of the troupe. Ellen understood entirely. He had gambled heavily on the Lyceum venture and was striving for perfection in a myriad of nagging details. He hoped thereby to avert the kind of first-night calamity that had made Bulwer-Lytton's *Last Days of Pompeii* a laughing-stock only a year before, when the earthquake refused to quake, the volcano refused to erupt, and the tightrope-walker at a pagan banquet fell off his rope.

Ellen did all she could by herself. To prepare for her mad scenes, she visited an asylum but found most of the inmates too "theatrical" to use as models for the gentle Ophelia. As she was leaving, she saw a young girl gazing at a blank wall. Her face was empty, but her body seemed to be waiting, waiting to escape. Abruptly, she flung her hands over her head and darted across the room like a bird. Ellen used this low, skimming motion in several different roles; it was called her "lapwing" flight. But from her asylum visit she concluded that it was useless simply to ape real life on the stage. The actor must first imagine a character as deeply as possible. "It is no good observing life and bringing the result to the stage without selection, without a definite idea. The idea must come first, the realism afterward." With this comment on the art of acting, Ellen came close to Whistler's dictum on the art of painting: "Nature contains the elements, in color and form, of all pictures, as the keyboard contains the notes of all music. But the artist is born to pick and choose, and group with science these elements, that the result may be beautiful."

For all the study and thought she gave to Ophelia, she finally bearded Irving: "I am very nervous about my first appearance with you. Couldn't we rehearse *our* scenes?"

"*We* shall be all right," he insisted, and then he spilled out what was really troubling him: "but we are not going to run the risk of being bottled up by a gas man or fiddler." Irving dreaded having a show stalled by a bungled light or musical cue.

Another Lyceum newcomer who shared some of Ellen's apprehension and felt even more like a fish out of water was the athletic young Irishman Bram Stoker, whom Irving had hired as his new business manager, secretary, and troubleshooter. Ellen and Stoker were the same age, and together they were the most important additions to Irving's enterprise.

A civil servant in Dublin, Stoker had doubled, without pay, as a theater reviewer. He wrote so glowingly of Irving in an earlier *Hamlet,* touring in 1876, that the actor summoned the critic to a supper party with several other friends. Keyed up by Stoker's approval, Irving volunteered to recite a gruesome poem, *The Dream of Eugene Aram,* which he rendered so powerfully that at the end Irving himself half-fainted, and Stoker—nothing halfway about him—had a fit of hysterics.

Thus reassured of Stoker's good judgment, Irving eventually persuaded the Dubliner to ditch his civil service job and move with his new wife to London. Stoker was to remain Irving's indispensable adjutant until the actor's death, although he did steal enough time to write a few gruesome tales of his own, including, in 1897, the celebrated *Dracula.*

Stoker's first glimpse of Ellen Terry was on a dark winter day in a backstage passage at the Lyceum, but the darkness could not shut out "the radiant beauty of the woman to whom Irving, who was walking with her, introduced me." To Stoker her face had beauty, color, animation; her form was fine, and he commended "the easy rhythmic swing, the large, graceful goddesslike way in which she moved." Having been a guest in her husband's lodgings in Dublin, Stoker assumed that Ellen already had some knowledge of him. But he was not prepared for her warm welcome, as if already she regarded it her duty to make him feel at home where she hardly felt so herself. "From the very first," Stoker said, "she took me into the heart of her friendship."

Two days after the opening of *Hamlet* had been announced in the press, all tickets were sold for the premiere, and the Lyceum was in the traditional state of frenzy that the theater not only generates, but adores as well. Workers were nailing wooden back planks onto the rows of benches in the pit and gallery so spectators could lean back without capsizing. The walls were being repainted in lush tones of sage green and turquoise, and all the more expensive seats were getting extra padding.

By 7:00 P.M. on December 30, 1878, Bram Stoker in formal elegance stood in the Lyceum lobby. Already, through a side entrance the younger hence poorer intelligentsia, after queuing for hours, were surging toward the cheaper seats. Stoker then began to greet the first platoons of consequence. Gloved, muffed, furred, caped, top-hatted, fragrant, rustling, and chirping, the guests rolled up in their hacks and hansoms, stepped out with cautious feet, and advanced through the Lyceum's lordly pillars.

After the orchestral overture, when the gas man dimmed the lights and the curtain rolled up on a darkened Denmark, Irving stood in the wings, as he always did, straining to control everything.

His first worry was Bernardo, acted by a Mr. Robinson, due to relieve the midnight guard at Elsinore. Irving had rehearsed him over and over, training him to put the right chill into "Who's there?" *Hamlet* must begin in a high state of tension in order, as Irving said, "to start the play as a living thing." Bernardo came on and did his two words just as his master had instructed. Now the vast, mysterious mechanism of the theater began to stir. Memory cells in the actors' skulls began to provide thousands of syllables in correct sequence, and Shakespeare's words were reproduced aloud. Actors' bodies moved according to rehearsed patterns. Almost at once the audience became part of the apparatus, reacting with their laughter, their attentive silences, and their applause. Emotions of wonderment and anxiety were manufactured. The *Hamlet* machine with its millions of interlocking parts was in full operation.

When the scene shifted to "A Room of State," Irving

made his first entrance at the end of a procession. "He was always a tremendous believer in processions, and rightly," Ellen once reflected. "It is through such means that Royalty keeps its hold on the feeling of the public, and makes its mark as a Figure and a Symbol." At the climax of a courtly parade, with the music boiling up anxiously, Hamlet walked in slowly, regally, and desperately alone. The lights dimmed as if already his too, too solid flesh had started to melt.

That night Ellen recalled little of her own performance, except that she felt she was acting poorly.

At midnight, as the play ended, the applause was tumultuous, but Ellen did not appear at the curtain calls. Irving was heaped with flowers and laurels, and he vowed to the audience that as long as he was manager of the theater he would "do nothing that was not aimed to elevate his art and to increase the comfort of the public."

Still more applause, and still no Ellen.

After the fourth act, Ellen had slipped out by the stage door and in despair drove up and down the Thames embankment in a carriage. On the same evening her husband was playing nearby at the Haymarket Theatre in James Albery's drama *The Crisis.* But it is not known whether he called for her at the Lyceum, or whether they saw each other at all that night. It was said, however, that Irving drove to Ellen's house in Longridge Road after the theater to pay his respects.

In the next day or two the verdicts were in. "Miss Terry is without a rival," said the *Times,* adding that she was "unapproached by any other actress on the stage." The comic weekly *Punch* was soberly rhapsodic about her third act in particular, when she pronounced Ophelia's epitaph to Hamlet's reason, "Oh, what a noble mind is here o'erthrown." Calling it both "intellectual" and "exquisite," the critic stopped searching for more adjectives and said simply, "Nothing like it has been seen on the English stage in *Punch's* memory."

Ellen's sudden eminence as first lady of the Lyceum

did not awe her. Backstage at *Hamlet,* Irving caught sight of her descending from her upstairs dressing room by sliding down the banisters, as if his Ophelia had really gone mad—or were still a teenager. He smiled and made no comment.

Most of Ellen's arrivals, by banister, foot, or carriage, were late, exasperatingly so when she dashed into the theater only a few minutes before curtain time, while her dresser, the call boy, and Irving himself stiffened with anxiety. Yet he refused to reprimand her. He knew that once Ellen was onstage, no matter how casual she had been about getting there, she performed with the utmost care and pains. He also saw and appreciated her influence on his entire theater family. Irving made punishing demands on his staff, and in the end he always grabbed the limelight for himself. But while Irving was a taker, Ellen was a giver, of sympathy, money, or advice, to any stagehand or bit-player who was in need. The staff, seeing how much Irving and Ellen respected and enjoyed each other, felt more secure, even as children do with congenial parents.

Ellen, on the other hand, had no compunction about trying to reform Irving. She scolded him for being so self-conscious about his spindly legs that he padded them: "What do you want with fat, pudgy, prizefighter legs!" Irving discarded the padding. She persuaded him not to lurk tensely in the wings ten minutes before his entrances, but to relax in his dressing room until the call boy summoned him, thus saving his energy and fire for the next scene and coming onstage with more ardor. During one Shakespearean revival, Irving mumbled a passage so badly that nobody could understand him. His colleagues told him to speak more distinctly, but it did no good. Finally, Ellen, right before he went on, gave him a list of words that he was stumbling over. He studied it for ten seconds, went on, and spoke the passage perfectly. He never had trouble with it again. It was the same kind of medicine she had once been given by Charles Reade.

Yet Ellen's best donation to Irving was her understanding of him. Half by intuition, half from hearsay, Ellen knew what forces had shaped the driving actor-manager. Behind the man, she sensed the small boy separated from his parents, then the lanky adolescent called "Spindleshanks." On her own tongue she felt the stutter that he lived to conquer while all dressed up in front of everybody. By now all the professionals in the theater knew something about Henry Irving, the hard worker and late bloomer, so from this common knowledge she could fit together the biographical details that filled out his story.

Nine years older than Ellen, Irving was born February 6, 1838, in Somerset in southwest England and was named John Henry Brodribb. His parents being poor and unsettled, he moved to the Cornish coast to live with his mother's sister, Sarah, and her husband, a hot-tempered, jovial giant who managed four tin mines. It was a good start for an actor, for John Henry whooped and ran with his two cousins, filling his lungs with sea air and building up the stamina that all show people need. Sarah bombarded him with Bible stories and moral precepts and somehow implanted in him the idea that he might recite stories and poems himself.

When Sarah's tin miner died, the boy rejoined his parents in a dismal London flat, where certain events, in retrospect, seemed to be leading him toward the theater. First, he had a schoolteacher, Dr. Pinches, who stressed elocution and found an eager pupil in John Brodribb. After triumphing in a school play, John went to Sadler's Wells and heard the popular actor Samuel Phelps being loudly applauded for his *Hamlet* at Drury Lane. By now the boy had discovered that on certain sensitive eardrums applause is the world's sweetest music and that the loveliest sirens never sing, they clap. For practical considerations, John got a job as junior clerk with Thacker, Spink and Company, East India Merchants. But he still favored the theater over commerce.

John's Methodist mother knew that her idiot son was heading for hell, but John's uncle (on his father's side) came into money and gave the boy one hundred pounds to squander as he wished. Now eighteen, John decided to outfit himself for his future and spent his money on the proper dress for the realms of illusion. Because actors were expected to pay for their own costumes and personal props, John stocked up on basic items that every young performer should possess: wigs, capes, robes, buckles, belts, swords, daggers, boots, fake jewlery to indicate status, and rakish hats with a stock of additional plumes in different colors. What good was an actor if he couldn't bow to a lady and doff his hat with a circular whoosh so the plumes fluttered behind it like a comet's tail? The only basic gear he lacked was a name; Brodribb, of course, was unspeakable.

To capitalize on the craze for amateur acting and bouts of elocution, some London theater owners put on a single performance of a play with an all-amateur cast—for a price. A bashful aspirant could buy a mute walk-on role for a few shillings. John, now brimming with courage, paid the maximum fee of three guineas for full exposure, and went whole hog by paying for printed playbills which announced, "FIRST APPEARANCE OF MR. IRVING AS ROMEO." He had decided to salvage "Henry" from his own name and chose "Irving" mainly because he admired the writings of Washington Irving.

Within the next few weeks Irving refused a bit-player's job at Sadler's Wells and, showing almost supernatural common sense, joined a group in remote Sunderland because he figured it would give him much broader experience. Like a second Molière, he stayed in the provinces for ten years, playing more than six hundred different roles.

Irving was not really well designed for the stage. He was too lanky, too angular; his plumes and silver buckles might easily mock him. Laboring still to overcome his stutter, he developed an aggressive way of speech that made

114

every consonant seem a separate victory. Because he had to play many comic roles, he picked up a jerky walk from provincial comedians, a puppety jiggle that he never quite lost. In earlier years his face was not comely, though it did have an eager, intelligent look, with more humor in the eyes than in the delicate, almost girlish mouth. If his own visage had been more of a masterpiece, he might not have grown so skilled in covering it with makeup. His face, it may be said, was a blessing—in disguise. It got better-looking as time went on, and Ellen enjoyed gazing at it, stealing a peek at "the noble set of his head" or the creamy skin at the back of his neck.

What she understood, as only a veteran trouper could, was the prodigious amount of toil and hardship that went into his work. To an actor, every playscript is a bundle of orders—orders to carry out at exactly the right instant—and every performance is an act of obedience to these demands, not to mention the duty to strike a spark from his own personality. It is entirely possible that Henry Irving memorized more hundreds of thousands of words, more cues and intricate actions, assumed more identities, and created more counterfeit realities than any performer in stage history. As if that were not enough, he always took on the extra burden of being stage director, treasurer, artistic consultant, business manager. Yes, he had helpers, but he was always the boss. If Irving had been Atlas, he would not have been satisfied to support the world on his shoulders but would have wanted at the same time to dance a jig to please the gallery gods.

Looking for feats to perform, Irving joined resident companies in Edinburgh, Dublin, and Glasgow. He made a stab at London with a troupe that flopped at the old Princess's Theatre, where Ellen had made her childhood debut three years before him. Then, refusing to leave the city under a cloud, Irving rented a hall and gave a one-man show, acting all the parts in Bulwer-Lytton's popular thriller *The Lady of Lyons*, which not only pleased the audience but also impressed a London critic who saw in Irving "the fire of genius."

In Manchester where he settled for nearly five years and acted well over a hundred roles, he fell in love with an angelic little actress, Nellie Moore, who combined piety and gaiety. The romance hit a snag. When they resumed it later in London, Nellie's death cut it short.

During Irving's Manchester period (1860–65), half of Europe and America it seemed was still excited by spiritualism with its parlor séances and table-tipping. The theater contributed to the rage, with almost every melodrama boasting a gauzy apparition or two and ghosts dissolving back into the cellar in a puff of red fire. Among the leaders in such antics were two American brothers, Ira and William Davenport, bogus mediums on a four-year European tour who got a warm welcome in England. Their act began, as Irving saw it in Manchester, when a member of the team claiming to be the Reverend Dr. Ferguson made a spiel about the immortality of human souls and the fun they were having in the next world. Then he introduced the two solemn Davenports, who entered a large roofless cabinet and invited a committee from the audience to rope them tightly to two chairs, while around them on the floor were placed an assortment of bells, horns, a tambourine, and sometimes a trumpet and guitar.

As soon as the cabinet doors were closed and the lights lowered, a faint jingle issued foom the tambourine, bells began to ring, horns tooted, and the trumpet or tambourine sailed over the top and crashed onto the floor. When the committee opened the doors, the brothers were found in a deep trance, still tightly roped. A large majority of the viewers suspected no fraud and apparently never wondered why the souls of the dead stooped to take part in such a childish uproar. Irving was fascinated, thoughtful, and not fooled for a minute.

Gathering around him two of his actor friends, one of them a practiced magician, Irving hired a hall and announced that he would duplicate the Davenports' séance, altogether by trickery. Five hundred spectators turned up in the library hall of the Manchester Atheneum on February 5, 1865, and were welcomed to the demonstration by Irving—without makeup. Then he went off for a few seconds, and after clapping on a wig, false beard, and a frock coat, he returned as the "Reverend Dr. Ferguson." The likeness was hilarious, and so was his sanctimonious ballyhoo, which ended up with Irving asking the audience to have faith "in the greatest humbug of the nineteenth century." The two actors as "the brothers" gave a dead-ringer imitation of the Davenport séance, from being roped to their chair to the last tinkle of the tambourine.

Irving was not alone in exposing this hocus pocus—others, such as Harry Houdini, were to have a go at it later—but Irving was the first to handle it humorously. His godson, Gordon Craig, wrote that the Davenport affair was a crucial point in Irving's career, for he discovered then the mesmerizing effect he could have on an audience, even when they knew he was teasing them.

Irving's fortunes took him back to London where the rising actor-playwright Dion Boucicault cast him as the polished villain, Rawdon Scudamore, in his new play *Hunted Down*. Irving was admired by such assorted personages as George Eliot, W. S. Gilbert, and the powerful critic of the *Sunday Times*, Clement Scott, who saw him as the first actor "to undermine the artificialities of the old school." Irving was still only a half-hatched eagle, yet he was invited to meet artists and men of letters at the Arundel Club; Clement Scott asked him to a Christmas party at his home in Linden Gardens.

Irving went to a wrong address and was met at the door by a Miss Florence O'Callaghan, who, it turned out, was an old flame of Scott's and was going to the same gathering. Irving escorted her to the party; nineteen months later he escorted her to the altar. Whatever favor Irving owed Scott for his kind review, he more than repaid by taking the ill-tempered Miss O'Callaghan off Scott's hands.

While the nuptials were pending, Irving found another juicy role as Digby Grant in *Two Roses* by James Albery. Digby is an outrageous snob, short on cash and long on pedigree, who depends on handouts from friends who are beneath him socially. When a windfall makes him rich again, Digby snubs his old friends without mercy.

To a nation enjoying the industrial leadership of the world, when wealth and status and social climbing were as uncertain as English weather, Digby was a familiar type, and Irving squeezed all possible fun out of him. Year by year, Irving was creating a gallery of eccentrics, men who might have stepped out of Dickens—as, in fact, many of them had: Jingle from *The Pickwick Papers*, Bill Sikes from *Oliver Twist*, Dombey from *Dombey and Son*, and Nicholas from *Nicholas Nickleby*. The tremendous growth of the English reading public was whetting a corresponding interest in the theater, just as nowadays people who have "read the book" want "to see the movie."

A direct result of Irving's Digby was his alliance with Colonel Hezekiah Linthicum Bateman from Baltimore, who attended the 291st night of *The Two Roses* which Irving acted as a benefit for himself. After the play, Irving made a quick change from his Digby costume and reappeared before the curtain in elegant evening clothes. Then he recited Thomas Hood's *The Dream of Eugene Aram*, the same poem that was to devastate Bram Stoker. Aram was another English eccentric, a mild-seeming schoolteacher who killed a feeble old man for his gold and dumped his corpse into the river. Irving knocked himself out in the violent action of battering the old man to death and evoked in detail how the corpse is exposed when the riverbed dries, and how the murderer hides it again under heaps of leaves, only to have the wind scatter them away, as if the very forces of nature were bent on exposing his crime. At last, after agonies of remorse, and in full awareness that his soul is condemned to eternal hellfire, Aram gives himself up to the law and the hangman.

Overwhelmed by the audience's response, Colonel Bateman decided that Irving was exactly the actor he needed in his new company at the Lyceum Theatre which he had just leased. His enterprise was strong on the female side because Bateman had a wife who was both actress and playwright and four stagestruck daughters. Irving agreed to join the Batemans; they were cordial, southern gentlefolk, whose hospitality he enjoyed.

To Irving the future looked auspicious. At the moment, his marriage to Florence O'Callaghan showed signs of being successful. His son, Henry, born in 1870, was flourishing, and his haughty wife, after several periods of estrangement, was eager for reconciliation. A second baby was expected. To provide for his growing family, Irving had signed a three-year lease on a house in West Brompton.

Under its new management the Lyceum opened in September 1871 with *Fanchette*, a tale of a witch girl, taken from the French of George Sand and revamped by Mrs. Bateman to suit the mediocre talents of her daughter Isabel. *Fanchette* failed, and Irving was rushed into a jerry-built comedy, *Pickwick*, which was well received but not substantial enough to fill the Lyceum. In despair, the Batemans discussed calling it quits and returning to America until Irving convinced them to let him have a crack at a melodrama called *The Bells*, based on the Parisian play *Le Juif Polonais* (*The Polish Jew*). Bateman had already turned down an adaptation of it, but at Irving's urging, he reluctantly agreed to its production, with Irving tinkering and tampering to make it fit his needs.

The Bells was the towering success of the Victorian theater. In theme it was almost identical with Hood's *Dream of Eugene Aram*. The murderer, instead of being a respectable schoolteacher, is a respectable Alsatian mayor, a devoted family man named Mathias. In each work the victim is a hapless stranger, the motive is robbery, and the killer is ultimately exposed by the thrashings of his own conscience.

What made these similar works so appealing to Victorian audiences? A partial answer lies in the fact that in both of them the wrongdoers were neither kings nor courtiers committing high crimes of state, nor were they lowly ruffians, but ordinary middle-class citizens, average mortals with whom the audience could easily identify, thus bringing the crime closer to home, making it cozier, planting the guilt right in the domesticated heart. It was thrillingly horrible to observe that nice people like themselves were capable of such villainy.

Another partial answer is embedded more deeply in the Victorian sense of self, the self holding itself responsible for its own acts and struggling for its salvation. In the words of Cardinal Newman, "Unless you are struggling, unless you are fighting with yourselves, you are no followers of those who through many tribulations entered into the Kingdom of God. A fight is the very token of a Christian." Eugene Aram and Mathias both fought the battle of conscience and lost to the devil, which is what made their plight so terrifying and such a rip-roaringly good sermon. If today the torments of conscience seem obsolete, it is perhaps because conscience itself—like the free will it presupposes—has grown obsolete.

Forty-one London periodicals commended Irving for his stunning performance, and many were impressed by the production. A cinematic use of flashbacks and "visions" revealed how the innocent Jew, after taking shelter at Mathias's house during a snowstorm, departs with his sleigh bells jingling and is ambushed by Mathias himself, who strikes him down with an ax and carries his corpse to be burned in a limekiln, crying, "Into the fire, Jew, into the fire!" Years later, Mathias is still haunted by the bells, faintly jingling like the Davenports' tambourine, and at the play's end he falls ill and has a ghastly nightmare in which a sinister mesmerist puts him in a trance before a tribunal of judges. He admits his crime and in his sleep actually blurts out the truth before his horrified family at his bedside.

At the opening of *The Bells,* Irving arranged for his wife to sit in a box with their friends, the Hain Friswells. After the final ovation, his wife waited outside in a carriage while Irving in his dressing room scrubbed off his makeup and accepted further congratulations. When he joined Florence they rode to the Friswells' for a small champagne supper where Irving was toasted under his wife's baleful eye. As they drove home, Irving, still aglow, promised that soon they would have their own coach and pair. Florence could stand it no longer. Tired and antagonistic, she asked, "Are you going on making a fool of yourself like this all your life?"

Irving did not speak, except to order the driver to stop as they passed Hyde Park Corner. He got out and strode away, leaving Florence to continue on alone. It was a more dramatic exit than Henry Irving ever made on the stage; he never went home or spoke to his wife again. Irving walked to the Batemans' house where he was always welcomed like a member of the family.

His seven-year hitch with the Batemans was shaken in 1875 by the death of the colonel, but Mrs. Bateman immediately took command, and Irving stayed on. A major complication developed when the third daughter, Isabel, fell in love with Irving. Never much of an actress to begin with, Isabel grew stiffer and more uneasy than ever when she had to play love scenes opposite her idol. Her mother hinted that she would not object if Isabel lived with Irving until his divorce came through, but Irving was skeptical about Isabel's qualifications, offstage as well as on. When plans were afoot for the new 1878 *Hamlet* revival, Irving seized the chance to take a stand. He wrote to Mrs. Bateman saying he could not accept Isabel again as Ophelia and asked permission to hire an actress of his own choice. Mrs.

Bateman reacted with exemplary common sense. She explained that if she refused to support Isabel it would have a crushing effect on her daughter's career. On the other hand, she quite understood Irving's objections and felt that the only wise solution was for her to relinquish the Lyceum and sell her lease to Irving. She would be glad, she told him, to make reasonable financial arrangements. Irving leaped at the opportunity. As for choosing an Ophelia and a leading lady to join his company, he lost no time in recruiting Ellen Terry.

If any evidence is needed of Ellen's importance to the Lyceum, it can be found in a short business letter written to Henry Irving from 33 Longridge Road, on January 21, 1879, three weeks after her first night.

Dear Sir,

I write at the request of my wife (Miss Ellen Terry) to say that I shall be happy to enter an engagement with you on her behalf for the season 1879–80 at the Lyceum Theatre to commence, say, on Saturday 25 October, 1879, and terminate Saturday 31 July, 1880, on the following terms, a weekly salary of forty guineas (42 pounds) and a half clear Benefit.

Should this suit your views, may I ask you to write me accordingly? Believe me

Yours faithfully
Charles Wardell

And so, with her first season barely started, Ellen was already signing up for her second. For the first time in her life, she was to have steady security over a period of eighteen months and could confidently expect it for longer. Few women in England had ever, with their own regular earnings, achieved this kind of sustained financial independence.

With Ellen as an assured asset, Irving began to exercise his genius for making the Lyceum an institution almost as imposing as Buckingham Palace. He developed an astonishing gift for institutional promotion that in today's world would have landed him at the head of any major advertising agency

A year before he took over the Lyceum, he wrote and read a paper at a social science congress, stressing the need for a national theater, describing the great benefits of such an organization, weighing its dangers, but proclaiming that sooner or later it had to come. Meanwhile, he set out to make the Lyceum the nearest thing to it. Starting with minor improvements for public convenience, he abolished the usual fees for programs and cloakrooms. He did sell, however, handsome souvenir programs that could be taken home and displayed in Victorian drawing rooms. Most impressively, he published his own acting versions of Shakespearean texts, so that for a small sum, a student could see how much cutting or fiddling was being done. This created an impression of institutional integrity and lifted the theater above the level of frivolous diversion. At one time he tried to end the queuing and scrambling for bench seats in the pit and the gallery. These cheap seats had never been numbered and were sold on a first-come-first-served basis, the early birds getting the best locations. Irving's attempt to sell only numbered bench seats in an orderly fashion met with such howls of protest that he had to go back to the old messy method where cunning and strong-arm aggressiveness paid off. But at least Irving got credit for trying.

In his campaign to create an image of respectability and rectitude, both for the theater and himself, Irving made a big point of honoring important visitors. In the summer of 1879, when the Comédie Française came over from Paris for a short season at the Gaiety Theatre, the company included its greatest stars, Sarah Bernhardt and Coquelin. Arriving at her London quarters, Bernhardt found it full of plants and flowers all from her admirers back in Paris—with one exception. The only Englishman to send floral tribute was Henry Irving. He proceeded to entertain the French visitors at banquets and receptions as if he were the queen's official greeter.

Ellen and Bernhardt immediately took to each other, and although as unlike as a tiger lily and a primrose, they remained friends for years. Speaking a linguistic goulash which they both pretended to understand, they gabbled together like housewives, Ellen more or less keeping the upper hand by reducing the Divine Sarah to a pet name, "Sally B."

As *Hamlet* neared the end of its run, Irving was preparing a new offering, *The Lady of Lyons*, a cinch for him because he had enacted it twice in one-man recitals. Irving's policy at the Lyceum was to present a balanced mixture of Shakespeare, new works, and revivals from the stockpile of Victorian hits. Audiences seemed quite happy to see these proven crowd-catchers over and over, with new actors and sometimes new twists in the text. Irving also had to provide good showy parts for himself—not difficult because of his versatility—and for Ellen Terry. Ellen could be a problem. Lacking Irving's relish for melodrama and caricature, she was generally restricted to being witty, lovable, and noble in spirit. Irving figured that in *The Lady of Lyons* Ellen could shine as haughty Pauline, who spurns the love of Claude, a dashing but humbly born gardener, played by Irving. In a plot that is pure operetta, Claude tricks Pauline into marriage by disguising himself as a prince. When Pauline learns the truth she reviles her fake prince so bitterly that, with chin up and eyes flashing, he rushes out the door and joins a detachment of soldiers marching off to war.

Irving jumped at the chance to turn this scene into high spectacle and hired 150 soldiers at a shilling a night from the Brigade of Guards. Seen through a big open window of an interior setting, the soldiers paraded four abreast against the backdrop of a village street, with a band playing the *Marseillaise* and French drums beating up a storm. When Irving joined their ranks as the curtain fell, the audience demanded encore after encore, just to hear the drums and drink in the martial razzle-dazzle. Irving had arranged for the soldiers, after crossing the stage once, to run around backstage and return in a seemingly endless column, which the audience could have watched all night. By the end of the play, Claude had been promoted to colonel and had won Pauline's kisses and forgiveness.

Ellen never felt easy as proud Pauline, the girl's snobbery being too much at odds with her own nature; but she admired Bulwer-Lytton's surefire dramaturgy and liked to hear his old warhorse snorting again. She and Irving revived *The Lady of Lyons* in many years to come. Their first season ended with a flurry of benefits and crazy-quilt programs made up of short scenes and excerpts, which every ripened actor had in his memory and could piece together on short notice. The popularity of these mixed programs testified to the Englishman's affection for the theater. He had sentimental memories of the scenes being revived, and he liked seeing them in bits and snatches like listening to a medley of favorite songs.

For a single performance, Ellen played with her husband in a benefit, *All Is Vanity*, to aid an actor's widow. It was the only time Mr. and Mrs. Wardell ever acted together at the Lyceum.

The Lyceum's first season was a solid success, clearing some seven thousand pounds after all expenses and salaries had been paid, including those of its two principals. The most troublesome matter—it still persists in today's theater—was the lack of worthwhile new plays. Irving tried to prime the pump by paying some authors as much as nine hundred pounds ($4,500, worth perhaps $45,000 today) in advance—commissions for works in progress.

The summer plans of Ellen and Irving separated them from each other by thousands of miles. For the first time in his life, Irving took a full-scale vacation as one of the guests of his old friend the Baroness Burdett-Coutts, in her chartered steam yacht, *Walrus*, while Ellen was barnstorming on her second summer tour with Charles Kelly, playing *New Men and Old Acres, All Is Vanity,* and *Butterfly.* With her she had her brother George, who was learning the ropes as an actor. While she was bestowing her talents on Glasgow, Manchester, and Liverpool, Irving turned his eyes to Spain, Tangier, and the Greek Islands. By August he was growing restless. He wrote to his stage manager, Loveday, in London, suggesting what hats and furnishings he should round up for the revival of an old melodrama, *The Iron Chest,* and telling him to stir up his musical director, Hamilton Clark, about some entr'acte music and "get him to write some vague and mysterious bits for the change of scene." He politely expressed his hope that Ellen Terry was doing well on her tour. Then he added anxiously, "When can she be back at the earliest?"

Chapter Six

"MY OWN DEAR WIFE"

"When can she be back at the earliest?"

One reads the question twice, wondering why Irving did not know when his leading lady was due in London or why on his vacation he suddenly grew anxious.

The answers may be simple enough. Since he was starting his second season with plays that did not require Ellen's services, he had not bothered to fix the exact date for her return; and his abrupt desire to know her plans doubtless stemmed from something that happened on his trip.

While he was port hopping on the Mediterranean, getting whiffs of Morocco and Tunis, Irving was often struck by the stately Jewish merchants, robed and bearded like Bible patriarchs, standing guard over their bazaars. As a man of the theater, he imagined himself in their guise. Then a stopover at Venice again roused his sense of the dramatic, for the city itself is a vast stage, with great palaces for backdrops, dark alleys for sudden entrances and exits, open squares and balconies for showing off actors. Now he knew what he must do. Shylock! *The Merchant of Venice*. What's more, there was Ellen Terry, a proven Portia, waiting in the wings. So naturally he wrote to track her down. They had to make plans.

Back in London he fulfilled his first two commitments: a brief revival of *The Bells* (with Ellen's sister Florence playing the unimportant female lead) and *The Iron Chest*, which flopped. Of more consequence, Irving had ordered renovations to be made backstage during the summer in a dusty lumber room that was once a club for the Sublime Society of Beefsteaks. Its first members had included one duke, another lord, assorted men of the arts, and the Irish playwright and politician Richard Brinsley Sheridan. Irving was determined to restore something of the room's former atmosphere, using it to entertain friends and celebrities, giving the Lyceum an added prestige that no privately owned theater had ever achieved before—or ever has since. Irving installed a wine cellar; a chef was on call for midnight suppers; and the room was given a museumlike appearance with portraits and mementos of former stars— Garrick, Mrs. Siddons, Fechter—along with Whistler's portrait of Irving and, later, Sargent's of Ellen as Lady Macbeth. It was a new claim that the theater had its own heritage, its own aristocracy. To be invited to dine after a play in the Beefsteak Room carried with it the privileged touch of going backstage, meeting actors, identifying oneself with the arts. It was enjoyable to boast later that one had visited this sanctum.

The first meeting there was not a social affair but a supper of chops at which Irving announced to his henchmen, Stoker and Loveday, that they had to present *The Merchant of Venice* in three weeks. Showing his ideas of scenery, he tore up and bent several pieces of paper and arranged them like a house of cards on the table. The next day three scene-painters were put to work simultaneously. Irving broke the news to Ellen and began the most successful of all the Irving-Terry collaborations. It was given more than a thousand performances, at the start 250 of them consecutive.

The first-night ovation certified that *The Merchant* was a winner, but, equally important, the acting gave rise to scholarly disputes that were all to the good; they indicated that what went on at the Lyceum had to be taken seriously in cultured company.

Both Irving and Ellen had departed from orthodox interpretations. Irving's Shylock was designed to suggest dignity and arouse sympathy. Earlier portrayals of the Jewish moneylender made him a malicious rascal, steeped in an alien religion, and, like the devils in early church plays, a clownish lout whose downfall was greeted with glee. Shylock often wore red wigs, not only for their comic effect, but because they symbolized the red hats that the Jews of Venice were once ordered to wear.

The gradual humanizing of Shylock on the stage began when Edmund Kean, flouting tradition, had acted the role in a black wig and put genuine, understandable passion into his animosities; his son, Charles Kean, went further by stressing Shylock's tenderness to his renegade daughter. But it remained for Irving's Shylock to inspire sympathy on a broad humanitarian basis. Irving did not abandon his exaggerated gestures and eccentric diction. But he toned them down, breaking his speeches with anguished pauses, hunching his shoulders as if he were being beaten by the world's cruelty, and glancing up sideways at his tormentors like a man who has often been brought to his knees and is ready either to plead or to snarl. Irving discovered more possibilities in Shylock than any other actor had ever imagined.

It is hard to know to what extent the presence of the prime minister Benjamin Disraeli, whose grandfather had immigrated to England from Venice, influenced Irving's Shylock; but undoubtedly Disraeli's eminence induced Irving to risk a more sympathetic portrayal. Then, too, there seemed to be a physical, and perhaps psychic, resemblance between the actor and the statesman. This was noted by Irving's godson, Gordon Craig, who wrote of them both, "They glide, they are terribly self-possessed, their eyes dart flame: you *have* to look and listen to them whether you want to or not." This likeness was also observed by Sir William Fraser in his book, *Disraeli and His Day:* "The only person whom I have met who reminds me in any way of the manner of Disraeli in private life is Mr. Henry Irving."

One had the feeling that Irving and Disraeli might have switched roles and each been quite expert at the other's game.

Ellen Terry's liberties with Portia, she said, were dictated by Irving's decision to underplay certain scenes, which in turn obliged her to overplay to maintain the necessary contrast and balance. Yet in one instance she defended her robust interpretation, not as a counterweight to Irving but because she felt it was true to Shakespeare. This was a love scene with her suitor, Bassanio. Casting aside what she called Victorian prudery, Ellen let her ardor ring out as only an aristocratic, self-confident young woman would dare to do. To benefit herself alone, she assures Bassanio she does not aspire to greater worth or virtue. But to make herself worthy of him, she proclaims boldly, "I would be trebled twenty times myself, a thousand times more fair, ten thousand times more rich; that only to stand high in your account, I might in virtues, beauties, livings, friends, exceed account."

Ellen Terry was made for these tumbling words.

And her frankness, far more Elizabethan than Victorian, was bound to bring charges of "indelicacy" against her. John Ruskin was not pleased with either Irving or Ellen. It might be mentioned that in the previous year the great critic had been the defendant in the famous art trial when James Whistler had sued him for libel. Ruskin was not able to attend the trial because of a prolonged attack of brain fever, and his continuing ill health may have contributed to his cantankerous mood. Some years earlier he had cited Shylock as typifying the evils of mercenary commerce, so he would hardly approve of Irving's sympathetic interpretation of the Jew. But the bulk of Ruskin's complaint, which he wrote to Irving after seeing the play, was that Irving was "not careful enough" with his other actors, especially with Ellen Terry. He scolded Irving for not teaching Miss Terry "a grander reading" of Portia, and, in her speech to Bassanio, Ruskin desired to see more "majestic humility." Presuming to instruct Irving on the details of stage direction, he advised that she stand at least a half-dozen yards (eighteen feet!) away from her suitor "with her eyes on the ground through most of the lines."

Henry James, writing for *Scribner's Monthly* in America, likewise complained about the same scene: "Miss Terry's mistress of Belmont giggles too much, plays too much with her fingers, is too free and familiar, too osculatory, in her relations with Bassanio . . . in truth there would be a great deal to say upon this whole question of demonstration of tenderness on the English stage, and an adequate treatment of it would carry us far. The amount of hugging and kissing that goes on in London in the interest of drama is quite incalculable, and to spectators who find their ideal of taste more nearly fulfilled in the French theater, it has the drollest and often the most displeasing effect."

As for her kissing, the only other critic who commented upon it was the Shakespearean scholar Dr. Frederick James Furnivall who wrote to her, praising her wifely "touches" with Bassanio: ". . . when you kissed your hand to him behind his back in the Ring bit—how pretty and natural they were! Your whole conception and acting of the character are so true to Shakespeare's lines that one longs he could be here to see you. A lady gracious and graceful, handsome, witty, loving and wise, you are his Portia to the life."

The long, lucrative run of *The Merchant of Venice* was marked by two unusual events. One was a London fog of such density that it invaded the Lyceum stage and obliged the actors to grope for each other in the darker scenes and kept the audience squinting through the smog in sunny Venice. The other event was a party to celebrate the play's hundredth performance.

After the play ended on Valentine's Day, February 14, 1880, some three hundred guests entered the backstage entrance and were guided through a passageway, carpeted for the occasion, to the new Beefsteak Room and were greeted by Henry Irving and Ellen Terry. Meanwhile, an army of stagehands dismantled Venice and erected in its place a tentlike pavilion of white and scarlet canvas, with two glittering chandeliers hung overhead. Nine long tables were set up on the stage, eight at right angles to the footlights and one across the back. Flowers and palms were scattered all over, along with lanterns and candelabra on the tables.

Once the stage had been transformed, the caterers prepared to serve a five-course banquet, to be washed down with Piper Heidsieck '74. At this point the guests, summoned from the Beefsteak Room, sat down to eat. As souvenirs, copies of the play bound in white vellum and lettered in gold were presented to the guests. Irving had rounded up two admirals, a major general, and a cluster of knights, artists, journalists, and authors, including young Oscar Wilde over from Oxford.

In most respects it was similar to the grand bash given in honor of another famous actor, Charles Kean, twenty-one years earlier, with one significant difference: Irving was not the guest of honor but the host, entertaining in his own theater like a king in his castle; and Ellen Terry was unmistakably his queen.

The speeches included one remarkable address given by Lord Houghton, formerly Monckton Milnes, the first biographer of Keats, a familiar figure in London society, nicknamed by his friends "The Bird of Paradox" and "London Assurance." Evidently intending to be bold and sassy, Houghton ended up being sour and embarrassing. He praised the players for the recent improvement in their manners, holding out hope that if they remained mannerly, "families of condition were ready to allow their sons, after a university education, to enter the dramatic profession." He rebuffed Irving for producing long-run plays, claiming that frequent changes of bill made playgoing more amusing, and he deplored the tendency to whitewash the villains of history, implying that he regarded Irving's portrait of "the Old Jew" as quite tiresome. Irving rose to defend himself with good humor and better manners than Houghton had learned at Cambridge. Altogether, the evening was a victory for the Lyceum.

Near the close of the second season, Irving jettisoned the last act of *The Merchant* with its lyrical get-together of lovers and substituted a short play, *Iolanthe*. A repertory item in England and France for thirty years, *Iolanthe* was a sleeping-beauty tale, which Irving chose as a romantic showcase for Ellen. She played a blind princess, dwelling in a paradisaic garden and having her sight restored by a kiss from a count in golden armor: Henry Irving.

To audiences, *Iolanthe* was a valentine, but to the reigning Shakespearean scholar, Dr. Furnivall, who had stoutly defended Ellen's Portia, the amputation of Shakespeare was "damnable barbarism." In a letter to Irving, he wrote, "May you and your accomplices in this treason, this crime of lèse-majesté, soon repent and come to a better mind." Furnivall carried on his anti-*Iolanthe* campaign in the press, but Irving never repented.

As usual, summer brought no proper vacation for Ellen. With Charles Kelly, she resumed for the third time her annual tour, the main event of which was her first bow as Beatrice in *Much Ado about Nothing*, with her husband as Benedick. Although Beatrice became her most celebrated role with Irving, Ellen always looked back at this provincial debut with satisfaction. "I never played Beatrice as well again," she declared, leaving us to wonder what combination of reasons produced her best performance of her best role.

Did the real-life friction between herself and Kelly give added mettle to their skirmishes? Did they enjoy reviling each other without the restraint they might have felt offstage? And when it came time to kiss and make up in the fifth act, did they take a wry comfort in displaying how lovable they could be, as if to taunt each other with what a treasure they might soon lose?

Ellen's marriage with Kelly was deteriorating rapidly.

When the couple married, neither could foresee that Ellen would become Henry Irving's leading lady, holding forth at the Lyceum as his partner and hostess. She tried doggedly to live up to her side of the matrimonial bargain, going on annual tours with him. But it simply was not working. Kelly, always inclined to drink too much, now drank too much too often. He had fits of jealousy. This might, or might not, be consistent with the rumor that their marriage was never consummated. Soon after this latest tour, Kelly asked for a divorce.

Ellen was distressed. It could mean a revival of public gossip and disfavor. Practically speaking, she did not need to be divorced from Kelly, since Irving himself was still shackled to a woman who swore she would never free him. Why couldn't Ellen and Kelly settle for a legal separation?

In 1881 they did. Writing to Bernard Shaw years later about her separation from Kelly, Ellen said, "I should have died had I lived one more month with him. I gave him three-quarters of all the money I made weekly, and prayed him go." Both Ellen and Irving, it should be remarked, were punctilious about financial payments to business and family associates.

While Ellen was touring with Kelly, Irving was reviving *The Corsican Brothers*, which, along with *The Bells*, was another formidable standby of the Victorian stage. The male star always acted two roles, twin brothers separated since childhood but still clairvoyantly in tune with each other. Based on a novel by Alexandre Dumas, the play was thirty years old when Irving took hold of it; but he knew he could do wonders with the double role and trade on the public's appetite for the supernatural. Altogether, it was a grab bag of bloodstained ghosts, a riotous masked ball at the Paris Opera House, and a duel to the death in a moon-lit snowy forest.

Thanks to *The Corsican Brothers*, the Lyceum company won the staunch support of Gladstone, who accepted Irving's invitation to be hidden onstage during the opera-ball scene. Gladstone was instructed to watch it through one of the openings in a row of stage boxes painted on a large flat, a position that gave him a side view of the stage but concealed him from the audience. Gladstone got excited, however, popped his head out in plain sight, and was roundly cheered by the whole house.

Gladstone was permanently stagestruck. Time after time at Lyceum performances, Irving set up a special chair for the prime minister in the wings from which he could watch the show and feel part of the backstage hubbub of actors and scene-shifters. While it was surely a nuisance to have the great statesman stationed in their midst, the Lyceum company could hardly help feeling honored. Irving ordered that the Gladstone "throne" be draped in red; and two stagehands, dressed in their Sunday best, were appointed to watch over him, to puff up his pillows, keep him out of draughts, and not let him get hit on the head when the big curtain rolled down.

When Ellen Terry was giving one of her benefit performances, she dropped Gladstone a note: ". . . If it should but chance that you are not engaged for the evening it would make me very happy if you would come and beam upon us as you always do in the theater. I should feel prouder of your presence than any other Englishman. . . ." It is not known whether the prime minister could accept her invitation, but it is noteworthy that she felt free to ask him.

In many ways, the Lyceum was a substitute home for Ellen and Irving. Away from the theater, Irving lived for twenty-seven years in a modest little bachelor flat at 15-A Grafton Street, using it mainly for a night's sleep or for an occasional late snack with a friend or two. More often he supped with companions at the Garrick Club. On Longridge Road Ellen had her ménage for the children, aswarm with faithful servants, whom she could not pay much but who were proud to be her ladies-in-waiting. In contrast to these two rather specialized domiciles, the Lyceum was where Ellen and Irving did their important living together. Lord and lady of the house, they were attended by a large devoted staff, always greeted by the stage doorman, Barry, a chatty old Irishman, who, like everyone else in the family, called Irving "Guv'nor." Their dressing rooms were side by side on an upper floor in their own corner of the building and reached by their own stairway. Each had a separate dresser. Customarily, Ellen took a carriage home, and, weather permitting, Irving walked.

A major portion of the letters between Ellen and Irving were destroyed, perhaps because they revealed too much of their private life, or, equally possible, because they were subject to being misinterpreted. But in a few scattered words Irving's ardor is evident. In the early 1880s, following some unspecified upset, Irving apologized to Ellen for "the misery my thoughtlessness has caused" and assured her of his reverence for "your truth, your beauty, your genius and yourself." While *Faust* was in its final dress rehearsals, he left her a note which may, in its simple wording, suggest their intimacy. "No rehearsal for you this morning my darling. Tonight at seven dress."

Irving looked forward to times when they could be together away from the theater. "Soon—soon! I shall be near you on Sunday. God bless you, my only thought. Your own till death." On another occasion, after he had sent her a schedule of Lyceum plays, he added, ". . . we must bring the summer to ourselves by being together." And again, he declares his love in the closing of a letter, "You gave me a lovely letter to take away with me on Monday.—My own dear wife as long as I live."

All their close associates knew that, from time to time, the couple spent weekends together at one of Ellen's cottages, although always with friends. Once, while Irving was contemplating a production of *Coriolanus*, several years before he actually put it on, Ellen said that after staying up at night to cut the text, "the next morning he called out to me from his bedroom to mine, 'I shan't do that play' " which testified at least that Irving was within shouting distance. Their concern for each other's welfare was so great that once when Irving's feet were cold she warmed them by holding them against her stomach.

But whatever forms their intimacy took, they could not permit a hint of scandal to jeopardize their professional status. Irving had lifted the stage to a new level of respectability, and Ellen could not take the slightest chance of getting pregnant or damaging in any way the Lyceum's fair image. At one point it was said that Irving seriously contemplated risking the unpleasant publicity of getting a divorce from his wife in order to marry Ellen Terry. But that idea was abandoned, probably because Ellen felt the gain was not worth the gamble. The only solution, finally, was to go on living as before, being intimate in their fashion, and accepting the demands of the Lyceum, with its sacrifices and rewards, as part of their "marriage contract."

The hours they spent in the theater, more often than not, were enthralling. Working together, they saw each other in countless moods, simulated or genuine. Night after night, they confronted one another in different disguises, different costumes, sometimes extraordinarily beautiful ones. Because they admired each other, they took pride in each other's applause. They played an abundance of love scenes, but the pleasure they took in touching each other had nothing to do with memorized words. Though they had no family library in which to settle down, they had a hundred stage settings in which to feel at home— never long enough to get bored. They had shared so many remarkable experiences that they never ran out of things to talk about after hours. And they had the satisfaction of being indispensable to each other, not totally—that would have been intolerable—but enough to bind them close together.

Irving added to the Lyceum's homeyness by filling it with several generations of employees, like a large Victorian household teeming with old-timers and youngsters.

Whenever possible he hired veteran actors such as Henry Howe, who stayed and toured with the Lyceum until he died in Cincinnati at eighty-three. Then there were up-and-comers like the author Arthur Wing Pinero, who at twenty-two joined the Lyceum acting company and had several short plays done by Irving. Ellen told how her dresser, Sarah Holland, had two small daughters playing walk-on parts in *Romeo and Juliet*. One night after the show, Ellen and Irving came downstairs from their dressing rooms and found a forlorn little girl sitting on the step. "Well, my dear," asked Irving, "what are you doing here?"

"Waiting for my mother, Sir."

"Are you acting in the theater?"

"Yes, Sir."

"What part do you take?"

"Please, sir, first I'm a water carrier. Then I'm a little page. Then I'm a virgin"—one of those who awaken Juliet on her bridal morn.

The Lyceum family was multitudinous, and neither Ellen nor Irving could quite keep track of them all. Irving was hospitable to the Terry family, always welcoming Ellen's mother to the theater and hiring the rest from time to time. When Florence Terry retired to marry, Irving arranged a benefit for her. It included a scene with Ellen as Portia, Irving as Shylock, Florence as Nerissa, and Marion dressed in male attire as Clerk of the Court.

During the season of *Romeo and Juliet*, Irving and Ellen may have envisaged a more orthodox home setting for their personal drama. Irving bought a dilapidated house in a village called Brook Green, surrounded by neglected lawns and shaded by poplar and chestnut trees. He set out to restore the house and replant the gardens in the hope, so some people said, that Ellen Terry might live there with him as Mrs. Irving. But whether real trees and gardens could compete with the painted trees and gardens at the Lyceum remained to be seen.

As soon as Irving had packaged *The Corsican Brothers,*

he turned to a riskier project, Lord Tennyson's poetic play called *The Cup*. Ever since Irving in 1876 had acted in Tennyson's *Queen Mary*, the poet laureate had had an itch for the theater, an itch reinforced by the general passion of the nineteenth-century poets to emulate Shakespeare. Tennyson felt it even more keenly since he had learned to like and trust Irving, and Irving, in turn, appreciated the value of the queen's official bard to his enterprise. The poet had submitted an overlong drama, *Becket*, which Irving pronounced "magnificent," but he felt it was too costly to produce and needed drastic cutting. To soften the blow, Irving suggested he try something shorter that could be given at once. In a surge of excitement, Tennyson wrote *The Cup*, a subject taken from Plutarch. Irving saw its advantages at once, including fat roles for Ellen and himself and opportunities for a dazzling production. To supply the needed blend of archaeology and artistry, Irving asked Ellen to write Edward Godwin and invite him to supervise the scenery and costumes. Godwin accepted the job. Probably Ellen saw little or nothing of him during the work, but it is characteristic that she would not begrudge his being consulted.

Early in the preparations, Irving requested Tennyson to read his play aloud, a solemn event that took place at the poet's house in Eaton Place before a group that included Ellen, Tennyson's son Hallam, the actor William Terriss, and Irving with his terrier, Charlie, at his feet and Ellen's daughter, Edy, on his knee. Tennyson read the female parts in a high squeaky voice, which reduced Edy to smothered giggles. Irving himself began to laugh, and only the stern glare of Ellen, who had apparently forgotten that she had once giggled at Tennyson's reading on the Isle of Wight, restored decorum among the listeners.

There was no problem of decorum, though, on the opening night of *The Cup*, when a fashionable and reverential audience came to honor the poet laureate. When the curtains parted on a rocky landscape in Asia Minor, a villainous Irving entered. He was the tyrant, Synorix, who coveted a nobleman's beautiful wife, Camma, played by Ellen. To create a blend of Roman decadence and barbaric lust, Irving had seen fit to throw a tiger skin over his gold armor; thin scarlet lips were painted on his corpse-white face, and topping all was a bright red wig. "Henry looked handsome and sickening at the same time," wrote Ellen. "Lechery was written across his forehead." Ellen never imagined that her Henry could look so depraved: "I flamed with outraged modesty. . . . I could strike him—he licked his lips at me—as if I were a bone and he a beast."

After murdering Camma's husband, Synorix prepares to seduce the widow, who has become a priestess in the temple of Artemis of Ephesus. She was a foreign edition of the chaste Greek goddess and flourished in Asia Minor. The temple setting with its twenty-foot statue of the many-breasted divinity riveted the Victorian audience, who might have been shocked at an orthodox two-breasted goddess but who evidently felt there was safety in numbers. Ellen pretended to encourage Henry's advances while offering him a cup of poisoned wine. After he drank half, she downed the rest, no longer able to exist without her beloved husband.

The audience applauded the play, mostly for its visual splendors, and Irving made a happy curtain speech, regretting that the author had to be absent but promising to telegraph him how warmly his work had been received. *The Cup* was Tennyson's most popular foray into show business. That it ran for 127 performances was due in part to its sharing the bill with *The Corsican Brothers;* but it had its own enticements. As Tennyson's grandson wrote, "A hundred beautiful girls were carefully chosen to represent the choir of the Vestals, the massed color of their costumes and their well-drilled movements being something quite new in stage production." The presence of a hundred well-drilled beauties clearly suggests that Britain's poet laureate, in a sense, was the godfather of Radio City's Rockettes.

Among the actors in *The Cup*, Ellen as the noble wife ran off with the press notices. Irving's old friend Henry Labouchère, writing in *Truth*, jestingly praised Irving for his shrewdness in engaging Miss Terry who was the idol of the artists "at a time of affected aestheticism, of rapture and intensity, of sad wallpaper and queer dadoes. . . ." Then Labouchère, whose wife was Henrietta Hodson, Ellen's old friend from her Bristol days and a less important actress, went on to observe, "The age that gave us the Grosvenor Gallery must necessarily adore an Ellen Terry, for she is the embodiment of the aspirations of modern art. With her waving movements and skill at giving life to drapery, she is the actress of all others to harmonize with gold backgrounds and to lounge under blossoming apple trees."

Labouchère's amusing put-down of Ellen points out correctly that she was in harmony with the new aesthetic and could well embody its ideals. Yet, oddly, none of the Pre-Raphaelites or their followers ever painted her portrait, nor did her friend Burne-Jones ever ask her to join the angelic girls that he painted on stairways, perhaps because he feared she might break loose, as she did at the Lyceum, and slide down the banister. Ellen could assume aesthetic languor and wistfulness, but she could not sustain them.

Her interest in art and artistic people led her to exhibits at the Royal Academy where she was painted in a crowd scene of celebrities by the famous W. P. Frith; and she turned up at the gala openings of the Grosvenor Gallery, the hub of the new aesthetic agitation, to inspect the latest works of her friends Rossetti, Whistler, and Holman Hunt. Her heart was with these innovators, and she defended them sanely: "The aesthetic movement, with all its faults, was responsible for a great deal of enthusiasm for anything beautiful." Still, she could hardly qualify as their bona fide goddess. While she was acting in *The Cup* at a nearby theater, Gilbert and Sullivan were ribbing the "greenery-yallery, Grosvenor Gallery" boys in their wicked

new operetta *Patience*. Ellen, for all her love of the aesthetic, would not have felt at home with the chorus of
maidens bewailing their unrequited love for a willowy
poet and singing "twenty love-sick maidens, we." Her
taste in men was eclectic, but she favored dominant, masculine males.

The changes in Ellen's private life are scantily reported
at best. From her neighbors, the D. S. MacColl family, who
lived across the street from her on Longridge Road, one is
grateful for glimpses suggesting that the MacColls often
peeked out through their curtains. Apparently, not knowing her name at first, they called her the "Greek Lady,"
probably from a Hellenic hint in a cloak or scarf.

Recounting Ellen's daily departure for the theater, Mr.
MacColl wrote: "She raised and kissed two little tots who
were to be known as Edith and Gordon Craig. She greeted
the next-door neighbors, the family of a rabbinical scholar
who had promptly become slaves of her apparition and
stood ready on the pavement. Her cushions were brought
out, placed and patted in the open carriage; herself installed, the air became tender and gay with wavings and
blown kisses; the wheels revolved and greyness descended
once more on Longridge Road."

A jarring presence, according to Mr. MacColl, was
Charles Kelly, who did not fit in with this "phantom of
delight." It is easy to see why he might not and easy to
sympathize a little with his irritation during a morning-
after hangover at the clamor of Ellen's daily adieus with a
full cast of admirers waving her off.

"When a year had passed," Mr. MacColl went on,
"that too substantial figure disappeared and a new figure
was seen in Longridge Road," spare and grim—jaunty in
close-fitting short jacket and tilted wide-awake: Henry Irving.

If and when Henry Irving ever became Ellen Terry's
lover is still a subject of argument and speculation. Old
friends and family descendants take sides on The Question

as if it were a debate on papal infallibility. Rumors hint at telltale letters being destroyed, and there is worry about a batch of letters from Henry Irving, now carefully guarded in California, which allegedly refer to their physical attachment. Both camps convey an impression that they are protecting Ellen Terry. To one group, the claim that she was Irving's mistress must diminish her respectability. To the other, her abstinence during twenty-four years of close and affectionate contact would equally diminish her humanity. Several of her oldest friends declared that Ellen admitted her sexual relations with an open "of course." Others quote her as saying, "Irving never sees further than my head." If Ellen could know that this hassle persisted after her death, one can imagine her asking, "How can it possibly interest anybody?"

It can and does only because Ellen Terry was an exceptional woman who handled her human relations with courage and originality. She lived for other people as much as for herself, which invites one to question exactly how she managed it.

Ellen and Irving alike were loyal to old friends. Ellen hung on to her early friends like the Casella sisters and Alice Comyns Carr; and Irving always kept tabs on old-timers like his teacher, Dr. Pinches, and the bandy-legged comedian J. L. Toole, who had befriended Irving in the provinces. Irving was able to bestow a great favor on another early friend, Edwin Booth, with whom he had acted when the great American star toured England back in 1860. Irving had admired Booth for his "fierce concentration . . . the blazing of his tempestuous eyes." Now the tragedy-haunted Booth, whose brother had shot Abraham Lincoln and whose insane wife was dying in London, was playing Shakespeare at the Princess's and doing badly. Irving saw a chance to help. "Why don't you come and play with me at the Lyceum?" he asked Booth. "I'll put on anything you wish, or if there is any play which we can play together, let us do that."

They picked *Othello,* taking turns playing Othello and Iago, with Ellen as Desdemona to each. Fascinated by such a novelty, audiences packed the Lyceum for six weeks. As Othello, Booth was better than Irving—Ellen in her *Memoirs* accused Irving of ranting—and both actors were at their best as Iago. For one of the rare times in her career, Ellen was satisfied with herself: "Some nights I played it wonderfully."

A few cynical observers accused Irving of buttering up Booth in order to incur favor for his coming American tour. But although it is very possible that such an idea crossed Irving's mind, it hardly detracts from his good deed. Favors with a dash of self-interest are sometimes the best kind; they do not make the recipient feel too abjectly grateful.

Now that Ellen was no longer obliged to tour with Charles Kelly, Irving planned a late-summer provincial tour of nine Lyceum productions. He would have been ill-advised to risk them without her, for her reputation was spreading across Britain and her absence would have been deplored. To date, it was the most elaborate tour in theatrical history; the advances in railroad travel had made it possible to transport the gigantic load of scenery on a special train, along with a company of fifty-five.

Irving demonstrated the abiding truth that the only way to conquer the provinces is to give them the best. Wherever they went, the two stars were greeted like visiting royalty. Irving spouted speeches about the nobility of high drama, Ellen radiated beneficence, and in ninety-one days they made a profit of 18,000 pounds.

Back in London, the couple screwed up their courage to play *Romeo and Juliet.* Irving knew that at forty-four he was on the verge of being too old to act a fiery lover and that Ellen, nine years younger, was already a bit mature for the fourteen-year-old Juliet. So it was a case of now or never.

Preparing for Juliet, Ellen read everything that had

been written about her, boned up on the opinions of critics, and Irving provided a production that rushed from one enchanting tableau to the next. Perhaps to offset the critical drubbing they might get, he wrote Ellen a note on the day after the dress rehearsal: ". . . beautiful as Portia was, Juliet leaves her far, far behind. Never has anybody acted more exquisitely the part of the performance which I saw from the front. . . . Your mother looked very radiant last night. I told her how proud she should be, and she was. . . . The play will be, I believe, a mighty 'go', for the beauty of it is bewildering. . . . Now you—we—must make our task a delightful one by doing everything possible to make our acting easy and comfortable. We are in for a long run." Then he added, "I have determined not to see a paper for a week—I know they'll cut me up, and I don't like it!"

Irving guessed right on two scores. The production had a long run: 180 performances. And a majority of the critics did cut him up. Among the detractors was his wife, keeping her first-night vigil over him from her complimentary box. Before turning off her bedside lamp, she wrote in her diary, "First night of *Romeo and Juliet* at Lyceum—jolly failure—Irving awfully funny."

Ellen fared little better in the press. In reply to a friend who evidently defended her against the critics she wrote: "A thousand thanks for your letter. The fact remains that Juliet was a horrid failure. *And I meant so well!* I am very sad, but I thank you. *It is not the critics.* I knew it all on Wednesday night."

As usual, once the strain of an opening was over, both Irving and Ellen improved. Catching her later in the run, Sarah Bernhardt on a second visit to London came backstage. Embracing her friend, she exclaimed, "How can you, dear Madame, act like this night after night?"

"I cannot," Ellen answered. "But you were in front tonight and that inspired me."

Ellen liked to play for one sympathetic person in an

audience, as many actors do. But to an unusual degree, all acting for her was a personal relationship and she needed to feel that the entire audience was "with her." "I love my audiences," she once said, "and I want them to love me." In later years, when she made a few movies, it was hard for her to adjust to the impersonality of a camera.

Irving celebrated the one hundredth performance of *Romeo and Juliet* with another banquet on the stage. The afterdinner oratory side-stepped the current offering and dwelt on the Lyceum's hopes and goals. One goal was a North American tour to be undertaken the next season.

It was probably in anticipation of this trip that Ellen appointed the Honorable Stephen Coleridge to be Teddy's legal guardian. Her platonic dalliance with Stephen had settled into a firm friendship; now he was a budding diplomat and married. His first duty was to advise Ellen to send the boy to a school in Kent, run by the Reverend Mr. Wilkinson and his wife. At eleven, Teddy scorned this little academy on sight because most of the boys were not "gentlemen," but he soon admitted to having "fine larks." Separated from Teddy longer than ever before, Ellen began to shower him with letters. In an undated specimen, probably written as he was winding up a term in 1883, she struck the archetypal "mother's tone," mildly admonitory and hopelessly devoted:

Ted, my darling—I never know whether you receive things or not that I send you—so there's not much encouragement to send 'em!

Now that your time at Southfield Park is coming to an end, I'll send you one *jolly good Hamper*—I'll send (if you'd like them) a *Cake* (2 cakes)—*3 boxes of Sardines*—*Some biscuits*—*Bon-Bons* (to pull)—some *Jam*—*Toffy* (or some kind of sweet) and some *Oranges*—Now *I* think that will be a splendid Hamper!! *Don't you?* Are you getting on better with your work now? Keep your record for *"good conduct"* clean at *least,* to the very end of your stay with Mrs. Wilkinson. . . . Shakespeare! Why surely you *have* a Shakespeare with you—You shall have the Walter Scott when you come home. . . . Best regards to Mr. and Mrs. Wilkinson. Boo is well—so is Fussy and Puffy and the bird, but I have one of my severe colds, and cannot sleep.

God bless you my darling boy,
y^r *Mum.*

Events were shaping toward the projected trip. While Teddy was happily installed at boarding school, Edy became a boarder at Miss Cole's School, and Irving was getting ready to present *Much Ado about Nothing*, enabling Ellen to repeat her earlier success as Beatrice and stacking the cards, he hoped, so his company could leave Britain on a high note of triumph.

Of all her roles, Beatrice represented the quintessential Terry, playful, independent, thoughtful, passionate in derision and, later, in love. As she acted her, Beatrice pointed to the changing position of Victorian women, veering toward great self-reliance and expression, using their wit to tame stuck-up bachelors. Ellen took pains not to make Beatrice too shrill, her belief being that the lines should be spoken with the lightest raillery, "with mirth in voice and charm in manner," as a reminder that women's liberation need not entail the loss of women's grace.

Much Ado was unanimously commended, racking up an unbroken run of seven months. During the run, the pageantry of its cathedral scene was painted by Ellen's old admirer Johnston Forbes-Roberston, who had visited her back at Taviton Street and joined her in *The Wandering Heir*. Since Irving had hired him to play Claudio in *Much Ado*, it seemed only sensible to take advantage of his brushes and palette; his painting now hangs in the Players Club in New York City.

Before embarking for America, Ellen and Irving were given a send-off at the Lyceum, the audience singing *Auld Lang Syne* across a sea of waving white handkerchiefs. Just before leaving, the company took a short provincial tour to test their new stage equipment. At Glasgow, Ellen was joined by her two children and was invited by Sir William

147

Pearce, along with Irving and Bram Stoker, for a weekend cruise on his elegant new steam yacht, *Lady Torfrida*.

In a raging storm the little party was transported by night in a rowboat to the yacht. Blue flares were lighted to attract the attention of *Lady Torfrida*, which seemed to be lost in the dark, while mountainous waves slammed against the little craft and drenched the passengers. To keep Teddy from being frightened, Ellen chatted with him as if they were watching some of Irving's stage effects. When the party was hauled aboard, Teddy was thrilled. "It was a wonderful fine, luxe yacht," he wrote in his diary. "I went down to the cabin. The storm seemed to have vanished—had a most wonderful supper and went off to bed—to bunk. Rose about eight the next day. Saw to right and left signs of wreckage. There had been a very devil of a storm." Being Ellen Terry's son was manifestly all he needed to be to outride a tempest and be welcomed into a world of privilege and luxury.

Later during the cruise, when Ellen and the children stood on deck, the captain pointed out a magnificently rugged rock called Ailsa Craig ("craig" is a Scotch variation of crag). The name so appealed to Ellen that she said she might bestow it on Edy. Teddy said he wanted it too. In time, both her children took Craig for a last name.

On October 11, 1883, Ellen and Irving sailed on the S.S. *Britannic*. Flocks of friends came to see them off, including Lillie Langtry and Oscar Wilde; Irving in the final flurry had managed to have a farewell lunch with Gladstone. The rest of the Lyceum troupe, as well as the scenery and costumes, followed in a slower ship, *The City of Rome*.

Many other English actors had crossed the Atlantic before, but never in a single company of such magnitude, carrying tons of equipment for twelve plays, nearly a hundred performers and technicians, including three wigmakers to tend eleven hundred new wigs. Ellen Terry was treated like royalty. Part of the ship's drawing room had been screened off for her private use, and for her comfort two cabins had been rebuilt as one.

During the months that Ellen had contemplated the trip, she worked up some suitably dramatic forebodings; she knew she would "never, never return." Boo would be dead, the children lost. But once she sniffed the open seas she was exhilarated. It was the same kind of excitement she had first tasted when at thirteen she took a summer tour with her mother and father and Kate, going from town to town playing *Home for the Holidays*. The difference was really not so great. Then she walked from Bristol to Exeter; now she was sailing from Liverpool to New York.

Chapter Seven

ALMOST HALF-AMERICAN

When the *Britannic* came to anchor in New York harbor, two welcoming craft approached it on opposite sides. One was the chartered river steamer *Blackbird*, carrying thirty reporters who had boarded her late Saturday night and napped in the ladies' lounge in order to be ready to pounce on Irving and Ellen at dawn. Also aboard the *Blackbird* was a little group of late revelers from the Lotus Club, hell-bent on paying homage to the distinguished visitors, and an Italian band, provided by Irving's American manager, Henry B. Abbey, who was opening the new Metropolitan Opera House in a day or two and presumably could conjure up a band at any hour.

The other welcoming craft was Colonel Tilden's luxurious yacht *Yosemite,* carrying two of Irving's actor friends and America's foremost dramatic critic, William Winter, who had fallen under the Irving-Terry spell in London. Neither Ellen nor Irving appeared on deck at first, and somebody shouted that Irving was still shaving. But never one to keep an audience waiting, Irving showed up presently, looking pale and imposing, and, while the band played *Hail to the Chief,* started to cross the precarious little gangplank that had been laid between the *Britannic* and the top of the *Blackbird*'s paddle wheel. Halfway across, Irving was hallooed by the *Yosemite* greeters who had clambered aboard the *Britannic* on the other side and were beckoning him back to their yacht. What might have been an embarrassing social dilemma for Irving, in the position now of a woman between two beseeching lovers, was solved when it became known that the *Yosemite* was well stocked with chicken and iced champagne. Irving turned backwards, and the *Blackbird* crowd transferred to the *Yosemite* for the press interviews and refreshments.

After Irving had won over the reporters with his modesty and excellent cigars, Ellen entered while the band played *Rule Britannia*, looking too frightened to rule a cup of tea. She had been warned that American reporters were devils who asked terrible questions and sometimes went so far as to disguise themselves as bellboys and sailors in order to spy and pry. When Irving introduced her, he whispered to her to say something friendly; but when a reporter began by asking if he could send her friends back home a message from her, she broke into tears and sobbed, "Tell them I never loved 'em so much as now."

When she was asked, "Do you appear in one of your best characters in *Charles I* which Mr. Irving has chosen for your opening night?" she replied grumpily, "No. I do not like the part, and I really don't see quite why I am to make my first appearance here in *Charles I*." As for her clothes, one reporter struggled to describe her bows, scarf, and sash, her color scheme of "greenish-brown . . . and peculiar shade of red," and ended in panic by comparing her to both "some eighteenth-century portrait," and "some Pre-Raphaelite saint." Though she certainly did not put her best foot forward, nobody could accuse her of false cordiality. She aired her emotions freely, as she usually did, and no harm was done.

She and Irving rode off in separate carriages to their hotels, Ellen depressed at first by "the muddy sidewalk and the cavernous holes in the cobble-paved streets." While Irving put up at the Brevoort on Fifth Avenue off Washington Square, Ellen went farther uptown to the Hotel Dam (named after its proprietor) on Union Square almost next door to the Star Theater on 13th Street where the Lyceum company was booked for six weeks.

With a week free before their stint began, Ellen had time to sample New York theaters and inspect the city. On their first night, Irving took her to a blackface minstrel show. Ellen did not understand the comedians' jokes but said she liked "their cool, dry way of making them." During the Lyceum engagement other theaters were offering Joseph Jefferson, escaping from his famous success, *Rip Van Winkle,* to play *The Cricket on the Hearth;* Sardou's *Fedora;* the great comic team Harrigan and Hart in *The Mulligan Guard Picnic.* A whole catalog of Irving's mannerisms were being lampooned at Tony Pastor's music hall, while in another playhouse the comedian Henry E. Dixey, dressed up as Irving, "convulsed" the audience. There is no record of anyone joshing Ellen Terry; she was not so easy to caricature.

The season's major event was the opening of the new Metropolitan Opera House with Gounod's *Faust* on the night after Ellen and Irving arrived. When asked if he expected to attend, Irving replied, "I do not wish to appear before the public in any way until I have made my own appearance at the Star. . . ." He and Ellen did slip quietly in to see their old friend Joe Jefferson and also Laurence Barrett, who, with young Otis Skinner, then twenty-four, was playing in the popular tragedy *Francesca da Rimini* at the Star, just before the Lyceum troupe moved in.

Waiting for their booking to start, Ellen found time to drive in Central Park, admire the new mansions being built on Fifth Avenue, and survey the city's inhabitants. "Of course, there is poverty in New York, but not among the Americans. The Italians, the Russians, the Poles—all the host of immigrants washing in daily on the bosom of the Hudson—these are poor, but you can't help feeling that in their suffering is hope. The barrow man of today is the millionaire of tomorrow! Vulgarity? I saw little of it. I thought that the people who had amassed large fortunes used their wealth beautifully."

Ellen was entranced by the Brooklyn Bridge, which

had been open only since May and was the subject of a popular song, *Strolling on the Brooklyn Bridge*. She visited it many times and liked it best when it was coated with ice and snow, "a gigantic trellis of dazzling white. . . ."

Ellen responded more graciously to America than did her countryman Matthew Arnold, who arrived in New York a week later on a lecture tour and upset his audiences, according to the theater historian of the New York stage G. C. D. Odell, with his "high and rather condescending tone." Arnold mentioned in passing that he was glad Mr. Henry Irving, whom he knew well, had arrived safely in America and pronounced him an able actor "in spite of certain mannerisms and peculiarities of elocution." Still another lofty Englishman, Lord Chief Justice Coleridge, with his son Gilbert, joined the British invasion of Manhattan at the same time; he referred to his friend Irving as "eminent in dramatic art."

For the star opening, Ellen did not act but sat in a box with young Gilbert Coleridge and watched Henry perform *The Bells*; he had been advised to offer it first in America since it was surefire. Act 1 went badly, and Henry in his dressing room ranted that the Americans were "icebergs." But things picked up and swept to the hoped-for ovation at the end. After the show, as Irving and Coleridge were walking Ellen back to her hotel, she broke into a dance on the sidewalk and then all three linked arms in a jubilant caper.

On the next night, Ellen had her innings as Henrietta Maria, who married the Stuart king Charles I. This was the part Ellen did not like—understandably, since it gave her little to do but display wifely devotion and shudder at the rumors of Cromwell's plot to overthrow her husband. Yet such roles, now and then, were immensely important to her image as a star. Queen Henrietta personified all the noble docility that good wives up to recently hoped to possess and that every husband liked his wife to display in public. That she was a queen to boot made it still more exciting to a queen-dominated empire, and even to Americans. She suggested, not too logically, that every virtuous woman was a queen and every queen, a virtuous woman.

Ellen Terry never lent herself cynically to these idealized portrayals. Once the curtain was up, she believed in what she was doing. When the play took a sad turn, her eyes overflowed, and she made the audience weep along with her. Looking back on Ellen's teary role as Queen Henrietta, her son, Gordon Craig, held forth on how the English public loved a good cry "and likes it best very soppy, and to last very long. How my mother used to laugh when anybody was like that—what astounding virility and power in her healthy sense of humor! And yet, *faced with the public,* rather than carry the public along or fight it, she would side with the cowlike animal and begin to imitate its face and to drop tears all over the place."

Calling the public "the cowlike animal" came naturally to lordly Gordon Craig; but not to Ellen Terry. Although she saw the comic side of people, their weaknesses and pretenses, she was simply incapable of condescension. In a statement remarkable for any young woman, she once said, "I have always thought it hard to find my inferiors." This must not be mistaken as an expression of humility. She was not selling herself short—or anybody else.

Victorian audiences were proud to unleash their emotions, to roar with glee or anger, to shudder or hiss, and, above all, to cry. These were, to be sure, age-old rewards in the theater. Shakespeare's rustic buffoons boasted that they could make the ladies cry. Greek audiences heaved tragic sighs over Electra's woes. And Japanese audiences, reports Clement Scott, wept so copiously in Tokyo that he feared they would flood the little cooking fires in all the private boxes. Like Alice in Wonderland, Ellen herself shed pools of tears deep enough for a mouse to swim in, and she was satisfied only when the audience kept up their end.

In her first New York engagement, Ellen played only one important role, Portia. Her reviews left no doubt that she created a favorable impression; but, as usual, the critics struggled to convey "her strange fascination" and her "spiritual majesty." Once again, the star was outshining the actress, which helped promote the false impression that her gifts as an actress were of lesser account.

As company boss, Irving had many more official duties than Ellen. He was always addressing various civic groups, paying calls on newspaper editors and patrons of the arts, spreading goodwill with ambassadorial largess. Scrupulously, when speaking on behalf of his Lyceum group, Irving paid homage to Miss Ellen Terry as "my sister in art." But Ellen kept herself in the background where she felt she belonged, and where she preferred to be. Meetings bored her, and Henry handled them so well.

An exception to the rule was an invitation from the famous pastor Henry Ward Beecher. At seventy, Beecher had never been to a theater until, with his wife, he saw a Lyceum production of *Louis XI*. As he wrote to Irving later, "It burst upon my ripe old age as June would to a Greenlander." The upshot was that he invited Ellen and Irving to attend one of his Sunday morning services in his vast Plymouth Church in Brooklyn, to be followed by lunch at the Beechers' house.

Beecher was a spellbinder like Irving; in fact, with his long gray locks falling to his shoulders, his erect carriage and proud head, he looked distinctly actorish. But in spirit he was closer to Ellen. At heart a rule-breaker, he liked to romp with children at Sunday school picnics and was as casual in his clothes as he was cordial to everyone he met. Accused of seducing a friend's wife, he was finally cleared in court after lengthy litigation; but a cloud of scandal still hung over him, which put a crimp in the spectacle of his sanctity but not his popularity. His wife, Eunice, who bore him ten children, was steadfastly loyal and held hands with him, Ellen noticed, at the dinner table.

Beecher had a sensualist's yen for rich colors and rare objects, and he sometimes kept precious gems in his

pocket to fondle and to feast his eyes on. He offered Ellen
an aquamarine. Before accepting it, Ellen turned to Mrs.
Beecher and asked if it would be all right. The hostess
granted her permission—what else could she do?—and in
due course Beecher had the stone set into a Venetian ring
for Ellen to wear as Portia. At first, Eunice Beecher was
polite but aloof, probably in the belief that all actresses
were sinful. But before the visit ended, Eunice was reminiscing freely about her own strict girlhood, when her father
once threw scalding soup at her neck because she was
wearing a new blue silk dress with a modestly open collar.
As the two women said good-bye, they both honored the
occasion by crying. "That a woman who had been brought
up like this," Ellen reflected later, "should form a friendship with me naturally caused a good deal of talk. But what
did she care? She remained my true friend until her death,
and wrote to me constantly when I was in England."

When the company set out for Philadelphia, their private train consisted of eight coaches, two boxcars, and an
immense open "gondola," all packed with poles and rig-
ging, 150 stage baskets full of costumes and small props,
and a fold-away wonderland of palaces, parapets, churches,
gardens, balustrades, stairways, and snowy landscapes.
By the time this cargo had been unloaded and carted
to the Chestnut Street Theater, Irving and his henchmen realized that they could not handle all these bulky
wonders on tour. They used them in Philadelphia, but before the troupe rolled on to Boston, they sent a huge portion—twenty-seven drops, sixty wings, eighty flats—back
to New York. Thus it turned out that only two cities saw
the Irving shows in all their grandeur. In other cities the
troupe used simplified settings, augmented by pieces of
scenery ordered in advance from local carpenters and scene
painters. There was no skimping on costumes, however,
and the actors rose to the challenge of reduced scenery by
doing their best.

Ellen approved Philadelphia's "red brick sidewalks,

the trees in the streets, and the low houses with their white marble cuffs and collars." Boston was more stimulating. She played there so many different times that her memories were not always in chronological order; but she vividly recalled the witty, exuberant Mrs. Jack Gardner whose art treasures were housed in her incredible palazzo with its lofty indoor courtyard transported stone by stone from Venice. Ellen gave special eye to John Singer Sargent's portrait *Mrs. Jack,* in which she is dressed in tight-fitting black, with no ornament except a rope of pearls wrapped twice around her slim waist. A year after Sargent did Mrs. Jack, he painted Ellen as Lady Macbeth in an outfit as daringly elaborate as Mrs. Jack's was daringly plain.

A favorite Boston oasis for "rest and peace" for Ellen was Oliver Wendell Holmes's house on Beacon Street: "Oh, the visits I inflicted on him." Since it was usually winter, they moved their chairs close to the fireplace and, as Ellen said, "at once it was four feet on a fender." Holmes belonged to a group of American authors, including Henry James, Mark Twain, and Bret Harte, who made periodic stabs at playwriting, usually with dismal results. The basic difficulty seemed to be that they wanted to flirt with the hussy, the Stage, for both pleasure and profit, without bothering really to learn the craft of the profession and without serving the long, and often grubby, internship that produces an effective dramatist. Whatever the case, Holmes's interest in the drama made him a stimulating host to Ellen Terry, who, after all, represented the most distinguished element in the English-speaking theater and could be welcomed safely to a gentleman's hearth. As for Irving, he also met Holmes, and such literary figures as Mark Twain and William Dean Howells, at a dinner given in the actor's honor at Boston's Somerset Club.

Privately Ellen responded to a wider variety of people than Irving could; he felt most relaxed after a night's hard work with a group of theater cronies drinking port and swapping tales. At other times he was always aware of his position as an eminent actor, and although he did not put on imperial airs, he remained unshakably onstage. Ellen, on the contrary, was never onstage when she was off. In fact, considering her outstanding ease of manner before an audience, some people felt she was not sufficiently "onstage" onstage.

From Boston, the Lyceum caravan proceeded through blizzards and snow-blocked tracks to Baltimore for Christmas. Remembering from her own youth how strolling players like treats, Ellen's mother had baked and sent a plum pudding. Then the troupe looped back to Brooklyn and, after a week there, headed for Chicago in a train provided by the president of the Erie Railroad. The entire crew was armed because of a train-robber scare.

Ellen was pleased to find that the youthful Prairie City was not as barbaric as it had been painted. The Chicago audience reacted ecstatically to *Hamlet,* and Ellen felt that her Ophelia had never been better. The company's erratic schedule, designed to take advantage of available bookings, obliged them to play in Chicago two weeks, then dart off to Cincinnati, Columbus, and Indianapolis, and then to come back to Chicago for a third week. But despite this exhausting zigzagging, despite the coldest winter in eleven years, despite the fact that during their Chicago run the ubiquitous Mark Twain, at the height of his popularity, was a rival sellout attraction, Ellen and Irving liked Chicago and always looked forward to returning.

After two days in Detroit, the company took a day off to sightsee, and Ellen began her long love-hate relationship with Niagara Falls. She wandered off to look at it in solitude. "It became dreadful. . . . I was *frightened* by it . . . felt queer . . . wanted to follow the great flow of it." At another time she was staggered by its beauty, "with pits of color in the waters, no one color definite. All was wonderment, allurement, fascination." At her final visit it was "wonderful, but not beautiful any more. The merely stupendous, the merely marvelous has always repelled me."

In Toronto, Ellen abandoned herself to nature again

and went tobogganing. "I should say it was like flying! The start! Amazing! 'Farewell to this world,' I thought as I felt my breath go. Then I shut my mouth, opened my eyes, and found myself at the bottom of the hill in a jiffy. I rolled right out of the toboggan when we stopped. . . . Henry Irving would not come, much to my disappointment. He said that quick motion through the air always gave him the earache."

After a week in Washington, where Ellen and Irving dined at the White House with the luxury-loving President Chester Arthur, the company toured three cities in New England, while Ellen, needing a rest, stayed in the capital city in the home of her new friend, Miss Olive Seward, the adopted daughter of ex-Secretary of State William H. Seward. Almost wherever she went, Ellen scooped up new admirers, especially among intelligent women who were charmed by her forthright, emancipated attitudes.

The American tour wound up with return bookings in Brooklyn and New York, followed by a flurry of farewell speeches and two breakfast parties at Delmonico's. At one of these, the critic William Winter read sixty-four lines of his own execrable verse in praise of Henry Irving, including a fleeting reference to Ellen Terry. After declaiming that Irving would have heavenly powers "to guide him," the poet added, "and blessings pour like diamond dew on her that walks beside him!"

The metaphor of diamond dew was relevant to the whole Lyceum tour, although it might have been altered to golden rain. To see the English actors, Americans paid over $400,000. After expenses, some £11,700 remained to plow back into future Lyceum productions. Weeks before Irving left, he was mapping out his next American tour under his own management. Most of the troupe, with Bram Stoker in charge, sailed home in late April; three days later, Ellen, Irving, and Mr. Loveday left on the *Aurania*. In a shipboard benefit for the Liverpool Seamen's Orphan Asylum, they recited scenes from Tennyson's *The Cup*.

To call the tour a honeymoon for Ellen and Irving may

be as metaphoric as "diamond dew." Yet in the context of their special "marriage," the tour served some honeymoon purposes. They began to store up a wealth of shared adventures, enough to keep the embers of reminiscence glowing for years. They proved that their affection for each other was sturdy enough to survive the ordeals of travel, the demands of being punctual—train time, curtain time, interview time, packing time—the disrupting shifts of climate, diet, sleeping hours. Also, they survived the stresses of being in an alien land, uprooted, deprived of familiar faces and landmarks, which just by their absence can make travelers feel forlorn, cranky, and sometimes illogically hostile to each other. Ellen discovered that Irving could be a martinet, stiff and pompous, but she loved him anyway. Irving discovered that Ellen could be wayward and foolishly flippant, but he saw that she was invaluable to him. As he wrote to a friend in England, telling of Ellen just before their tour ended, "She was even better than she was in dear old England and has had a glorious success."

A few weeks after their return to London they staged *Twelfth Night* with Irving as Malvolio and Ellen in a role Shakespeare might have written for her: Viola. *Twelfth Night* was a flop. Irving tried to be both comic and tragic, which might have worked if he had had strong comic support from the play's other zanies. And Ellen contracted an agonizing case of blood poisoning from a scratch on her finger which necessitated having her arm in a sling on the opening night and tortured her so that through most of the play she had to sit. A night or two later, Bram Stoker's brother, a doctor, came backstage and lanced the finger. With any more delay, he said, it would have been necessary to amputate the arm. An understudy took over Viola, and Ellen was bedridden in her home. To make it easier for her to rest, Irving ordered the street in front of her house to be covered with straw to muffle the clatter of carriage wheels.

During their absence, Ellen and Irving discovered that

their respective sons had developed identical interests—in the theater. For a charity show, Irving's two boys, Henry, Jr., and Laurence, had done a scene from *The School for Scandal;* and in a school play, Ellen's son, Teddy, was acting Bluebeard. Irving did not want his boys sidetracked into the theater before they had a good education. Ellen was worried by Teddy's presumptuous tone in ordering his mother to have Arnott, the overworked property man at the Lyceum, "make me a wooden sword nicely finished and curved a good shape and give him something—a present for making it." Already little Teddy was serenely secure in his lifelong belief, "Ask Mother and ye shall receive."

Both Ellen and Irving were beset by parental worries, and each desired to be helpful to the other. At this stage, Ellen had no contact with Irving's two boys; they saw little of their father, and their mother instilled in them a contempt for Ellen Terry, whom she called "the serpent, scarlet woman" and "wench." So Ellen had to wait several years before she could overcome the boys' prejudice and be useful to them. Irving had no such obstacle in befriending Ellen's children. Ellen was immensely gratified by Irving's concern, especially for Teddy, who, being virtually fatherless, needed an older man to respect and love.

The illness from her blood infection weakened Ellen for many weeks. Though she managed to sail in September 1884 for the second American tour, she dropped out of several Canadian engagements. In Boston, Philadelphia, and New York she felt better, enjoying her reunions with American friends and having her first success in *Twelfth Night.* As the Christmas season drew on, she longed for her family and telegraphed Stephen Coleridge, "Bring over one of the children."

It was a wisely worded wire, leaving the choice to Coleridge, making the children feel she loved them equally, and would be happy to see either one.

Coleridge picked Teddy, who was twelve at the time.

161

The crossing was rough; Teddy was seasick and walked in his sleep during the day. He might have toppled overboard, he liked to recall, if the captain had not grabbed him by the elbow just in time. He was met in New York by Irving's private secretary, Lewis Austin, who wrote his wife that Teddy "looked like a peach . . . never was a nicer lad . . . pursued by all the little girls in the hotel. One of them wanted to be introduced, so Teddy told a waiter that he would be glad to see the young woman, but she ran away." In the future, not many young women would run away from Gordon Craig. Teddy noted in his diary, "December 24: Arrived in Pittsburg in time for Christmas Day with Xmas pudding." He might have added that the pudding had been packed with Ellen's furs and, as she said, it "simply reeked of camphor balls." It could not be eaten.

In Chicago, Irving gave Teddy the small part of Joey, a gardener's boy in *Eugene Aram*. Ellen was blissful when a local critic wrote: "His eyes are full of sparkle, his smile is a ripple over his face. . . . This Joey is Ellen Terry's son and the apple of her eye. On this Wednesday night, January 14, 1885, he spoke his first lines upon the stage. . . . He has the instinct and the soul of art in him. . . ."

Two days later, on Teddy's thirteenth birthday, Irving gave him *Robin Hood*, illustrated by Howard Pyle. Pyle's rigorous style had an enduring influence on the boy, especially evident in his woodcuts and costume designs. For years he diligently clipped and pasted Pyle's magazine illustrations in a scrapbook. Perhaps Pyle's greatest value to Teddy was psychological rather than artistic, leading him into new realms of art, distinct from the theatrical art of his mother. At the same time, Teddy began to find a father in Irving, which was all the more beneficial because the boy saw the love and respect between Irving and his mother. In this cluster of emotions, Ellen loved Irving still more because of his concern for her son.

Teddy toured more than three months, playing walk-on roles in several plays. Somewhere along the line he acquired a sled. When the train stopped on a stretch of snowy track, Lewis Austin took Teddy out on a sled ride, pulling him with a rope. Then Ellen joined them, and Austin pulled her about. In turn, Ellen ordered Austin to sit on the sled while she, the reigning actress of Britain, acted a sleigh horse. Irving ventured out on the steps of his train to watch these capers but refused Ellen's offer to give him a ride.

In April the tour ended on familiar ground, and Ellen announced that by now she felt almost half-American. Henry lectured at Harvard while Ellen revisited old friends in Boston. In New York, Ellen introduced Teddy to the Brooklyn Bridge; she now considered it as if it were her personal property. In a photograph taken on deck of the homeward-bound S.S. *Arizona*, Teddy, with an ear-to-ear grin, sits in a group that includes Henry Irving, Ellen Terry, and the ship's captain. It is the first known picture of Teddy in what looks like a happy family party. Teddy lived to be eighty-four, but he never returned to America.

A day or two after Ellen returned to London, a pretty but poorly dressed young woman, who called herself "Mrs. Wardell," paid her a visit. Mr. Wardell, she said, was seriously ill and begged to see his former wife. The woman took Ellen to their shabby quarters where Wardell, comforted by a last glimpse of Ellen, died in her presence. Ellen admitted to a curious sensation as she stood by Charles's deathbed; she felt she was playing the tomb scene in *Romeo and Juliet*. As often happened with Ellen, fantasy and reality blended, and by projecting herself into an imaginary death scene, she was better able to bear the painful reality of the actual event. It was natural for Ellen to feel some guilt about Charles Wardell, for to some extent, she had used him to give her children a legal status. After his death, she settled all his debts and for years supported his first wife's sisters.

Immediately upon arriving home, the Lyceum company put on a week of *Hamlet,* and then Irving prepared a revival of *Olivia,* Ellen's first great success seven years earlier at the Court. Since *Olivia* was an easy show to produce, it gave Irving a chance to plan ahead for his most ambitious production, *Faust.*

Olivia was like a family reunion. William Terriss, better known as "Breezy Bill," was back at the Lyceum, enchanting Ellen as he had before with his rakish charms, and both Teddy and Edy were back, not for just an evening or two, but as full-time villagers. Sir Arthur Sullivan (between his productions of *The Mikado* and *Ruddigore*) contributed a new song, and an extra scene was added in the last act so Ellen and Irving could stand outside the old parsonage on a snowy winter night and gaze through the window at a happy family gathering inside. Irving loved snow scenes; he knew that audiences marveled at seeing winter weather conjured up inside a warm, cozy theater.

Irving had trouble trimming his sails for the bland role of Dr. Primrose, the Vicar of Wakefield. During rehearsals he trotted out his specialties, his eerie looks, fateful pauses, and masterful twitches. Nobody dared to object until Ellen's fearless Edy, now fifteen, cried out, "Henry, don't go on like that." Not for years had anyone spoken so bluntly to Henry Irving. In the horrified silence, Edy pressed on: "Why don't you talk as you do to me and Teddy? At home you *are* the Vicar."

Contrary to what anybody expected, Irving listened attentively, and then proceeded to follow Edy's advice and reduced his theatrics. Recalling the episode later, Ellen wrote, "A terrible child *and* a wonderful critic."

Olivia was even more cordially and weepily received than it had been the first time. Ellen's portrayal was called "more profound," and Irving was commended for "a performance more carefully restrained and modulated, a study more innocent of tricks and less disfigured by characteristics of marked style and individuality than anything he has attempted before." Irving's subduing, however, did not come easily. In the wings during a performance, he was observed letting out a secret melodramatic snarl, "Bah—ahhh," just before stepping onstage to radiate muted holiness.

In August, *Olivia*'s reign was interrupted while Ellen and her two children joined Irving on a trip to Germany to scout for ideas—for scenery, costumes, props—for the new *Faust*. With them were two of Ellen's oldest friends, Alice and Joe Comyns Carr. Alice was a costume designer, and her husband was director of the Grosvenor Gallery and editor of the *English Illustrated Weekly*. Their base of exploration was the medieval city of Nuremberg, which allegedly was Faust country. When word got around that Irving was preparing *Faust*, shopkeepers and castle-owners brought out their treasures, and bands played in the visitors' honor. Most of the time, they were welcomed. But on one occasion, when Joe Carr, Teddy, and Irving were prying into the Nuremberg slums, they were faced by a menacing band of hoodlums who assumed that the visitors were rich enough to rob. As the thugs came closer, Irving refused to retreat. Instead, he assumed the most hideous expression and terrifying posture in his whole repertory, and the attackers ran off in terror. Teddy was so impressed by this show of theatrical prowess that years later he tried it on a harmless crowd in Italy, brandishing a stick and shouting, "I am the demon dwarf of blood!" The crowd fled.

Irving had been brooding over *Faust* for several years. To take care of the wordage, he enlisted the dependable W. G. Wills, who, under Irving's guidance, began patching together an acting script. Billed as "Wills's version of Goethe's *Faust*," the play, in its operatic flamboyance, owed a lot more to Gounod's *Faust*. It certainly owed next to nothing to Goethe. Goethe's name was an asset, though, for it added an aura of intellectuality, the perfume of high culture which the Lyceum customers loved to inhale.

Ellen Terry knew from the start that in playing Margaret she faced two sources of formidable competition.

One was Irving himself. From the moment he towered out of a billow of sulfurous smoke in Faust's study caparisoned in crimson from his sandals to the cocky feather in his hood, Irving was in malevolent command. The swirling of his cape was in itself an act of sorcery. Critics marveled at his flashing white teeth—probably the only time that Irving, who performed with every other part of his anatomy, acted with his teeth. Unlike the French portrayals of Lucifer with their amusing hints of a wicked roué, Irving was all evil. Audiences cringed in terror at his outburst:

> . . . I'd tear you limb from limb,
> your blood I'd dash
> Upon the wind like rain
> And all the gobbets of your mangled flesh
> I'd seize up in a whirlwind
> And hurl them worlds away
> With your crushed quivering spirit under them.

Ellen was also in danger of being outshone by the scenery. Never had such stage effects been crowded into one drama. When Irving started out, like a tour guide, to show Dr. Faust "every sensual pleasure known to man," the pair were hoisted into the air, disappearing out of sight, and from then on there was no solid ground under anybody. Pits opened in the stage as apparitions appeared and vanished, fogs and fenny hazes blurred the border lines of reality. When Faust dueled with Margaret's brother, their swords emitted sparks, a sensational new effect created by having the weapons connected by invisible wires to sources of electric power—which obliged the duelists to wear rubber gloves or else be electrocuted. Most arresting of all were the Walpurgis Night revels when "forms weird but squalid begin to congregate and gibber . . . and Mephistopheles, seated on a rock in front, is fondled by two queer juvenile-seeming creatures, for whom he appears to have, and they for him, an affection that curdles the beholders."

Yet, despite all these counterattractions, Ellen held her own and liked playing Margaret, at least for a while, better than any other non-Shakespearean role. To a sugary character whose soul is damned by Faust and the devil, Ellen brought such depth of emotion—innocent joy, passion, and agonizing remorse—that audiences were overwhelmed. In essence, it was the same kind of tosh that Irving played in *The Bells* and in Wills's adaptation of *The Dream of Eugene Aram;* a decent human being succumbs to sin and is doomed to eternal hellfire. As she awaits the hangman in prison, after causing the death of her brother, her mother, and her illegitimate baby, Ellen's grief was profoundly moving. There was probably no sadder moment in Lyceum drama than her last instructions for her burial:

> Tomorrow I must die,
> And I must tell thee how to range the graves.
> My mother the best place—next her my brother,
> Me well apart, but, dearest, not too far,
> And by my side my little one shall lie.

Wills's *Faust* lifted Ellen to her full glory as a star. People waited at the stage door to see her enter and leave. As Margaret she embodied all that was wholesome and bright, yet she was human enough to err and devout enough to repent. Her admirers from then on would care less and less what parts she played or who she really was than about what they chose to make of her.

Faust, in its resplendently trashy way, was also the apogee of old-fashioned Victorian theater. Henry James regarded it, rightly, as a defilement of Goethe and no better than a Christmas pantomime. Its continuing popularity dissuaded Irving from touring America in 1886. So Ellen was in London when she received word that Edward Godwin had died on October 6. A mutual friend had brought the news to her so she would be spared the shock of reading it in the paper. The friend said she never would forget the look on Ellen's face, as she cried, "There was no one like him." Among her belongings, she always kept a picture of Godwin on which she had inscribed, "Better to have loved and lost than never to have loved at all."

Ellen's grief was less for Godwin's death—she had already lost him—than for his unfulfilled life. After their separation, Godwin had pursued his career with moderate success. He did several stage productions that were distinguished: *Helena in Troas*, a *Hamlet*, an outdoor *As You Like It*. He was the architect of a few more exceptional buildings, including the "White House," a home-studio in Chelsea for his friend Whistler. He was considered a genius by many connoisseurs, but there was no escaping the impression that his life had somehow misfired, that his talents had not fully flowered. Suffering from a painful illness, he booked himself into a hospital ward and announced, "The next ward may be six by four by two. I feel completely done with life." He was. After an operation, he never rallied from the anesthetic, and he died at the age of fifty-three.

His funeral was a strange, sad affair. His wife and two of his closest friends, Whistler and Lady Archibald Campbell, accompanied the coffin by train to Oxfordshire. When it was placed in an open farm wagon, they crowded in beside it, and as the rustic hearse jolted through the autumnal country lanes, they used the covered coffin as a table for a makeshift meal. The burial, as Godwin wished, was "in the corner of a field" near a church.

These melancholy events added to Ellen's resolve to give all possible attention to her boy, Teddy. Entering a period of what might be called intensive motherhood, Ellen was determined that he should have a happier, more fruitful life than his father's, and fearing, perhaps, that his father was a bit equivocal in business matters, Ellen tried to imbue Teddy with a sense of honor and responsibility.

Just before she and Irving began their third American tour, Ellen sent Teddy to a prep school in Heidelberg College. "I don't know who it was who gave my mother the

idea that it would be good if I went to a German town."
Ellen had also sent Edy to Berlin to study music. She might
have felt it would benefit her children to escape for a while
from her engulfing presence, that they might profit by the
discipline of German schools, and, away from England,
feel less handicapped socially.

Chapter Eight

A GOOD MOTHER? A GOOD QUEEN?

In November 1887, Irving and Ellen opened in New York for a five-week run, with *Faust* as the main draw. Since taking *Faust* on a long American tour would have meant simplifying the scenery and putting a damper on the hellfires, Irving wisely decided to cut his itinerary, not his spectacular stage effects. After New York, the company proceeded only to Philadelphia, Chicago, and Boston, and then looped back to New York for a final five weeks, just in time for the historic blizzard of '88.

By late Monday afternoon, January 12, as Ellen and Irving sat down for dinner at the Hoffman House, a Broadway hotel, the city was frozen stiff and the wind reached eighty-four miles an hour. Most of Manhattan's electric light poles had been blown down, and frost had cut off gas supplies. Five new shows were expected to open that night, but all were called off. Ellen and Irving lingered over dinner, assuming that their performance had also been canceled. But close to curtain time, a messenger ran up to the table, announcing that their audience had started to assemble. Hearing the news, a dozen male diners formed a rescue squad and took turns carrying Miss Terry on their shoulders for twelve blocks, or what might have been across the snowfields of Alaska, to the Star Theater. It was a very small audience, which included New York's Mayor and his daughter, but the show was a roaring success, and for once the glowing coals of the Witches' Sabbath looked more cheerful than sinister.

Later that night the famous tragic actor Maurice Bar-rymore jumped on a table in the Hoffman House saloon and outshouted the storm by reciting from *Julius Caesar:* "Friends, Romans, countrymen, lend me your ears. . . ." When a more sober onlooker tried to muffle him, insults were bandied and the night ended in a violent fistfight. This has no relevance at all to the life of Ellen Terry, except that it reminds one how, at certain times, people who are gathered in one place in ignorance of each other, are yet destined to meet and play important parts in one another's lives. While Maurice Barrymore was raving on a tabletop, his little daughter Ethel, aged nine, was safely asleep in the family's new brownstone uptown on West 47th Street. Within ten years, Ethel, soon to become a great American actress, would be playing on the Lyceum stage with Irving, and offstage Ellen would be trying to act as matchmaker for Ethel Barrymore and Irving's son Laurence.

Compared with Ellen's two previous tours, the third was far less strenuous. The only hit-and-run engagement was at the West Point Military Academy where the company had been invited to perform *The Merchant of Venice* on a bare stage. Ellen was delighted by the fresh-faced cadet audience, who threw their caps in the air at the end. In a farewell speech, Irving told the cadets that there would be joy bells ringing in London because at last the British had conquered West Point. More seriously, a senior officer at the Point wrote to a friend declaring that the Lyceum visit was of "enormous benefit," both to the United States and to Britain. Although no measure is possible, it is prob-able that Ellen and Irving, spending a total of nearly five years on tour in America, did more in their informal way to promote friendship between the two nations than a dozen ambassadors.

Back in London, a perennial problem awaited them: what to do next? Finding worthy plays for Ellen Terry was difficult, just as it was difficult to find worthy plays at all. In his first four years as head of the Lyceum, Irving spent nine thousand pounds on advance payments for new scripts that the authors never finished to Irving's approval. He was determined to give every Shakespeare play that suited the talents of one or both the stars, but they were sometimes unsure of what was suitable.

Irving wanted to play Brutus in *Julius Caesar*. Yet he knew that Mark Anthony might run away with the show, and, worse, there was no good part for Ellen. *The Tempest?* Irving fancied himself as the fearful monster Caliban—but again, nothing for Ellen. *Macbeth?* Ellen tried to talk him out of it, reminding him that when he first acted Macbeth with the Batemans, he was only moderately successful. In the back of her mind perhaps was a suspicion that as Lady Macbeth she herself might fail. Whatever the case, Irving announced *Macbeth* and assured Ellen that he had complete confidence in her. They took a quick trip to Scotland to look for scenery that might suggest a "blasted heath," but they saw nothing but flourishing potato fields. In her diary Ellen wrote, "We must blast our own heath when we do *Macbeth*."

Ellen was rightly apprehensive. Lady Macbeth is the most awe-inspiring of all Shakespeare's women, and Ellen feared that her own strong points, her humor and gentle pathos, would be worse than useless to her. The very notion of Ellen playing the Killer Queen would strike some of her admirers as ludicrous, so she had reason to feel licked before she started. But once having agreed to take the risk, she began to study the role with painful diligence, to assess her own qualifications, whatever they were, and somehow create a Lady Macbeth à la Terry. Anxiously, she spent most of the summer of 1888 in the process.

Irving gave her an invaluable boost by calling her attention to an essay in the *Westminster Review* of 1843 quoting the views of Sarah Siddons on the character of Lady Macbeth. As a great tragedienne of the English stage, Sarah Siddons was noted for her fiendlike portrayal of the lady.

Ellen, therefore, was relieved and gratified to read that Sarah Siddons herself saw Lady Macbeth as a devoted wife, willing to commit foul murder to further her husband's ambitions. It was puzzling that onstage Mrs. Siddons, contrary to her own beliefs, had not suggested a tender wife in any respect. Ellen concluded that the actress, whose specialty was high drama, simply decided to stick to what she did best. This, in turn, encouraged Ellen to do likewise: play the role in the style natural to herself— with love or nothing. Although she realized the danger of turning the ambitious wife into an angel, now she felt secure in her basic motivation and could start to build the role on a congenial premise.

With their *Macbeth* project settled, Ellen and Irving scheduled a summer vacation together with their old friends Joe and Alice Comyns Carr in Lucerne, where they would be joined by Ellen's children, both studying in Germany. Ellen had been firing a barrage of letters at Teddy, telling him to obey his Heidelberg masters. "Remember, dear, it's *your* duty to please *them,* not the Masters duty to please you! It is perhaps rather more their duty to *dis*please you boys, for I fear it seldom pleases us (especially when we are young) to be told when we are not doing right. You are generally a sensible boy so *'think'* a little now and again, *all by yourself,* and argue *against* yourself, and you will do more good than by discussing your fancied ills with other lads. Remember, my darling boy, I look for more in *your* nature, of *fineness* and *nobility* than in other boys, for you have many advantages of life, which should not leave you a commonplace, ordinary lad, and you should rather *lead* towards good than be *led* towards bad. . . . You must never leave off pulling the rope, or the others will have you over the line, and it's a sight harder work to get back again. *Here endeth my Sermon!"*

For all his mother's fight talks, Teddy was often confined to quarters and blamed his misdemeanors on the

173

romantic old town with its castles and vineyards. "I could not study. I could not settle down. The romance and sentiment were too much for me. . . ."

The family reunion in Switzerland came off as planned, and Teddy had scarcely returned for a second year at Heidelberg when he was in real hot water. Ellen for the moment had retreated to Margate to study *Macbeth* when a letter from Germany announced that her son had been summarily expelled and was being sent home. His crime was not specified. Teddy went straight to Grandfather Ben in London, who wired Ellen, "Ted with me will be well looked after nothing serious but most idiotic write tonight."

The story, when pieced together, was tame enough. Teddy and two other students had climbed out of their bedroom windows at night and hopped onto their bicycles for a prolonged moonlight spin. Returning to quarters at 3:30 P.M., they found the school in an uproar. Of the three culprits, only Teddy was sacked because of his "very ill-disciplined nature with an impulsive temper."

As if Teddy's spree reflected somehow on his guardianship, Stephen Coleridge wrote Ellen an overwrought letter, hinting that the boys might have indulged in some immorality; and his wife, Geraldine, followed it with another outburst, begging Ellen to keep closer watch over her children, "Oh, Nellie, do forget yourself and think what you owe to them . . . you used to let me say things to you sometimes. . ."

While Ellen knew that Teddy could be an exasperating brat, she felt that the school was too severe and Coleridge too emotional. To Stephen she wrote, "Sometimes I think you are the silliest gentleman I ever met with."

The problem of Teddy's education was temporarily solved by sending him back to the Reverend Dr. Wilkinson, who maintained that Teddy was "a good boy. Flighty, but good." Henry Irving, seeing that Ellen was still perturbed about her son's future and aiming to minimize her strain before the *Macbeth* opening, proposed that Teddy join the Lyceum acting company, not right off but perhaps the following fall. This prospect had a soothing effect on both Ellen and Teddy.

As *Macbeth* drew nearer, Teddy observed, "Mother is in an agony over it." Still Mother found time to write, pursuing her usual policy of encouraging his talent for drawing, urging him to keep sending her his latest sketches, which she praised or panned according to her best judgment. "Yes, one drawing is most careful but I can say nothing whatever good for the rest. . . ." Yet she conceded, "Your tree in your last sketch was good." As a whet to his visual sense, she promised to send him all the bound copies of the new *English Illustrated Magazine*. "Then I will see that you get the fresh number every month. . . ."

When Teddy wrote that he was soon to play a farce in a school entertainment, she offered her most professional advice: "If I were you, I should *recite* something, not play a farce yet, one of the most difficult things to do, requiring no end of careful rehearsals, and a fellow actor to 'play up' to one. Why don't you recite? I'll send you a list of things to choose from if you'll let me know. Just off to rehearsal . . ."

When Teddy picked two recitations, he asked her for tips. She replied: "Dear, I can't give you tips . . . for I haven't got the *book*. But one thing I remember in *The Tours* you must be rapid and convincing, and look pleased all the time. The other, *The Confession*, take in slower time . . . don't look all the time at the audience in this but sometimes at your fingers as you pause, abstractedly. When you come to "It's that confounded *cu*cumber' (or whatever the words are) speak the line *sharp—look* at the audience, and speak the line in a slightly higher key. . . ."

The same attention to details—pauses, tempo, pitch, inflections—that Ellen was drumming into Teddy she was applying concurrently to *Macbeth*. At the outset, when Irving published his usual acting version of the play, he had a number of copies bound for his company with blank pages inserted between the text so the actors and technicians could make their own notes, scene by scene. Ellen filled two copies of the leather-bound Lyceum texts with comments and instructions to herself. No known actress before her had ever left so copious a record of her preparation for a role.

Most of these notes do not warrant reprinting because they make sense only in relationship to specific passages, just the same as musical terms such as *forte, adagio,* and so on, have meaning only next to specific measures or movements. But her general comments are another matter.

In a surprising remark on the nature of women, Ellen wrote: "Yes, Lady M. was ambitious. Her husband's letters aroused intensely the desire to be a Queen—true to a woman's nature, even more than to a man's, to crave power, and power's displays."

Ellen herself never appeared to be a power-hungry woman. Yet she felt women were the ambitious sex.

She labeled Macbeth a physically brave man, but one who was frightened of a mouse, "a man who talks and talks and works himself up, rather in the style of an early Victorian hysterical heroine." Lady Macbeth, she mused, was "a woman (all over a *woman*) who *believed* in Macbeth with a lurking knowledge of his weakness, but who never found him out to be nothing but a brave soldier and a weakling, until that damned party in a parlor—'The Banquet Scene' as it is called."

Ellen saw clearly that Macbeth's panic at the sight of Banquo's ghost augured the end for them both. Now Lady Macbeth knows her husband is unstable, uncontrolled, and will never rise above his crime. Then—Ellen wrote—her own "softening of the brain occurs—she turns quite gentle—and so we are prepared for the last-scene madness and death."

Speculating on the source of Macbeth's weakness, she

surmised, "He must have had a neglectful mother, who never taught him the importance of self-control."

While considering the effect of a neglectful mother on Macbeth, Ellen took a sterner, more adult tone with Teddy. He would not be allowed to stay with her during Christmas holidays, "for it will be just in the thick of my work and I want *helpers* instead of children who need help. The quicker you mature the better . . . your (our) bitter little experience of the last two months *I hope* will have had the effect of making you a little wiser. . . . You should have learned *one* lesson, that rebellion against orders is *only* childish—that the *manly* thing to do is to endeavor to obey them."

From her next letter it appears that Teddy was to be in London after all and to see *Macbeth*, thanks to the hospitality of Mrs. George Stoker, the wife of Bram's brother. "I am sending your shirt—tie—stud and all, together. . . ." wrote Ellen, preparing him for the visit. "I hope you'll like the stud—it is a beautiful pearl, and there are 10 wee diamond sparks, so learn to put it in the card in your box directly you have done with it, or you'll lose it, by having it sent to the wash."

Teddy's apparel worried his mother simultaneously with her own problems of queenly costuming. For her first entrance in *Macbeth*, Alice Comyns Carr designed what is possibly the most famous costume in stage history. A long, regal gown, crocheted out of soft green silk and blue tinsel, it was trimmed at the edges with rubies and diamonds and partially covered by a heather velvet cape, decorated with flaming griffins. But what made it memorable was that hundreds of real green beetle wings were sewn on the dress, giving it a metallic dazzle that has not dimmed to this day, where it is displayed in the Ellen Terry Museum in Smallhythe in Kent. After the murder of Duncan, Ellen wore another of Alice's masterpieces, a blazing blood-red cape. She wore it, that is, at a dress rehearsal, but never again. Henry Irving snatched it for himself.

Among the first-nighters on Saturday, December 29, 1888, was the American painter John Singer Sargent, who wrote on Monday to his friend in Boston, Mrs. Jack Gardner: "Miss Terry has just come out in Lady Macbeth and looks magnificent in it, but she has not yet made up her mind to let me paint her in one of the dresses until she is quite convinced she is a success. From a pictorial point of view there can be no doubt about it—magenta hair!"

All the reviewers agreed that the show was worth seeing, but some had reservations about both Irving and Ellen. Still, Ellen had no regrets that she had tackled it. Her mood speaks in a letter to Edy in Berlin: "Oh, it's fun, but it's precious hard work, for I by no means make her 'a gentle, lovable woman' as some of 'em say. That's all pickles. She was nothing of the sort, although she was not a *fiend*, and *did* love her husband." A vivid evocation of Ellen's portrayal came from a Liverpool critic, Sir Edward Russell, who covered the London performance and described the scene when Macbeth stabs Duncan in his sleep, then in his panic forgets to plant the bloodied daggers beside the sleeping grooms.

"Mr. Irving's dagger soliloquy is most searching in its ghastly truth. His exit to commit the murder is a living embodiment of the wonderful text, which, as it were, reels and yawns and rocks, a very abyss of moral dread and sickened horror. Then enters Lady Macbeth with a firm step, making a frank and meaning confession of one source of her courage. The words 'Had he not resembled my father,' etc. are presently given, not with the old groaning pathos, but with cursory half-sensibility and entire practical freedom.

"When Macbeth returns, the scene merges as far as she is concerned into a cool though anxious partner's solicitude. . . . There is no blenching when she snatches the daggers from him. It is with cold and perfect sincerity that this fierce, firm woman declares that the sleeping and the dead are but as pictures. Yet Miss Terry never misses the

178

greatness, the thrill, the suspense, the dread of the action."
Sir Edward watched her admiringly as she returned with
bloody hands from depositing the daggers, summoned her
nerve to greet Banquo and Macduff, and then, when the
crisis was over, fell in a faint and "is raised and carried out
with her fair head thrown back over a thane's shoulder,
and her red hair streaming in the torchlight."

From her father, Ellen received what perhaps was her
most cherished accolade: "Nelly dear your performance of
Lady Macbeth was *fine*. . . . Don't allow the critics to in-
terfere with your own view of the part. . . . There will be
thousands who will think otherwise. . . . I had no opportunity to tell you on Saturday how beautiful you looked,
how exquisite were your dresses. . . . My joy was prodigious: Always your loving Daddy." Another comment,
which Ellen never saw, was entered by Lewis Carroll in his
diary on May 11, 1889: ". . . went to *Macbeth*, Miss Terry
was *far* better than I had thought possible."

At the start, Ellen seemed to feel that she was not ade-
quately eerie in her sleepwalking scene and remarked that
Henry, whose "imagination was always stirred by the
queer and uncanny," would have been marvelous at it. But
there is evidence that in time Ellen improved. When she
played the scene in New York, the flame from the lamp she
carried ignited the ends of her hair and shot up the long
braid. Her lady-in-waiting, acted then by a young girl
(later Dame May Whitty), stepped up and smothered the
blaze with her cloak. Ellen appeared to be so uncannily
deep in her trance that she did not bat an eyelash. Once
offstage, she whispered to May, "Thank you, darling—
that was a narrow squeak."

By the end of January, Ellen felt sure of her success and
was posing for John Singer Sargent in his new studio in
Tite Street. Oscar Wilde, who lived nearby with his wife,
Constance, saw Ellen in her beetle-bedecked costume roll
up in a four-wheeler to visit the artist and wrote, "The
street that on a wet and dreary morning has vouchsafed the

vision of Lady Macbeth in full regalia . . . can never again be as other streets."

Sargent's first idea was to paint an imaginary scene of Lady Macbeth rushing out of her castle, her skirts swirling around her, to welcome the doomed Duncan. But after making several sketches, he gave it up in favor of another imaginary pose, a stately portrait of Ellen in her beetle-wing raiment, holding a gold crown over her head as a symbol of her ambition to be queen. Many visitors came to the studio to kibitz, including Teddy and Burne-Jones, who suggested some color changes that Sargent amiably adopted. Irving turned up one day and was talked into posing for a portrait, which he ended by hating—and destroying. Irving never liked his more interesting portraits, including those by Whistler and Bastien-Lepage, but he approved the sentimental likeness by John Millais.

Ellen's portrait was a theatrical eye-popper, not a penetrating study of Terry but an apotheosis of her dress. Exhibited first at the New Gallery, it was greeted by the *London Times* as "without exception, the most ambitious picture of our time." *The Magazine of Art* called it "a noble portrait," while the snooty *Athenæum* slapped it down as "a painting for the pit." The picture, when not on exhibit in several countries, hung in the Beefsteak Room. Eventually, it was bought by Joseph Duveen and presented to the Tate Gallery.

Macbeth was a milestone in Ellen's career. No other play challenged or stretched her talents as much or induced such profitable "agony."

In the ensuing period of doldrums, motherhood became her most absorbing role. By today's Freud-inspired standards, Ellen was in many ways a typical enveloping mother, too much in love with her beautiful son. But the case was not a stereotype. Ellen Terry felt peculiarly responsible for her offspring because of the circumstances of their birth, and she was especially worried by Teddy because he appeared to lack totally the self-mastery to get

When Ellen joined Irving at the Lyceum,
he was forty-seven, his hair was slightly
gray, and he wore a winged collar
and cravat with magisterial style.
"I doted on his looks," said
Ellen. His famous roles ranged
from Satan, for which he wore
one feather in his hood, to his lanky,
sword-swinging Hamlet. His vast repertory
of melodramatic disguises and gestures made
him irresistible to caricaturists. Though
Ellen was seldom caricatured, at top
she appears as Juliet with Irving.

Ellen as Juliet

The Lyceum, one of London's grandest old theaters, was illumined with blazing torches for special occasions. For over two decades it served Ellen Terry and Henry Irving as head-quarters and home, where important people from all over the world saw them perform and mingled with them socially at lavish midnight parties in the Beefsteak Room. Here Ellen played all her great roles, including a few that she had created earlier and polished up at the Lyceum. Most of them, as shown on these pages, were from Shakespeare, whom she once called "my sweetheart."

...as Lady Macbeth

...as Tennyson's Camma

...as Portia

...as Ophelia

...with Irving in Olivia

In his portrait of Lady Macbeth, John Singer Sargent created a pose
not in the play: Ellen holds the crown as a symbol of ambition.

Left: Ellen's son, Teddy, at thirteen sails home from America, where in 1884 he had joined his mother and had done a bit of acting. The lap beneath the dog belongs to Henry Irving. Below: On a later trip to America, Ellen had her picture taken in New York—not in a play, just looking smart.

Left: Ellen and her son, now twenty, act together in a short play, Nance Oldfield. *She portrays a mature actress, and Teddy is a young playwright who is smitten by the star. A bit of fluff, it was given on special occasions, mostly for fun.*

Left: *Ellen, as Queen Katherine in* King Henry VIII, *played this little domestic scene with her daughter, Edy, as a lady-in-waiting, strumming a lute. Edy at twenty-three was a competent actress, but she later proved her real talent as a costume designer and play director In this 1892 production, Irving created a magnificent historical pageant, but with such costly costumes and scenery that it shoved the Lyceum close to bankruptcy.*

Right: Ellen is honored at a mammoth Jubilee given at Drury Lane in 1906, celebrating her fifty years on the stage. The program resembled a glorified music-hall show, involving a greater galaxy of international stars than anybody had yet seen. Ellen performed her favorite Shakespearean role, Beatrice (center), in the first act of Much Ado about Nothing, *with over twenty members of the Terry clan as extras and in supporting roles and with scenery by Ellen's son, Gordon Craig. By this time, Ellen was portly, but she slimmed down by and by.*

NIXEY'S BLUE

FLANNELETTE BAGS

"The Purest I have ever used" (ONE OF MANY TESTIMONIALS)

MISS ELLEN TERRY AS MADAME SANS-GÊNE
THE ORIGINAL PAINTING IN THE POSSESSION OF W. G. NIXEY ESQ.

Left: The custom of ac-
tresses and ladies of fashion
endorsing commercial
products was just beginning
when Ellen Terry in 1897
was recruited to endorse
a "blueing" to make laun-
dry look brighter. Since
she was playing a laun-
dress in Sardou's hit,
Madame Sans-Gêne, her
role was at least appro-
priate to the merchandise.
The role of the spunky
laundress who stood up to
Napoleon was the last
rewarding part Ellen had
at the Lyceum.

In Alice Sit-by-the-Fire, *written for her by James Barrie, Ellen comforts her daughter's beau, acted by A.E. Matthews. Right: In later years she toured widely reading Shakespeare. Below: In her Smallhythe cottage, she lived briefly with her third husband, James Carew.*

along in the world. Gifted Teddy was the kind of son who would drive almost any mother frantic. Yet Ellen kept her head and did her best to discipline him with her long and honest plain speaking.

While waiting to join the Lyceum in September, Teddy was installed in a tutoring establishment run by the Reverend Dr. Gorton at Denchworth, about fifty miles from London, where he did a lot of "Shakespearean readings." But Ellen's letters did not advise him to concentrate solely on high art. "If you get a chance of a billiard table at Mr. Gorton's, practice properly and so you can play Grandad or Master Fred—learn the *science* of it, for like some other things it does not come by *chance*. I'll send you on the banjo song book when I go back to town."

For his school reading of *Twelfth Night:* "Mind you make Malvolio the essence of *complacent,* UNCONSCIOUS conceit."

"Pray keep *your best character:* YOURSELF, and play the part *well,* and with pride and care to *succeed each* and *every day,* and then you will. God keep you in his care my sweet heart—*Your old Mummie.*"

"Ever so many lovingest thanks for your drawings on my birthday [she was forty-two]—Edy made me something very pretty and I had lots of presents—the best of 'em all was a sweet little parrot!! . . . He is very tame, and goes with me in the open carriage or a 'hansom'—and to the theater and out visiting."

At times, Ellen attached more importance to animals than human beings. She wrote twice to Teddy about a reading she gave for the benefit of the Dogs' Home. "It was a great success and made nearly 500 pounds!" But apparently she forgot to mention to her son that, several weeks later, she, Irving, and the Lyceum company were invited to the royal residence at Sandringham, where they gave *The Bells,* followed by Ellen's big courtroom scene from *The Merchant of Venice.*

The queen, before the death of Albert in 1861, had invited several troupes to perform for her friends at court. Now, twenty-seven years later, she was reviving the custom. Irving set a new precedent by refusing any payment for transporting his seventy-six troupers, for building special scenery to fit the small stage, and for money lost at the Lyceum during his absence. It was a grand and lavish gesture, which, in effect, put the queen in Irving's debt. After the performance, Ellen and Irving had an audience with Her Majesty and dined with the royal guests. On behalf of Victoria, the Prince of Wales gave Irving a pair of gold and diamond cufflinks and Ellen a diamond brooch depicting two small birds.

If Ellen failed to convey this impressive news to her son, she did indulge in a casual bit of royal name-dropping in a letter written as *Macbeth* was closing for the summer: "Did I tell you the Princess gave me a splendid diamond bracelet the other night with her name and mine written on a gold plate in her handwriting?"

When Ellen took off for Germany to visit Edy, Irving invited Teddy to visit him at a Ramsgate hotel for a week, directly after the boy's school was over in early August. Ellen was delighted by Irving's fatherly interest and wrote her son repeatedly to behave himself. ". . . Remember to go every night to bed *not later* than between 10 and 11—for of course Henry may have friends, and go much later." In anticipation of Teddy's Lyceum debut she added, "It will be very good for you to be with Henry for he will go through your part with you and then it won't be a bother to him (& you . . . ?) when we come to rehearse in September." Ellen evidently worried how Teddy might measure up to Henry's sons, for she wrote, "The 2 young Irvings have been staying at Ramsgate with their father—and I want you to be very attentive and show that you can be a *nice young gentleman*—your heart is all right, but your lack of—what is it called—'style' rather stands in your way sometimes. . . ."

Then she offered her own definition of style. "This will

come to you more by consideration of other people, and their feelings. . . . For when one is, *and tries to be,* in little things, *unselfish* (that is to say, thinking of others and not of oneself), a Gentleness comes to one—and then style becomes innate."

When Ellen returned to England Teddy and Boo were off on a visit to the Norfolk coast where Boo had relatives. Ellen dipped her pen in ink and was at it again. "Be careful not to get a chill . . . be very prudent when you swim." Then came a capsule sermon on success. "You have the brightest of futures before you *if* you will slave for it a bit—'Success' means so much—it means friends, money— honour amongst fine people—*peace* and sweetness—and a failure means dismal repinings, discontent, poverty and unrest with sourness! I guess my lad has more sense than not to bid for the former state of things!"

As a junior arrival at the Lyceum, Teddy felt he had acquired another family. Old-timers like the Master Mechanic, known simply as Arnott, made much of him and reminisced about magical stage effects in the old pantomimes, and the young actors gabbed with him in the greenroom. Teddy especially admired Breezy Bill Terriss, who used to lunch at Rule's restaurant and regale friends with tales of his early years as a midshipman, sheep-herder, tea-planter, and horse-breeder. Terriss still did cowboy stunts riding in Richmond Park. Ellen, who had a fine gift for sketching her friends in a few deft words, summed up Terriss beautifully: "He had unbounded impudence, yet so much charm that no one could ever be angry with him. Sometimes he reminded me of a butcher-boy flashing past, whistling, on the high seat of his cart, or of Phaethon driving the chariot of the sun— pretty much the same thing, I imagine!"

Teddy had an important role in *The Dead Heart,* an exciting piece of claptrap with traces of Dickens and Dumas which Irving revived for the one hundredth anniversary of the fall of the Bastille. Nightly at the Lyceum, the Bastille fell for 183 performances amid stage fire and bogus cannon smoke. Ellen, who aged from coquette to crone during the play, called her role "small beer." She acted the mother of Teddy, who was saved at the guillotine by Irving volunteering to substitute his own head under the bloody blade. On the program Teddy was listed as "Mr. Gordon Craig," and on opening night Irving gave him a fine Malacca stick with a silver-gilt head. Lest Mr. Gordon Craig assume he was already God's gift to the theater, Ellen made him study elocution, fencing, and grace of movement from various masters of the Lyceum staff.

Back in June 1888, Ellen had written to Teddy that she was moving from Longridge Road: "I have taken a new house (we enter it in August) *No. 22 Barkston Gardens, Earl's Court.* It's close by here . . . and it's *nice,* I tell you." The house where Teddy now lived looked out on tidy lawns and trees, and with window boxes at every window, it appeared to be festooned with vines and flowers. "But ours was not planned as a sociable house," wrote Teddy, "or a society house—it was a working house. It was E.T.'s house, and run for her, and for her alone, and this demanded quiet."

On the parlor floor were two pianos (which everybody played) and comfortable chairs and settees. Ellen's quarters occupied the entire second floor: her bedroom at the front, a big dressing room at the back. Ted and Edy had their own rooms above, and in addition there were quarters for Boo, Miss Harries, and three servants. "A home full of women," recalled Teddy, "and I in the midst of them. . . . Ring at the front-door bell—another woman; ding-a-ling-aling—a girl this time; they trickled in all the time and out again."

But if Barkston Gardens was not "a sociable house," Ellen had a way of making all of London seem like her own sociable house. When she and Teddy rode to the theater, she might stop her carriage at Jackson's food shop on Piccadilly. Seeing her stop, a clerk ran out in the street holding a big tray of cheeses that he knew she liked. Taking his silver knife, she would slice off tiny samples, taste them reflectively, and give Teddy a nibble. Then she would decide on her favorites, order them to be sent home, and drive on, as comfortably as if Piccadilly were her pantry. When she got to the Lyceum, if she saw a queue lined up for tickets, like as not she would stop to chat with some stranger who looked attractive.

On one occasion, she caused a near-panic backstage by arriving only two minutes before curtain time, explaining to the tight-lipped Irving that she had been in a slum area looking up a stranger who had written her for money. A mob of men had surrounded her carriage and, of course, she took time to lower the window and shake hands with each of them, as if the slum were her living room. When Irving reminded her that she might have been attacked, she laughed him off by saying that every man Jack of them had heard of her, and she had the situation under control.

Did she enjoy playing Lady Bountiful? She never thought of herself in those terms. Cordiality came naturally to her, and she enjoyed airing it. Almost every day in her mail she received requests for money from strangers, and almost automatically she slipped a ten-shilling note into a letter, along with a few words of cheer and advice, and rushed it to the needy one. In later years, her companions tried to stem this largess, reminding Ellen she could no longer afford it. But she kept it up secretly. One friend called her "the furtive philanthropist."

Usually, after the theater, Ellen and Teddy were driven home together. Ellen had boards put up between the facing seats so she could stretch out and snooze on the way. Arriving home at Earl's Court, Teddy dismissed the coachman, telling him what time to return the next day. Inside the front door, Teddy bolted it behind them and went to the dining room on a lower floor, where the table had been set for a simple supper. In the winter, a fire glowed and the food was kept hot. They dined alone, Teddy at the head of the table and Ellen at the side. Both were too sleepy to talk much. Ellen sometimes read the mail that had accumulated during the day, stuffed it back into her big chaotic hand-bag, and they climbed the long stairs to bed, Teddy turn-ing off the lights along the way and pushing his weary mother from behind. After leaving her in her second-floor domain, he climbed another flight and quickly fell asleep.

The household had its big meal in the afternoon, with Edy, Miss Harries, and the ancient Boo. Teddy presided again at the master's place and carved the roast. After Boo's plate had been filled, it was Ellen's turn to be served, and she was shamelessly greedy. She could tell by the way Teddy aimed and twisted the carving knife what piece of mutton he planned to cut for her and, if she disapproved, she would run around behind him and point out her pref-erence.

Recalling how well his mother had taught him to carve, Teddy paid loving tribute to "her rather large, but white and speaking hands . . . like a physiognomy, they lighted up with expression. . . . Useful as she made them, they were so much more than that . . . they were lovely in themselves. In repose—closed across her breast, they still seemed alive—the hands of *Beatrice, Imogen* and *Portia's* right hand.

"She could play the piano well—she touched the notes with much surety, and without assault: her hands could grasp without snatching—without a tremor—hold firmly, ready to let go at the first sign—and hold up, sign or no sign.

"All her life lay in these strange, fine hands—and when she held the carving fork and knife and showed me how to cut a leg of mutton or a sirloin of beef, I learned from her performance in a trice."

Without this description, it would be easy to assume that since Ellen herself was often lighthearted and festive her hands were also light and fluttery. But Teddy has provided a clue to his mother's secret strength: hands that were gentle and sensitive, but also strong and competent.

As if Irving were aware that now Teddy's life was too sheltered, he advised him to join a small touring company during the summer, so he could benefit by some rugged barnstorming. Irving had a mutually helpful arrangement with the Haviland and Harvey troupe, which kept him informed of any promising talent they might be hatching, and he, in turn, might toss them one of his neophytes, like Teddy Craig, for extra training. In Teddy's case, Irving reserved the right to say what Teddy should play, parts that would further the boy's development. In the same summer months that Teddy was farmed out, Ellen and Irving were touring major British cities, giving readings of *Macbeth*, lucrative enterprises because they cost almost nothing to put on. Irving acted every role except Lady Macbeth. He fought himself to death in the duel between Macbeth and Macduff and had an inordinately fine time playing the three witches.

Toward the end of Teddy's tour, when he played in Northampton, Ellen reminded him that his father had designed the town hall there, eleven years before Teddy was born. Ellen enjoyed making Teddy aware of his heritage and background. In her London house she kept several pieces of furniture that his father had designed, and from time to time she took Teddy to Harpenden to see the scenes of his early childhood and the romantic gabled house his father had built. On these jaunts she called on her old friends, the Gibsons, from whom she and Godwin had rented their first cottage and whose daughter, May, was once Teddy's playmate. To May, now a pretty, strong-minded girl with a modest talent for painting, visits from Teddy must have seemed like the return of a prodigal adventurer—after all, he had acted on the stage in America, not to mention the famous Lyceum in London—and Teddy must have basked in her esteem. Sometimes she was allowed to go to a theater with him, if chaperoned by her small niece, Maud.

Ellen played Teddy's older sister in *Ravenswood*, the first offering of the new season. The play was based on Sir Walter Scott's novel *The Bride of Lammermoor*, which had already adorned the stage a half-century earlier as Donizetti's opera *Lucia di Lammermoor*. Though Irving's version was still operatic in spirit, it seemed forlorn and empty without its music. Ellen was "touchingly beautiful," and Irving never looked handsomer. "He may be fifty-two," said one spectator, "but he can teach all the young ones how to make love." Despite its amorous interludes, Ellen's mad scene, and a death in quicksand, *Ravenswood* was a failure, and Irving had to fill out the season with favorite revivals. The only novelty was *Nance Oldfield*, a trifle by Charles Reade for which Ellen bought the rights. Dealing with a popular eighteenth-century actress, the playlet showed how clever Nance cured a lovesick young playwright, acted by Teddy, and in the end inspired him to work hard for his future success. This was a smart investment for Ellen, for it presented her in several guises and left a charming impression of a worldly, tender, and wise woman. It hardly extended her talent or nourished her intellect, but she made use of *Nance Oldfield* for years, and it paid off nicely. For its Lyceum debut, Ellen and Ted got it up so quickly that neither of them knew all their lines and had to read them furtively from scraps of paper pinned to the furniture. When Teddy, with Irving's approval, signed up with another summer troupe, Ellen had a sudden impulse to join the little company and play a matinee of *Nance Oldfield* with him. It was such a surprising gesture from the foremost actress of the British stage that at first Miss Sarah Thorne, who ran the company, did not seem to believe it. But once the offer was confirmed, Ellen swept into action and ordered the necessary costumes and prompt book sent from the Lyceum to the Theatre Royal at

Canterbury, where on the afternoon of August 26, 1891, Ellen and Teddy packed the house.

Toward the end of the year, the whole Lyceum troupe again invaded the provinces, with Teddy in most of the plays. Writing from Edinburgh to a friend, Aimée Lowther, Ellen spoke of her boy, "You see, he is quite a success, and has *no end* of engagements and I must see that he 'gets on,' must I not?" Her sense of responsibility was unflagging.

Ransacking the field of drama for works of sufficient bustle and importance to warrant the "Lyceum treatment," Irving settled on *King Henry VIII,* which Shakespeare had probably written, or collaborated on, to solemnize a royal marriage. Irving called it "a pageant or nothing" and added, "Shakespeare, I am sure, had the same idea, and it was in trying to carry it out that he burned down the Globe Theatre in letting off a cannon." The Lyceum suffered no such material damage from Irving's production, but the financial damage it inflicted was ominous. Despite a run of 176 performances, the season ended with an unprecedented loss of some four thousand pounds. Costs had soared so high that there was no guarantee that Lyceum pageantry could pay off.

Ellen played Katherine of Aragon, Henry VIII's first wife whom, after twenty-three years of marriage, he divorced for Anne Boleyn. Ellen could hardly forget that as a child at the old Princess's Theatre she was once "a top angel" in Katherine's deathbed vision and that the heat of the gas lights had made her sick. Now, thirty-four years later, she lay dying comfortably on a bed while another young "top angel" was getting dizzy among the gas jets.

The show had many assets: it had in Act Two Ellen's pithy skirmish with Irving, who was dazzling in Cardinal Wolsey's scarlet robes; it had Terriss playing Henry VIII, Johnston Forbes-Robertson as the Duke of Buckingham; it had Teddy handsomely bearded as Wolsey's

secretary; it had a superb production and Alice Comyns
Carr's costumes based on Holbein etchings. But for all
these pleasurable elements, Ellen confessed to herself, "I
am not interested in it, or in my part."

What interested her far more was the news about
Teddy. On his birthday—he was twenty—he wrote to one
of his old nurses, Essie, sending a photograph and a letter
saying, "You remember Mrs. Gibson, don't you—Mother's
great friend: well, her daughter and I hope someday to be
married—I thought you would like to hear this and perhaps from me. . . ."

Surely, this was not a complete surprise to his mother.
In letters to Teddy she had made friendly mention of May,
and she had eyes to see that the two childhood friends
were often together. Ellen knew also that, thanks to her
badgering, Teddy had banked some seven hundred
pounds by now, which was bound to give him a heady
sense of independence. Yet, regardless of May or money,
was Teddy mature enough to marry? Preferring as he did
to splurge on luxuries for himself—books, hats, fancy writing paper—would he be content to spend his savings on
dull household expenses? And at this embryonic stage of
his career, was it not best for him to be free to travel, to
take poorly paid engagements if they broadened his experience?

Then there were additional questions that might make
Ellen mistrust her own misgivings. After her two mar-
riages, both unhappy, was she now being unduly wary of
marriage in general? Was she hanging onto Teddy, perhaps
subconsciously, because he was her closest link to his father? And after the shock of seeing Godwin marry a
younger woman, could she really think sensibly now about
losing her Teddy to the young May Gibson? The parallel
was not precise, but it was close enough to be tormenting.

It seems that simultaneously Ellen and Irving were
worrying about their sons. Irving's youngest boy,
Laurence, after a brief stint in the diplomatic service in

Russia, recognized that he was irresistibly drawn to the theater and contracted to play minor roles in the Shakespeare troupe of Frank Benson, an alumnus of Irving's Lyceum. While the Benson company was in Belfast during a bleak January, Laurence retired to his room to study a part, and shortly before teatime a fellow actor in the same lodging house heard a pistol shot. Rushing to Laurence's room, he saw the youth sprawled on the bed, his Russian pistol on the floor and blood gushing from a chest wound. A hastily summoned doctor saved his life. Then Irving was notified in London and promptly dispatched a leading London surgeon, who reported from Belfast that Laurence was well taken care of.

Had Laurence attempted suicide? Although he had been deeply depressed at the time, his mother, flying to his bedside, was convinced it was a rehearsal accident, though why Laurence should have been rehearsing a Shakespeare scene with his Russian pistol remained a puzzlement. Writing about the incident years later, Laurence's nephew, also named Laurence, concluded, "Yet all the evidence, factual and psychological, led to the conclusion that Laurence had tried to put an end to his short life."

This near-tragedy was probably as distressing to Ellen as to Irving, for it suggested that young Laurence, like her own son, lacked stability and was perhaps the victim of his father's neglect. She might also imagine that her closeness to Irving somehow deprived Laurence of his father's attention. She had to try to find a way to compensate Laurence for some of his unhappiness.

A few weeks later Ellen's mother, Sarah, died on March 1, 1892. Ellen wrote to a friend, "Yes, my pretty Dear has left us and I pray we may never battle to live as she did." When Ellen returned to the Lyceum after a few days away, she found that Irving had filled her dressing room with daffodils, "to make it like sunshine," he said.

In the summer of 1892, while Teddy was at Margate, again with Sarah Thorne's troupe, Ellen's letters reported querulously that both she and Irving had severe throat trouble, he requiring surgery. "Henry went through the operation very well, but the poor dear has to lie on his bed all day and tomorrow . . . he's all bound up. I sent to thank May for the flowers. . . . Let me hear from you once a week and then I shall be satisfied and happy about you."

She was pleased, a few days later, that Henry was "much better and pegging into *King Lear*," but she was still ailing. In her longing to feel close to Teddy she asked for a detailed schedule of his engagements so that on the night he was acting a certain role she could be reading the same play at home.

Irving was preparing two productions: *King Lear*, followed three months later by the long-delayed Tennyson opus, *Becket*. Irving economized on *Lear*, hoping to compensate his public with superior acting. But at the opening, he deliberately injected an artificial quaver into his voice, which rendered him almost unintelligible and baffled the other actors, as well as the audience. In a day or two, with Ellen's help, he resumed his normal voice, but the disapproving reviews scared off the customers. Nonetheless, when the play shook down, Ellen and Irving provided their finest vintage pathos in the reconciliation scene between father and daughter. Seeing Cordelia weeping, the dazed old king asks, "Be your tears wet?" Then, touching her cheeks with his frail fingers, he puts a salty drop to his lips, and answers, "Yes, faith."

While Teddy was playing Oswald in *Lear*, he decided to move from Barkston Gardens and occupy his mother's little cottage at Uxbridge, a short journey from London by train. At first, Ellen wanted to give him the cottage rent-free, but she concluded that it might be better for his character if she charged him five shillings a week. Teddy commuted daily from Uxbridge to the Lyceum, and the marriage hung fire.

This was the start of a new life for Teddy; he was more

independent than ever before. On the train he met a young artist, James Pryde, whose sister, Mabel, was married to another young painter, William Nicholson. All lived in the hamlet of Denham near Uxbridge. Teddy found this trio, with their zeal for the arts, immensely congenial. For the first time he had his own circle of adult friends, apart from the theater world. Pryde and Nicholson worked as a team of artists, signing their works with one name, Beggarstaff. Teddy was aroused by their bold, decorative posters, as outstanding in their way as the great posters of Toulouse-Lautrec and Mucha, and from the Beggarstaff team he picked up the art of making woodcuts. After toiling as a boy to copy little pictures, Teddy began to feel he might produce his own original works and further follow Nicholson's example by taking a pretty young wife to keep him cozy.

On his twenty-first birthday, Teddy took the legal leap to manhood and was free to marry whenever he pleased. To help celebrate, Ellen gave him an original manuscript of Walt Whitman as well as his *Leaves of Grass,* and Irving presented him with a massive gold watch, inscribed "with love and remembrance." Teddy had promised Irving to join the Lyceum's fourth American tour, but now he talked of backing out.

Irving urged him to postpone marriage until he returned from America, or else to marry and leave the bride in England. To take May along, Irving said, would be "positively dangerous," evidently thinking that she might become pregnant during the strenuous coast-to-coast tour and could not be cared for properly. Irving went on to argue that Teddy's presence would give much comfort to his mother and, in addition, that he was bound to profit professionally; he would be given good roles to act and important roles to understudy.

Teddy's decision was still hanging fire when Ellen wrote to him on the day after his birthday.

"Well, my dear old Ted, you must pull yourself together now and choose a path. There is one simple, easy and straight path, which is the right path, and which you will *probably not follow*, but I must point out to you that your duty to May and yourself, and to your art, is to go like a man to America, make some money, for the first time in your life, bring it back to May, making her your wife in a little over a year. This is not *my* dictation it is your simple duty. . . . May's duty is simple, too—she should urge you by all means of affection to do this. . . . I have not yet said whether or not you are going to America to Henry—Take to the end of the week to think the matter over. Meanwhile, I have 'said my say' and will urge the matter no more. . . ." After assuring Teddy that he could save three hundred pounds on the trip, thus enabling him to marry with more financial security, Ellen wound up: "You are of age now—a man—and must look the matter in the face— not excitedly like an histerical girl, but calmly and dispassionately as someone guiding another person. Give my love to little May (who made me more fond of her on Sunday than I have ever been before). . . . Anyway, I am always the same loving old Mother."

A week later, after Teddy had made up his mind, Ellen wrote to May. She knew it would do no good, but she was hurt and worried and had to have another say.

"Yes, I *am* sorry Ted is not going to America—but it is for his sake, dear May, and for yours, and not for mine. . . . Ted's *well-being* and *success* is what I think about. I don't doubt his future happiness in regard to *you as far as you personally can contribute to it—and I never have*, but if you both think and act as if all worldly advancement had nothing whatever to do in helping towards happiness . . . all I can say is you are a couple of Geese, and I retire from the scene, in which, it is the opinion of *both* of you, I can be of no use. . . . I am very angry with you but nevertheless I am your loving friend, E.T."

One may be certain that Ellen could not retire from the

scene, and even more certain that if she did, Teddy would be outraged and lost.

On March 27, 1893, the couple were married in a registry office, an official rite by which Edward Gordon Craig did not so much acquire a wife as defy a mother—safely.

Chapter Nine

THE DWINDLING OF LOVE
AND OTHER DISASTERS

Tennyson's bulky verse drama *Becket* had gone unproduced for fourteen years while it was being revised, cut, shelved, and reconsidered. Now, four months after the poet's death, it was being staged with the pomp of a memorial service, with Irving as the heroic archbishop and Ellen wasting her "exquisite tenderness" on the dull role of Fair Rosamund. Even the poet's son, her old friend Hallam Tennyson, regretted that "Rosamund is so disconnected with the real story of the drama as to excite relatively small interest."

More and more, Ellen was obliged to take satisfaction in other people's fulfillment. Teddy, now married to May, was comfortably ensconced at the Lyceum until the season's end, and Irving was jubilant because *Becket* had been unanimously lauded. The Lyceum season closed again with a deficit, but *Becket* itself was a useful piece of merchandise; it could always be revived and counted on to bring prestige to the management. By royal command, *Becket* was presented at Windsor Castle, which made Teddy the third generation of Terrys to act privately for Queen Victoria.

To help fill his coffers, Irving booked a fourth tour to America in rather the same spirit as Pizarro when he went to South America for Incan gold. Before embarking, Ellen wrote to Augustin Daly, a leading American producer who was leasing the Lyceum during Irving's absence, to suggest he might hire Teddy for his company. (Daly, incidentally, installed the first full electrical stage lighting ever used at the Lyceum; upon their return Ellen and Irving disliked it and had it removed.)

Almost the minute she boarded ship, heading this time for Canada, Ellen wrote to Teddy, "In Daly's letter he says, 'I shall certainly try to bring out the very best in him, if he will be patient a bit.' "

Then her letter took a new tack, a confiding tone, as Ellen wrote to her son, perhaps for the first time, as if he were an adult who might understand her personal sorrows.

I feel better in my health after one night at sea—but I never felt graver in my life. If I'm not at the bottom of the sea, I wonder where I shall be this time next year! The look forward for me is pretty blank. I don't mean in the *Theater*—that's nothing—I care for that least of all.
Now the best of our love (Edy's and mine) to you and May—and I must leave writing, and send a word to Boo.

God bless you darling Ted
Darling little May

Let nothing concern you much but the biggest wickedness of all.
Giving Pain! to each other, or to others—
The dwindling of love is the only thing to be feared in this world. I am sure of that.

Amen—Your loving old
Mother

Eight days later, on an August morning with "Quebec in sight," Ellen wrote again to Teddy.

. . . a fine voyage in a steady ship . . . *even Edy* has enjoyed most of the time immensely. . . . I've no news except that we are well—"To be wroth with one we love, doth work like madness in the brain," and I am happy to say that the peace of the sea has . . . enabled me to cast out hate from my heart, and that makes a mighty difference to me.

Ellen's quotation ("To be wroth," etc.) is from Coleridge's *Christabel.* In her next sentence she notes that the peace of the sea also seems to have had a benign effect on Henry Irving.

The strong-weak man looks very much better, and says he's very happy now—he's very kind for a while, and so may it be, I pray. . . .

Some years later Ellen admitted to friends that Irving did develop a roving eye. To Shaw she wrote, "Henry is so nice to me lately that I'm convinced he has a new 'flame' (he is always nicer then, which I think is to his credit)"; and to Marguerite Steen she reminisced about Irving, recalling the period about 1894: "He began to get tired of me and to pay attention to other women. I wasn't jealous, but I said, 'I love you and adore you, and while you wanted it everything that was mine was yours. But when you ceased to want it, No!' "

Her denial of jealousy seems belied by her shipboard letter to Teddy, written when the future looked black. Mercifully, when she became an old lady she probably forgot her pangs of jealousy. In defense of closing her eyes to painful sights, she used to like to say, "God gave us eyelids as well as eyes," which could apply as well to the eyelids of failing memory.

After a coast-to-coast train ride across Canada, the troupe opened in San Francisco for two weeks, drawing their largest crowds with *The Merchant of Venice,* which in nineteenth-century America was the most popular of Shakespeare's plays. No matter how many times Ellen visited America, she reacted strongly to what she saw, for or against. In northern California, she wrote, "For, spite of fruits and flowers, the marvelous Bay and the Golden Gates, there is printed on the face of the people This-is-America-the-home-of-the-money-getter-Mammon-is-our-God and it spoils their faces and voices—although I *must* admit I don't think it spoils their *hearts,* for they are kindly to excess." In Mammon's hotbed she noted with comfort that while at the Lyceum the largest receipts for a night were 430 pounds, in San Francisco exceeded 1,000 pounds.

Next on the route were one- or two-night stands in Portland, Seattle, and Tacoma. From San Francisco Ellen wrote, "We leave here Saturday night after the Play and get to Portland on Monday morning—sleeping two nights on the Cars—(Oh, I don't like that) I shall be glad to get to Chicago." After playing in Minnesota, she arrived in October, at the time of the nation's first great World's Fair.

A familiar visitor to Chicago, she was met by a swarm of newspaper reporters who boarded the train as it neared the station. One of them wrote, "She persists in talking about her son, who has been naughty and married a very beautiful and adorable girl." Then, he veered from her family chatter, to rhapsodize, predictably, on her "vast vintage of youth which mellows, not fades; exults in her years, not shrinks at their approach"; she was "supple as a tigress," and her eyes were "turquoise stars." He marveled that this "breezy creature sitting on the dusty floor of the car . . . could have a marriageable family. In proof, she called a dark-eyed girl from the compartment and introduced her as 'my daughter.' "

Edy usually shunned interviews, keeping to herself with her needlework, sketching, or—her latest interest—photography. But this time she heeded her mother's call and as a reward was soon to read in the *Chicago Herald* that "the daughter is as rogueish and seductive as Miss Terry, but in a style so vastly opposed to every color and turn in her handsome mother that there is not the slightest trace of resemblance between them."

Then Ellen made a playful comment on Edy, which the reporter repeated in his story: " 'She is a dear child, if she only wouldn't snapshot me in the most alarming conditions,' said Miss Terry, with an injured glance from her throne on the carpet to her girl's pretty face. 'She has the most outrageous collection of Kodak pictures which she has taken of me exactly when I would least care to be perpetuated. I dream some nights that she is going to make me buy them, and I wake up in an imaginary financial panic.' " One must stop and wonder at the amazement of this midwestern reporter, confronted by this remarkably sprightly visitor arriving like Ariel on the Chicago and Northwestern Railroad.

Another reporter told that a carriage was waiting at the C. & N. depot for "the most picturesque figures in the world of English-speaking drama, and they are driven to the Grand Pacific Hotel, where Irving had a quick look at his suite. Then he accompanied Miss Terry to her hotel, The Virginia."

Here Ellen received the news she had been expecting. Teddy's wife was pregnant. "Darling Boy," she wrote back, "I've just got your letter and May's postscript—of course, I knew—but, oh————I'm wishing now nothing but that I were home—but that cannot be. Thank God, you are not both of you *here*—streaming about this unquiet galloping country. One wants extraordinary physical order to cope with America."

Ellen uncorked a geyser of maternal advice, mainly adjuring Teddy to be considerate of May—"You must forget yourself every minute . . . and think only of her. . . ." Important, too, was selecting the right doctor, not too young or too old. But Ellen added wisely that May's mother, Annie Gibson, "would know of this best of anybody." Ellen advised May to lead "a perfectly natural, busy, easy life . . . anything like tricycling, or horseriding would be absurd—but walking and driving, good. Oh, one might go on at this sort of thing for hours, and I'm sure I shan't." But she could not resist adding, "If you think of some particular and clever doctor and would like him for May, don't consider him expensive, because of course I will pay. . . ."

As for the great World's Fair, she merely said, "This Chicago has gone mad over itself and its fair—and certainly it has reason to be proud." Ellen made no mention that she herself, in Sargent's portrait, was hung and on view at the fair. In fact, the art exhibit might have seemed like old-home week to Ellen, including as it did a dozen paintings by her London friends Alma Tadema, Ford Madox Brown, John Millais, and her ex-husband, G. F. Watts.

Ellen had little mind for anything but Teddy. Now more than ever she worried about his being jobless, for Daly had dropped him, apparently for being late for a rehearsal; and another job fell through with Beerbohm Tree. Irving, in turn, refused to welcome him back to the Lyceum.

Ellen scolded her son for bewailing his ill fate and for making snide comments about luckier young actors. "You talk too much and find fault *too* much, my Ted. Go to the managers and try and get some work—any work for not less than five pounds [a week]. Only don't write too much to them. It bores them. And don't write except on business paper, *ordinary* paper—and cut it short!"

Her relations with Irving grew sunnier, perhaps because she had a chance to be of extra use to him. "Henry has been very ill," she wrote, "and for the future we must go to the same hotels—for I've had to do a great deal in the poulticing and Turpentine line, and rushing about kills me, and I expect to be ill next. The doctor absolutely forbids Henry sitting up late. . . ." Also, as an indirect kindness to Irving, she wrote to his oldest son, Harry, when she heard he had obtained an acting job, "to give him a bit of encouragement." Ellen did what she could to eradicate the animosity, instilled by Irving's wife, which turned his boys against their father and his "paramour."

Returning to England just before the baby was born, Ellen received a typical outcry from her son. He wanted to get costumes for a scene he was doing from *The Hunchback*—probably a one-night booking—and, as usual, regarded his mother as a supply depot.

201

Rosemary Craig was born on April 8, 1894, and almost before the cord was cut Ellen seemed to open another supply line to both mother and child. First Ellen pumped in Burgundy wine, and turtle and champagne jelly to restore May's strength, then she sent tiny bodices and pinafores curiously designed to keep babies warm and dainty. She requested that the recipient be taught to call her Nell, because it was easy to say.

But for all her joys in "the rosebud," Ellen was disturbed. On top of her American safari, she had to wind up the Lyceum season with three months as Marguerite in *Faust*, an emotional workout that further drained her energies. Impatient with Teddy for taking parenthood so casually, she even vented her spleen on his wife: "You're all playing instead of working! Be a *woman*, not a child. . . . Now you have taken a woman's responsibilities—help Ted to get an engagement."

Viewed in perspective, Ted was probably working out his salvation as best he could, feeding parasitically on his mother and at the same time searching for his own identity. Already he was attracted by the new wave of art, but as yet he was not ready to swim in it. In 1894, the year of Rosie's birth, an international poster exhibit was held in London where Beggarstaff posters hung among the works of Toulouse-Lautrec, who came over from Paris to help launch the exhibit; and in the same year the startling *Yellow Book* began to appear, offering works by Max Beerbohm, Walter Sickert, and Aubrey Beardsley (*Punch* called him Weirdsley). Among the characteristics shared by some of the contributors was a disdain for conventional embellishment and a mastery of outspoken design, both of which Teddy Craig was destined to incorporate in his own forceful art.

Ellen was always in sympathy with Teddy's artistic leanings, not only encouraging his work but buying and peddling the work of his friends. Yet at this juncture she was exasperated that Teddy, now twenty-two, with a proved and marketable talent for acting, was dawdling around when he should have been shouldering his own family burdens.

"I have been fully nine months out of harness," said Teddy, when at last he answered a newspaper call for actors and was hired by a Shakespearean touring group that gave him leads in *Hamlet, Romeo and Juliet,* and *The School for Scandal.* With immense relief, Ellen changed her tune from "How to Get a Job" to "How to Interpret Hamlet."

Realizing that she had been getting on his nerves, Ellen made a point of missing Teddy's *Hamlet* debut in Hereford, but she wrote to him on the same night, "I've been with you all the evening in spirit—with you and Hamlet." Then she admitted bravely: "My dear, we seem to get on better *in the spirit* lately, when our cussed bodies don't meet and wrangle. So perhaps it's as well that I am *here* and *you* are *there*." She confessed to him, though, that she would secretly slip in to see one of his performances somewhere on tour, without telling him where or when, and he would never know it. There is no record that she ever did it. Her notion that she, the celebrated Ellen Terry, could conceal her presence in a small audience, was absurd, like a scene from a chuckleheaded play.

In the autumn, Ellen made another provincial tour with Irving and regaled Teddy with her impressions. "What a rum place this Ireland is! *Filthy towns—Heavenly* in the *country.* Poetry just breathes down the lanes, and sings in the air. . . ." And then she addressed herself to five lion cubs in the Dublin zoo: "Such noble innocent little chappies—They looked like Rosemary Nell. I can't bear to think of Baby tho'—I've never had a proper cuddle with her in my life. It makes me sick—and miserable." A few days later, to prove that the strolling player was not yet dead within her, she mused, "If I had the strength and could do without a holiday, what fun it would be to go around, and, begging for a Theater, Hall, or Tent, act for nothing (you and I and Edy and a few who would consent) to give the poor people a treat!"

While Ellen was indulging in fantasies of humble bliss, Irving was heading for unprecedented glory. During the run of *King Arthur*, another W. G. Wills play that was closer to folk pageant than solid drama, Irving was knighted by Queen Victoria. He had prepared for this event, if not by any calculated strategy, with the instincts of a master showman. Some twelve years before, through the offices of Gladstone, Irving might have received this royal honor had he not indicated a reluctance to accept it on the grounds that he owed so much of his success to his fellow workers in the theater that it would be presumptuous for him to accept the reward as an individual. When rumors of Irving's refusal circulated around London, his stock rose even higher, and he was credited with a noble modesty that was not always evident in his deportment.

Only now, after gathering so many laurels at home and abroad, had he indicated that it might be forgivable for him to accept this ultimate tribute. It almost seemed now, by consenting to be knighted, that he was bestowing a favor on the queen.

When the great news from the palace was delivered in a letter to Irving at his flat in Grafton Street, he immediately summoned Bram Stoker, and together they took a carriage to Barkston Gardens to break the news to Ellen. Her instant reaction was never told, but a good deal is revealed in a long, chatty letter she wrote to Teddy two days later.

Sunday 26 May

Darling Ted,

I chanced to see your telegram to Henry—a very nice one— among the stacks of letters and "wires" he received. He had 5 men sitting down all day yesterday just answering them all, hard as they could write. He heard from India, New Zealand, Australia, America . . . Everywhere! I'm delighted for some things. He is *the first* (but he has a knack of being "first"—always would be!) and it's good for the dear work. Harry is pleased. A letter came amongst the first, "All congratulations from your Wife"! That was funny, I thought. It will be an early visit tomorrow to the Stationers to have the visiting cards altered—rather fancy! The Prince wrote a nice letter and so did some of the other Royalties. Labby [Labouchère] wrote that Gladstone wanted to do it in *his* Ministry.

The good folk at the Lyceum (who have no more logic than Cats) think it's too bad that "birthday honors" fall only to Henry's share, and so they have dubbed me *"Lady Darling,"* with which title I'm well content. It made my heart thump to hear the public reception of Henry yesterday. The dear old sweet was just as much pleased as he ought to have been.

It's a horrid day today. I'm going out to luncheon, and afterwards, thank the Lord, Henry takes me for a drive to Hampton Court, for the cities are stifling, and he will have some *quiet* with me, and we'll both be glad of it. It is pretty hard work just at present. Every day and all day rehearsing, and acting each night. Did you hear I got away to see little May and the babies? Edy went too. She won't admire *that* baby—*yet!!* He is a dear little velvety fellow. . . ."

Her letter continues with family matters: more about the baby, Robin, and her persistent admonitions to be considerate of May. "I'm giving her a little getting-up frock, or she'll have nothing decent. . . ."

Many people were pleased by Irving's honor, including G. B. Shaw, who felt, no matter how he rated Irving as an actor, that it was for the good of the theater. If knighthoods were given to poets, painters, and artists, why not to actors? But surely nobody was more delighted than Ellen Terry. She had an itemized memory of his labors over the seventeen years since he first called on her with his incontinent dog at Longridge Road, asking her to risk her future with him at the Lyceum. And added to her personal joy in seeing Irving's happiness and knowing how she had contributed to it was her awareness of the new prestige that Irving's knighthood would confer upon the ancient profession that three generations of her own family had embraced. Irving was the first modern European actor ever to be honored by his state. He had made an honest woman of the theater.

Max Beerbohm caught a glimpse of Irving riding in his carriage, off to board the train to Windsor Castle for his knighthood ceremonies. Beerbohm was charmed to see that Irving's hat was gaily tilted, his cigar was extra-long and perky, and the old bohemian wore "a look of such ruminant, sly fun as I have never seen equalled." Far from trying to transform himself into a figure of drab pomposity, Irving was looking more proudly actorish than ever.

The new prestige bestowed upon the Lyceum made no difference at all to the lives of either Irving or Ellen Terry. Socially, Irving had no ambitions higher than the ones he had already satisfied in the Beefsteak Room and at the clubs and universities where he had been honored. And Ellen knew, or could know easily, almost every notable in the Western world. Neither one, outside the theater, was a social climber or a conspicuous consumer. Ellen, unlike many movie stars-to-be in the twentieth century, or some of her own tribe such as Bernhardt and Lillie Langtry, had no craving for stately mansions or marble bathtubs. If Bernhardt had asked her to flop seductively onto her polar-bear rug, Ellen would have obliged; but she would have giggled. All she needed was solid comfort and willing minions.

Knighthood came to Irving as a last-act celebration in the long drama of his career, and he probably sensed, subconsciously, that he belonged to a disappearing era. Ellen knew that she, too, was in the doldrums, but she did not feel at all like disappearing. She was disturbed and challenged by new currents in the theater, by the shocking, muttered-about plays of Henrik Ibsen and the impudence of young Bernard Shaw.

In a series of articles, "Stray Memories," written in 1891 for the *New Review,* Ellen turned up her nose at Ibsen's plays: "I should not myself prefer to act in them." She dismissed Nora and Hedda as "silly ladies," popular with some actresses because "they were so extraordinarily easy to act." She was primly grateful that she had been "called upon to act very noble and clear characters." Ellen made a jackass of herself. When the "Stray Memories" was incorporated fifteen years later into her official memoirs, the anti-Ibsen nonsense was omitted.

As a champion of the new drama, George Bernard Shaw entered Ellen's life almost by accident in 1892 when she wrote to Edmund Yates, editor of London's bright weekly *The World*. She asked Yates for some advice about launching the career of a young singer. Yates passed on her letter to his new music critic, G. B. Shaw, who duly turned up at the girl's concert and after hearing her sing, wrote Ellen his honest opinion (not high), along with some helpful advice. Ellen liked his candor and wrote him a jolly note of gratitude, exposing her worst vice, an occasional weakness for baby talk: "Take my very bestest thanks." Shaw was hooked. In his next letter he reminded her of a speech Irving had recently given in Liverpool, damning Ibsen, damning Shaw for supporting Ibsen, and quoting Shaw incorrectly as calling Miss Terry an "ignoramus."

After a cheery answer from Ellen, brushing off the Irving speech, Shaw sent her his pamphlet "The Quintessence of Ibsenism," a powerful defense of the Wizard of the North. Shaw had already presented these views at the Fabian Society; later, with extra chapters, they became a landmark in dramatic criticism.

Ellen's response to the pamphlet is not known, but its contents must have shaken and refreshed her like a sharp wind. Although the Shaw-Terry letters apparently were discontinued for three years, Shaw had sown his salubrious mischief and would reap later. Ellen took the epistolary initiative, sparked off by a newspaper item saying that Shaw was lecturing to the Woman's Progressive Society on the subject, "Feminine Meanness." Ellen could not attend, so she wrote asking Shaw if he ever lectured on Sundays, her only free days. Nothing remains of any more letters until eight months later, when Shaw wrote to her in America.

The 1895 tour consisted mainly of familiar bookings, while Ellen suffered from familiar worries. Her letters to Teddy now were even more frantic since he had sired the second child and still relied largely on his mother's support.

Ellen broke the monotony of the tour by going into show business for herself on a very small scale. It began back in London when Irving's son, Laurence, wrote a short play called *Godefroi and Yolande* about a medieval leper colony. Irving turned it down as being too morbid for the Lyceum, but Ellen asked to read the script and found it "inspiring." She made Irving buy an option on his son's play and exacted his promise that he would produce it sometime in the future. Laurence was overwhelmed by this kindness from the Serpent and wrote: "My dear Miss Terry, I cannot tell you how deeply I felt all your generous enthusiasm over my play. Encouragement such as you gave me will spur me on to renewed efforts so I may hope to merit it again. I will have another copy of the play got ready, and then I will send it to you for the comments you so kindly offered to make. . . . I do not know in what words to tell you how honored I feel at such an offer from the first of English actresses." On top of that, Ellen also offered to play leprous Yolande herself.

How much did Ellen really admire the play, and how much was she swayed by compassion for the boy who had attempted suicide and by her desire to bring him closer to his father? No doubt Ellen herself could not have sorted out all her motives. And why should she? Certainly her compassion was involved. At the same time, she would not have gone to bat for the little play if she had thought it altogether lacking in merit.

Irving promised to let Ellen present the play on tour, but he insisted that she take full responsibilty for staging, directing—everything. She started rehearsing it in Baltimore, continued it in Washington, D.C. (where President Grover Cleveland and his party saw Ellen and Irving in *King Arthur*), then down into the Deep South—Richmond, Charleston, Savannah, Atlanta—and then to New Orleans where Ellen reported that the leper play in rehearsal was "getting on well."

The leper opus was not the only new script that Ellen carried in her luggage now. George Bernard Shaw had sent her his one-act play about Napoleon and a fictitious strange lady, which he titled *The Man of Destiny*, and hoped it would be acted by Ellen and Irving. It was, Shaw admitted, "not one of my great plays" and "hardly more than a bravura piece to display the virtuosity of two principal performers." But it was no worse, and somewhat better, than most of Irving's curtain-raisers. The female role, Shaw said, was tailored especially for Ellen, who, upon reading it, wired the playwright: "Just read your play. Delicious." She also reported, with injudicious enthusiasm, "H.I. quite loves it, and will do it finely." Henceforth, she nagged Henry to produce it, although for the time being, of course, she was absorbed in his son's play.

Ellen befriended two young actors in the company, Mr. and Mrs. Ben Webster III. Ben came from an illustrious old theatrical clan and had acted at the Lyceum before. His new wife was to become the popular stage and film actress Dame May Whitty, whose career was still bubbling when she died at eighty-three in 1948.

On tour young May Whitty was cranky. She grumbled justifiably about the smelly, muddy American streets, a live rat in her bathtub, and Ellen's little sideline project. "We're rehearsing that filthy leper play," she wrote from New Orleans to a friend, "takes up all our time, and it's such a muddle owing to the erratic Nell's stage management."

May Whitty liked to tease Ellen and poke fun at her, but all her life she admired her extravagantly and battered down anybody who tried to underrate her skill as an actress. Thanks to May, we see how Ellen faced a disaster that almost terminated the leper play altogether.

In New Orleans, after the Saturday night show, the troupe boarded their special train for Memphis, where they were due to open on Monday. Because of a sudden storm and washouts along the line, the train was delayed and rerouted on safer tracks. The next morning, high in the Mississippi Valley, the train came to a creek named Bayou Pierre. Over this marshy area, more than a mile wide, the cars had to crawl on a wooden trestle. Now an angry muddy flood, like a bursting sewer main, roared over the entire swamp and even covered the tracks.

In one car Ellen, Irving, Bram Stoker, and Loveday gazed out the windows at a grotesque parade of floating wreckage: fenceposts, chicken coops, pots and pans, roofs, logs, and upturned trees with their tangled roots held aloft like bony hands in prayer. Here and there, on stray planks, snakes were coiled.

All the passengers knew they were gambling with calamity, for at any moment the wooden trestle might buckle, the engine explode with a volcanic boom and sink with a sizzle, dragging train and passengers to oblivion. To comfort her mother, Edy came in from another car, only to find her with gloves neatly buttoned tying on her veil. Seeing her frightened daughter, Ellen chirped, "Edy, darling! Hurry and dress yourself properly, we shall probably have to swim."

The company finally arrived in Memphis too late for Sunday night dinner, starved but safe, and continued rehearsing through Nashville, Louisville, St. Louis, and Cincinnati, where Ellen received a heartsickening letter from Teddy, hinting that he and May Gibson might separate.

Ellen knew it was futile to protest, but she tried anyway. "I will only say *one* thing," she wrote back, "that it appears to me that utter wreck may be avoided if you and May will just try to think of some duty not to yourselves (Yourselves!!) but to the two who are at present helpless."

Inevitably, she saw in Teddy's separation from his little girl and boy a recurrence of his father's walkout on *his* little girl and boy and, just as before, Ellen would become responsible for the youngsters' welfare.

She urged May and Teddy to stick together, at least through the children's helpless years, and thus perform an honorable duty that would speak louder than all their arguments and self-justifications. "Do you remember what Emerson says?" she asked. " 'Don't say things. What you are stands over you the while and thunders so I cannot hear what you say to the contrary.' I wish you would have a try, my Ted, at forgetting yourself. . . ."

Grateful to settle in Chicago for four weeks, Ellen could submerge her family worries by concentrating on the final preparations for the leper drama. May Whitty was still writing home: ". . . all our days are spent in rehearsing the filthy leper play. . . . H.I. has taken it in hand and even he gets hopelessly mixed up."

Edy was in charge of costumes and helped with the scenery, all of which was patched together, from other productions. Stagehands and gas men were likewise pressed into service . . . bemused by the high-strung foreign ladies. The single performance, given along with other short plays, was a matinee on March 13, 1896. May Whitty feared the worst. How could it be anything but a mess? She describes how Ellen made her first entrance on a balcony, deathly pale as the leper-courtesan but dazzling in a crimson dress (part of her Portia costume), and wearing a bonfire of poppies in her tinted red hair. "I, as a lady-in-waiting," wrote May, "had to follow, but I stood there for a moment, transfixed by her strange loveliness and the scene itself, so rich, so beautifully composed." With astonishment May reported that it "went wonderfully well."

When Shaw heard that Ellen had portrayed a leper in a play by Irving's son, he wrote her in mock outrage that she had picked a boy's play to act in ahead of his. Shaw's first popular comedy, *Arms and the Man,* happened to be play-

211

ing in Chicago with Richard Mansfield in the lead at the time Ellen was there. Once more Shaw was irked because Ellen had not let her understudy take over her role for a night so she could attend Shaw's play and report how it was being received.

Two events saddened Ellen's last months on the tour. One was the abrupt report from England that Florence—"darling Floss"—her mischievous youngest sister, had died during premature childbirth. Ellen had adored Flossie's carefree spirit, for she never took her stage career very seriously and was happy to settle for married life and act only in amateur theatricals. To Teddy Ellen wrote, "I feel all is very black and cold for the news of my dear little sister has pretty nearly done me in." Accustomed to projecting her own imagination into other characters, Ellen did not stop at the barrier of death but speculated on how Floss might be feeling beyond the grave. "I wonder whether, when we are dead, we are conscious of our own forgetting us, bit by bit, more and more, as the months go by. . . . I'm *alive,* but I feel like that in regard to you and yours. I feel you are forgetting all about me."

Ellen's second source of distress was Edy's sudden aloofness. "I have scarcely seen her on this tour, when I most of all wanted her she avoided me like the plague!! When Flo died, I certainly did hope she would care to be by me. . . . Of course, I know it must be of free choice, but she didn't choose. I feel certain that she has something on her mind—some idea in her head. I hoped she might be in love! But she scouts the idea. . . ."

Then Ellen mentioned that Edy was taking "all her meals . . . with the Benny Websters and the Valentines . . . the Valentines appear to me to be common and uninteresting—harmless enough—but for Edy!!" Still baffled, Ellen began to muse on Edy's character: "I think she has a terrific temper, which she keeps pretty tight hold on, yet she is sweet enough to *me* at all events. At her worst and tryingest, I dote on her."

Light on the mystery was finally shed seventy-six years later in Margaret Webster's book about her theatrical family, *The Same Only Different*. Directly from Miss Webster's mother, Dame May Whitty, came the report that explained Edy's behavior. Edy had fallen "deeply and passionately in love with Sydney Valentine, who was married. When Ellen Terry found out, she reacted with violence. . . . She threatened to send Edy home to England at once."

Ellen's reactions were quite proper and understandable. Yet one wishes that Ellen somehow could have helped her daughter gain a deeper insight into herself. Edy, it appeared, had a tendency to bestow her love on ineligible men with whom, for one reason or another, she would not have to risk marriage.

Ellen, with her worries, found no immediate consolation from Irving. "I scarcely see much of Henry," she complained, "except in the confounded theater." But she felt better when Henry told her his intention of putting on one of Shakespeare's least-produced plays, the splendidly improbable *Cymbeline*, giving Ellen a run for her money as the adventurous princess Imogen. To make her even happier, he promised to offer Teddy a role as Ellen's brother, thus ending the boy's three-year separation from the Lyceum.

Now, in the last weeks of the tour, Ellen felt closer to all her dear ones. "Poor Henry," she wrote, "he has had a horrid lot done to his nose today—part of the bone cut away and he bled frightfully—he is sleeping peacefully enough now—" Then her admiration for him welled up: "He is a wonderful person—his ability, *executive ability*, is amazing."

This was followed by an easing of tension with Edy. Ellen wrote to Teddy that she was excusing Edy from making "the beastly hot English tour," which Irving had planned for the company immediately upon docking in Liverpool at the end of May. Instead, Ellen would give Edy a few weeks' rest, along with any friend of her own choosing, in one of Ellen's cottages. Edy, delighted, picked the one at Winchelsea. "She shall have a right-down good holiday—bless her old bones (for really she is little else but bones now). . . . I've just kissed her good night and tucked the dear thing up and she kissed me back so hard and I'm happy, too. So that's all right even if I'm drowned coming over and you never hear from me again! But 'my hope is better!!!' With a hug, your loving Old Mother."

Leaving the ship at Liverpool, Ellen was handed a message saying that her father had died while she was at sea.

Shortly afterward she received a letter from Shaw: "What I want to know is whether there was really anything serious in your notion that my Napoleon would be added to the Lyceum Knight's Entertainments. Or are you only a flattering story-telling Scheherezade? I do hate people who can't make up their minds: they remind me of myself."

If Irving did decide to do the play, Shaw said he promised to teach Ellen her lines by reading them aloud to her while riding across "the celestial plains" on a bicycle built for two.

Chapter Ten

THE PAPER COURTSHIP

"I really don't know what to say about this silly old *Cymbeline*, except that it can be done delightfully in a village school room and can't be done at the Lyceum at all, on any terms."

Shaw began to discuss *Cymbeline* in his letters to Ellen late in the summer of 1896. That he presumed to tell the first lady of the British stage how to act fair Imogen did not faze Ellen Terry. She heeded him intently, ignoring what sounded like poor advice and accepting what she liked.

Teddy always remembered that while he was rehearsing *Cymbeline* with his mother and used to ride home at night with her to Barkston Gardens how eagerly she opened Shaw's letters waiting for her on the supper table. In years to come, Teddy could not recall where his wife and children were at this juncture; but he never forgot his dislike of Shaw, which grew in time to a foolish hatred.

Shaw's disrespect for certain passages in *Cymbeline* probably served to make Ellen feel more relaxed with her role. For by ridding the play of its awesome Shakespearean aura, by daring to pick it apart, Shaw encouraged Ellen to think coolly for herself. He had obviously combed the script with care, deciding what should be trimmed, or cut, or juggled around.

"If you utter all that rubbish about False Aeneas and Dido's weeping, I will rise, snatch the nearest family Shakespeare, solemnly throw it at your head, and leave the theater."

Shaw was also worried about the famous scene when she wakes up and finds a bloody corpse lying beside her. Her line "A headless man!" came five lines too soon, insisted Shaw, and would spoil the climax when she unwraps the blanket around the corpse's neck and discovers that it really is a headless man—and thinks it's her beloved husband, too.

Teddy tried to discredit Shaw by saying that Ellen did not take him seriously. True, she was amused by his purposely wild exaggerations. She cooed over him for fun. But in matters of consequence she always listened to him with respect.

On the day *Cymbeline* opened, Ellen and Shaw exchanged notes. Ellen was exhausted. She complained of "no inspiration . . . no 'gold' tonight. Only dull mud. . . ."

Shaw shot back like a football coach bucking up his team. ". . . inspiration or no inspiration, tonight or never Imogen must be created. Next week is nothing to me or anyone else. Napoleon might have won the battle of Waterloo a week later. It is not your business to be happy tonight but to carry the flag to victory. . . . If you come on with seventy-seven sharp swords sticking in your heart, I should still say you must play as if you were never to play again, even if every word drove one of the swords an inch deeper."

Ellen carried the flag to victory. Both the play and her Imogen came off triumphantly. After the show, she went across to the Savoy Hotel, where she had been staying during final rehearsals because it was nearby, and with her first-night ovation still ringing in her ears wrote to Shaw: "Well, they let me down very kindly. . . . You were a great dear to send me that last letter. Oh, I'm asleep. Goodnight, goodnight. . . . They love me, you know! Not for what I am, but for what they imagine I am!"

The next night, after the show, she wrote again to Shaw from the Savoy. "Well, it was pretty bad again tonight. Only one scene better. . . . I think I'd rather never meet you—in the flesh. You are such a Great Dear as you are! And you are such a worker, and I work too for other people. My kids, and Henry, and my friends. And we both are always busy, and of use!"

The same day, Shaw was at her again for letting things drag in the cave scene and for shouting three words which should have been uttered in a "frozen whisper." In reply, she wrote: "I see now, and will try and try at it. . . . I shall delight to try at it. You must understand, I am the one person at the Lyceum who is never advised, found fault with or 'blackguarded.' . . . It is *frightful* not to be found fault with. Henry won't, can't find time, and the rest are silly and think me a very grand person indeed, and would not dare. Fancy! not 'dare' to *me,* and I never put on a ha'porth of dignity!"

In his review, Shaw called *Cymbeline,* for the most part, "stagey trash of the lowest melodramatic order . . . vulgar, foolish, offensive, indecent and exasperating beyond all tolerance," then he paid tribute to the aspects of Shakespeare he admired: his "enormous power over language, his humor, his sense of idiosyncratic character, and his prodigious fund of vital energy. . . .'"

Finding little to commend among the actors, Shaw called Teddy Craig and Ben Webster "desperate failures." Only two performers gained his full approval. Irving must have been stunned, considering how Shaw had lambasted him in the past, to read that G.B.S. viewed his portrayal of Iachimo "with unqualified delight. It was no vulgar bagful of points, but a true impersonation . . . varied on the surface with the finest comedy, and without a single lapse in the sustained beauty of its execution."

As for Ellen, having gone on record that he was "grossly partial" to her, Shaw now stuck to his guns by saying simply that Miss Terry "invariably fascinates me so much that I have not the smallest confidence in my own judgement respecting her." He murmured helplessly about

217

her "infinite charm" and "delicacy of appeal" and gave her credit for making certain cuts in her lines—which he had probably suggested himself.

Cymbeline was a spur to the Terry-Shaw correspondence. It inaugurated what might be called the Shaw period in Ellen Terry's life, a stretch of some three years, roughly between her fifth and sixth tour to America, tapering off with the finish of the nineteenth century. For Ellen, it was a painful period, when she felt herself growing less attractive to men, and her children were trying to escape her protection, even though they still relied on it. Most unnerving perhaps was the realization that her powers of love, her benevolent magic, seemed to be waning. Her capacity for loving was just as great as ever, but it wasn't doing her much good. At this time Shaw's interest came as a godsend, for she needed to be both admired and entertained by him. All told, Ellen wrote some two hundred letters to Shaw, probably more than he wrote to her, though the score is uncertain because some of the correspondence is lost. Shaw's letters to Ellen were generally longer, because he had weightier things to say and perhaps it was hard for him to stop once he got started.

These letters have become justly famous. But they are too often dismissed as light and frothy, the product of a mere paper courtship. Actually, they are the record of a moving and remarkable friendship that could have existed only under unique circumstances. As lovers in the flesh, Ellen and Shaw could not have accommodated each other for long. They were too busy, too tied up in separate worlds. Intimacy, moreover, did not come readily to Shaw. By his own account, his amorous ventures had been consummated sexually with only two women: Jenny Patterson, an older widow who had him in tow for ten years; and Florence Farr, a charming actress. Shaw's home was the world of ideas and words, and by means of his letters, he carried Ellen into the only home he possessed.

They spared themselves the problem of meeting furtively between their respective deadlines and curtain times. Shaw grabbed paper and pen wherever he was, even on the Underground where he complained of the "joggle-joggle." Ellen wrote in trains and carriages or propped up in bed with a writing board on her lap. Humor was their language, and they spoke it fluently to each other, knowing precisely how serious they meant to be. Although their lovemaking took only verbal form, it glowed with devotion. To Shaw, Ellen Terry was "the most beautiful name in the world; it rings like a chime through the last quarter of the 19th Century." She was "the most perfect lady in England . . . dearest and beautifullest." He called her to "come and pet me and console me" and signed good-bye with "a radiating aurora of love for my Ellenest Ellen." Instead of offering her any mundane gift like diamonds, he cried, "You may chop off all my fingers and toes for a necklace, and have my heart for a locket," which must have struck Ellen as rather savage, coming from a vegetarian. Ellen, in all her responses, never expressed herself more freely or thoughtfully to any other man. In her mailbox—signed, sealed, and delivered regularly—she found the most interesting mind in London.

Thanks to Shaw, Ellen was caught up in the cultural crosscurrents of her day. At the Lyceum with Irving, she represented the popular establishment, stoutly Victorian, dedicated to scenic beauty and moral uplift. With Shaw, she was linked to a redheaded Irish upstart and to his causes—social reform, destroying class privilege, women's rights, Superman, and the Life Force. As if Shaw himself were not wicked enough, he was crusading for Henrik Ibsen, trying to get Ibsen's obscene, subversive dramas put on at the Lyceum. Shaw accused Irving of holding Ellen a prisoner, forcing her to waste her talents on trash like *Nance Oldfield* and *Olivia*. Playfully, Shaw likened himself to Childe Roland rescuing the maiden from the ogre; but he meant it.

Ellen could hardly help feeling pleased having two

knights fighting over her; it was more interesting than half the plays she acted in. And especially now, when she was nearly fifty and was dubious about her future at the Lyceum, Shaw's attentions were pure oxygen.

Shaw, openly, had an ax to grind. He still wanted Irving to do *The Man of Destiny,* with Ellen as the Strange Lady. Irving would not guarantee a production, but he offered option money, which Shaw refused lest it appear that he, as a critic, were accepting a bribe in return for favorable reviews. Such deals were not unknown at the Lyceum. Irving and Shaw hassled for nearly two years over the little play, getting nowhere. One Saturday morning they agreed to meet in Irving's office. Ellen hid outside the door to eavesdrop on their arguments. But the thought of the two enemies glowering at each other amused her so that she feared she might laugh and be overheard. She ran away. Nothing was decided. Shaw reported to her later, "I like Henry, though he is without exception absolutely the stupidest man I ever met. Simply no brains—nothing but character and temperament."

Ellen finally broke her resolve not to see Shaw. Backstage at the Lyceum one night someone told her where Shaw was sitting in the stalls. She peeked out of a hole in the stage curtain and spotted him. Later she wrote, "I've seen you at last! You *are* a boy. And a Duck! . . . How deadly delicate you look!"

Shaw sent her his new plays, hoping to be praised, but also wanting criticism. Once he visited her house at Barkston Gardens to read aloud his *You Never Can Tell.* Ellen was not there, but the author read it to Edy and a young lady from America. Edy paid him so few compliments that Shaw said afterward that she behaved as if she had been married to him twenty-five years.

Later Ellen read it to herself. She pronounced it "tremendous. Frightfully funny," and ". . . INTERESTING." But she added that he had written a "wee bit too much of

Dolly," the dentist's pretty patient. "Too much of a good thing bores folk, especially a funny thing."

Shaw asked for Ellen's advice on *The Devil's Disciple*, his melodrama of the American Revolution, warning her that it might "possibly be the most monstrous piece of farcical absurdity that ever made an audience shriek with laughter . . . you will have to drudge conscientiously through it like a stage carpenter and tell me whether it is burlesque or not." After an obscure English production outside of London, *The Devil's Disciple* was done in New York with Richard Mansfield as the hero, Dick Dudgeon; it was Shaw's first big box-office success.

Shaw's ideal role for Ellen Terry, though it was first played by Janet Achurch, was Candida, the lively, tender wife whose love is split between an intense young poet and her doting husband, a worthy parson who needs her deeply. The similarity between this fictional triangle and the Ellen-Shaw-Irving triangle was not intentional. But Ellen was bound to catch the likeness and feel an emotional identity with Candida's dilemma. Shaw was dying to read it to her. To obviate their meeting each other, he suggested that she be blindfolded while he entered the room and sat down behind a screen. Then he would read. "This plan," he explained, "will have the enormous advantage that if you don't like the play you can slip out after the first speech or two, and slip back again and cough (to prove your presence) just before the end. I will promise not to utter a single word outside the play, and not to peep around the screen."

Eventually, Shaw consented to let her read it alone. "I've cried my poor eyes out over your horrid play, your *heavenly* play!" she wrote. "My dear, and now! How can I go out to dinner tonight? I must keep my blue glasses on all the while for my eyes are puffed up and burning. But I can scarce keep from reading it all over again. . . . Janet would look, and be, that Candida beautifully, but I could help her I know, to a lot of bottom in it. I could do some of it better than she. She could do most of it better than I. Oh, dear me, I love you more every minute. I can't help it, and I guessed it would be like that! And so we won't meet. But write more plays, my *Dear,* and let me read them. It has touched me no more than I could tell of. Yours E.T."

Ellen Terry was the prototypical Shavian heroine, the ideal interpreter of his liberated, humane women. If Ellen was more tantalizingly feminine than he wanted to cope with offstage, he thanked God that she *was*—onstage. At her prime, she could have played to perfection not only his Candida, but his Saint Joan, Major Barbara, Ann in *Man and Superman,* Lavinia in *Androcles and the Lion,* the Polish aviatrix in *Misalliance,* and probably half a dozen others.

Ellen tried to go along with Shaw in his zeal for Wagner and Ibsen. She did her best to interest Irving in Ibsen's dramas *John Gabriel Borkman* and *The Pretenders,* but when Irving recoiled from these alien, austere works, she understood his objections.

"You can't talk of Ibsen and Wagner in a breath," she wrote to Shaw, trying to organize her thoughts. "When jaded, ill-treated, *cheap*-treated Italian opera was at its lowest and dullest, Wagner (raising hundreds of fiddles and everything else to do it) made the air simmer with ravishing, expensive exhilaration. Now all the color and warmth we get into the Shakespeare plays would never, never (oh, I can't express what I mean), never be *made up for* to our audiences by substituting the tremendously powerful bare hardness of Ibsen's *Borkman.* As far as the Lyceum goes, it's much too big a theater to play delicately any of Ibsen's modern plays.

". . . Practically, the things you want to do won't work. A Theater supported by the State. Yes. Then it could be done, but in these dull, dull times in England to show grey instead of gold would not bring folk from their firesides. They would not come."

Ellen was more radically critical of Irving than Shaw

was. She saw him as a total egotist, "unwilling to appreciate the achievements of others." She winced at the naïve way he talked to painters and musicians about their work. She felt he was so self-occupied on the stage, that he hardly even saw the other actors performing with him. "He had precisely the qualities that I never find likeable," she admitted. But notwithstanding, through a quarter-century of, as she put it, "the closest friendship with him," she adored and admired him. Ellen Terry's capacity for love included her ability to come to terms with the faults of her loved ones, as she did notably with Godwin and her children. Her love did not demand perfection. When Irving fell sick in 1897, she wrote to Shaw: "If you worry (or try to worry) Henry, I must end our long and close friendship. He is ill, and what would I not do to better him?"

Ellen did not need Shaw to tell her that her future at the Lyceum was bleak. Imogen in *Cymbeline* was the last major role she played there, because it was the last major role for an actress that Irving provided. She did make a splash as the Napoleonic washerwoman in Sardou's *Madame Sans-Gêne*, which made a handsome profit when it went on tour. It also introduced her to a way of augmenting her income. The practice of commercial manufacturers paying for prominent names to promote their products had just begun. Pears Soap was being advertised by Sir John Millais's painting *Bubbles* and also by a portrait of Lillie Langtry. Now Ellen Terry, in her washerwoman's costume, endorsed a "blueing" for laundry.

Ellen was growing more interested in young playwrights than old plays. Irving's son Laurence submitted to his father a full-length drama, *Peter the Great,* dealing with the clash between the savage czar and his sensitive son, Alexis. Once again, Ellen went to bat for "my boy, Laurence." She told Shaw the play was "wonderful," urged him to read the script, and wangled a Lyceum production in 1898, with Irving and Ellen as Peter and Catherine. The beautiful Russian mistress of Alexis was played by Ethel

Barrymore, aged nineteen. During the play, Ellen had to slap her face, but offstage she treated her better.

The young American actress, whose soulful eyes and lovely long neck made her look like an aristocratic llama, had come to England in William Gillette's *Secret Service.* Jobless at the end of the run, she was packing up to sail home when a note arrived from Ellen Terry asking her to stop at the Lyceum to say farewell to Irving. As a result, Irving invited her to join *Peter the Great.*

Ellen was playing the matchmaker. She knew that Laurence was smitten with this husky-voiced beauty, who, in turn, admired his air of poetic melancholy. Between her performances at the Lyceum, Ethel played the piano for Laurence at her flat while he sang sad songs in Russian. After several proposals, she agreed to marry him, which made him so joyful that he lost his melancholy glamor and she broke the engagement. Laurence's play was no more successful than his engagement; it closed after four weeks, with heavy losses.

The troubles that befell Ellen and Irving began to come with the kind of baffling regularity that astrology is expected to explain. It was a time of omens and changes, most easily accounted for by some baleful conjunction, say, of Uranus and Saturn, or worse.

A shocking portent of change was the stabbing of Ellen's old friend Breezy Bill Terriss, whose verve always advertised the good life. Terriss was murdered by a demented actor outside the Adelphi stage door in Maiden Lane, where he was playing in a popular melodrama. His death was widely mourned; even the Prince of Wales sent condolences to the actress, Jessie Mitwood, who was his closest friend.

Another dreadful event, with more crippling consequences for Ellen and Irving, was the fire that broke out in the warehouse where nearly all the Lyceum scenery was stored. The flames destroyed 260 settings for 44 different plays, a priceless stockpile which permitted Irving to pick and choose a revival on short notice to fill in for an unexpected flop or emergency. Recently, to economize, the insurance had been reduced to cover less than a tenth of the scenery's cost. So there could be no thought of replacing it now, except for two or three major shows. All too patly, the disaster symbolized the end of Irving's regime and, by the lurid fire itself, the end of a whole era. The warehouse was built beneath two high railway arches, which framed the blazing inferno with Piranesi grandeur as the flames consumed the rooftops of Faust's Nuremberg, the Temple of Artemis, Canterbury Cathedral, and King Arthur's canvas Camelot.

Ideally, a phoenix should have risen from the ashes. But the Lyceum's next play was a different kind of a bird—a lame duck.

Irving picked *The Medicine Man*, himself playing a doctor who used hypnotism to gain control over a "fair society virgin," acted by Ellen Terry. Irving clearly hoped to mount a rival sideshow to the sensational new hit *Trilby*, another play exploiting hypnotism, based on George du Maurier's popular novel and put on by Irving's new competitor, Herbert Beerbohm Tree. Tree was a threat. He had just built an elegant new theater, Her Majesty's, with a banquet room up under its dome to rival the Beefsteak Room. It seems rash of Irving to have challenged Tree with a Trilby-type drama, thus inviting odious comparisons. But Irving was confident. Ellen wrote to Shaw of her misgivings. "It 'lunatics' me to watch Henry at the rehearsal. Hours and hours of loving care over this twaddle. He just *adores* his absurd part."

The play closed in three weeks.

Ellen saw other signs of shifting times. Teddy, after seven years as an actor, decided to abandon playacting and concentrate on the graphic arts. His first project was a monthly journal written and illustrated mainly by himself and called *The Page*. Once again, Ellen shared her news with Shaw: "I dispatched nearly one hundred copies,

N.S.E. and West," which meant that she had practically bought out the first run of 140 copies. Her enthusiasm was justified, for *The Page* was an extremely handsome little publication, with its rough brown paper cover, its bold typography, and a generous sprinkle of Craig's bookplates and other woodcuts. It included excerpts from Tolstoy and Marcus Aurelius. Teddy's enterprise was well received in the art world, which helped console Ellen when it came time to pay the printer; Teddy had talked him into producing the first issue on credit.

Between issues of *The Page*, Teddy was spending a few days in a seaside cottage with his actress friend Jess Dorynne, a serious young woman whom Teddy seemed to love and Ellen definitely liked. Their idyll was interrupted when, as Teddy reported, "two legal persons" employed by Teddy's wife came with pads and pencils and jotted down the information necessary to May's getting a divorce which was finally decreed in 1905.

Teddy expressed scorn for the whole crowd: "The moral wife, the moral mother-in-law, the moral lawyers— the moral friends and relations." He simply left it to his mother to perform what she thought was her moral duty to pay May's alimony and help support his children.

In this same unsettling year Ellen first got wind that Irving was seeking the company of Mrs. Eliza Aria, a journalist who wrote chitchat and fashion news for *Truth*. Predictably, Ellen confided her curiosity to Shaw. "But who is Mrs. A? . . . I never set eyes on her and she had no idea I knew of her. (This is fun, and would be better fun, if I knew something about her.) If you know her personally don't 'give away' that I know of her existence." Shaw replied that he had met her casually (she was the sister of Mrs. Arthur Frankau, a novelist who wrote under the name "Frank Danby") and that she seemed "a good sort." Mrs. Aria was also known for her pleasant social gatherings in her house on Regent's Park, attended by the likes of

George Moore, H. G. Wells, and Arnold Bennett. Her appeal for Irving, in contrast to Ellen's, may have been that she represented an escape from the worsening problems at the Lyceum, and there was little about her circle of friends to remind him of them. Ellen's desire to keep secret her knowledge of Mrs. Aria indicates how sensibly she intended to mind her own business. But can one believe that she really thought that finding out about Mrs. Aria was "fun"?

Ellen appeared equally unruffled by Shaw's marriage to Charlotte Payne-Townshend. To be sure, Shaw had always laid his cards on the table and kept Ellen well informed of his friendship with this rich, intelligent woman, for whom he claimed to feel no romantic attachment. Still, it was inevitable that after his marriage Ellen felt somehow demoted in Shaw's regard and missed the playful facsimile of passion in his early letters. Lovers sometimes miss words more than love. Ellen and Shaw continued to correspond, but with notably less sweet talk.

Irving's health was still another source of worry. A year before, according to Ellen, he had been close to "a frightful breakdown" and was saved from it only by enforced bed rest occasioned by a knee injury. Now, while on a provincial tour, he had collapsed in Glasgow with pleurisy and pneumonia and was confined for weeks to the Windsor Hotel and allowed to see no one but doctors and nurses. It was the most serious illness of his life. Ellen continued the tour without him, feeling poorly herself. "I'm laid up in bed the last fortnight just blooming on the stage for 3 hours daily and withering all the rest of the time." She told Shaw that she had little chance to write. ". . . oh, oh, oh, I've no time to call my own. It all belongs to the sick man in Glasgow."

When the gravity of Irving's illness became apparent, Stoker took a significant step and rented the Lyceum for part of the approaching season. Then a little group of Ir-

227

ving's friends, led by Joe Comyns Carr, decided the time had come to relieve Irving of the major financial responsibility for his playhouse by forming a syndicate.

It was an elaborate deal, with Irving receiving a sizable cash payment, along with shares in the New Lyceum Theatre Company. In return, he had to pay 60 percent of production costs and all "stage expenses." For a man in poor health and almost penniless, it seemed a sensible arrangement. Yet after twenty-one years of victorious autocracy, to Irving it was a heavy blow.

Ellen referred to the company now as "the farcical Lyceum Syndicate." Her emotions were torn between wanting to break loose and fend for herself—with more interesting plays, she hoped—and sticking by Irving in his dark hours. Optimistically, she tried a little of both. During the last two months of Irving's convalescence she went on tour with a member of the Lyceum troupe, Frank Cooper, playing in *Othello* and *The Lady of Lyons.* "The only reason for my doing it," she wrote to Shaw, "is that I've nothing in the way of any interesting part to look forward to for the next three years (which will I suppose see the end of me) and these two, Desdemona and Pauline, are easy, as I've done them before."

There were rumors, probably justified, of a flirtation between Ellen and Cooper. But writing to a woman friend, Ellen said, "No—I fear I can't snap up Frank Cooper (!) and marry him, for he happens to have a wife—and she's nice too. . . ."

Ellen Terry had little time, and less inclination, to worry about her social position as an actress. But sometimes she bumped up against the old attitudes. One morning she met her friend Lord Tennyson when he was shopping on Bond Street. "How very nice you look in the daylight," he greeted her. "Not like an actress." He probably meant it playfully, but it stung her.

Far more jolting was an outburst by the critic Clement Scott, for years an ardent admirer of Ellen and Irving. Writing of a woman's fate as an actress, Scott lashed out: "I do not see how she is to escape contamination in one form or another. There is no school on earth so bad for the formation of character, or that so readily, so quickly, draws out all that is bad in man and woman as the stage. . . ." Although Scott's diatribe drew an uproar of protest that cost him his job, it indicated that the antagonism toward players could boil up where least expected.

Ellen's old friend Lewis Carroll could never forget the "scandal" in her life. Whenever one of his young girl friends grew old enough to think of a stage career and begged him for an introduction to Ellen Terry, Carroll wisely, before he obliged, wrote to their mothers asking for parental permission. He liked to explain that at one time he himself had ostracized the famous actress because she had sacrificed her social position, but now he felt she had redeemed herself. One of Carroll's stagestruck young ladies was Dorothea Baird, who became an accomplished actress and married Irving's eldest son, H. B. (Harry) Irving. That Ellen usually remained indifferent to these undercurrents of prejudice testified to her strength.

Ellen's comeback under the new Lyceum regime was in *Robespierre*, written by the reigning French playwright, Victorien Sardou, on order from Irving, and "rendered into English" by his son Laurence. Ellen, as Robespierre's early sweetheart who bore him an illegitimate child, had little to do except grovel and beg him tearfully not to behead his own son. Edy came off better: besides having a small part, she designed all the costumes in the new atelier where Ellen had set her up in business.

On his first entrance, Irving had a thundering welcome, and then had himself an acting spree in a spooky scene where he confronted all the ghosts of the people he had guillotined. But Ellen muffed several of her lines and was dismayed. Two days later she wrote to Shaw, "I'm dead, a dulled thing from keeping on, on, on. . . ."

But if life was tedious at the Lyceum, Ellen could rely

on Teddy to keep her agitated, sometimes pleasantly so. He had once seen her do Ophelia's mad scene at a Drury Lane benefit for Nelly Farren, an ailing music hall queen. (As always in the comradely theater world, an Ellen Terry would not hesitate to help a Nelly Farren.) Ellen felt her Ophelia was "damnable," but Teddy called it magnificent and dedicated an issue of *The Page* to "The Divine Ophelia of Drury Lane."

When Teddy told his mother that he might discontinue *The Page* after the first few issues, she was distressed. "Do stick to the bitter end of *The Page*," she replied. "Nobody can believe in your bona fides if you don't carry out your one year. . . . Don't you see, dear, it will be dishonorable, for if you only had five subscribers to it for a year, you should fulfill your contract with them, or die in trying to do so." It pained her also that some subscribers were receiving no copies at all. As if trying to explain ethics to a ten-year-old, she went on, ". . . a contract is a contract, and whoever on either side breaks it is dishonorable, and I cannot get over my horror of that for you. I want to be proud of you all around."

Ellen was equally disturbed by his borrowing. "You think you have pride—you have none—or you could not borrow from your poor friends . . . and owe money to poor tradesmen, the people who can't afford to lend, and with whom you don't concern yourself in the least. I cannot understand how it has come to pass that up to the age of 21 you were so reasonable and had so much 'sweetness and light', and that you have suddenly become so *unreasonable*—so, almost, *outrageous*."

But Ellen was most troubled by Teddy's treatment of women. During the messy business of ending his marriage, May Craig forwarded to Ellen a letter that Teddy had sent to her. Ellen was shocked by its rudeness. "Very vulgar and very insulting and cad-ish. I'm quite ashamed of you."

Then Ellen became sharply practical about May.

"Thank goodness, she sends me your letters sometimes. Into the fire they go like lightning when I get hold of them. I wish you'd send me more of hers. They may be an excuse for you and a protection for you, in which case they would be well to be in my hands as in the hands of a counsel for the defendant. I should know what to keep and what to destroy—my Mother's eye would know."

Her mother's eye had also noted, and approved, Teddy's growing attachment to Jess Dorynne. Jess was smart, not too ambitious, and might be a stabilizing influence on Teddy. But although Teddy seemed to love and depend upon Jess, Ellen was apprehensive. Jess's mother looked askance at Teddy, and Ellen did not blame her at all. "Remember this, my dearest boy," she wrote. "I would rather *kill* you than see you grow systematically exacting and dishonorable to women."

Again and again, her despair over Teddy tore her apart inside. She tried to tell him about it. "I wish I was glass, and you could *see* how you can gladden or pain me." But no matter how acute the pain, she usually closed every letter on the same adoring note. "Bless you my dear. I'm missing you all most frightfully. Mother—with the same old love." Thus, she always managed to nullify her reprimands by assuring Teddy that in spite of his derelictions she would fight his battles, pay his bills, and be his doting "Mum."

Through all her misgivings and worries, Ellen continued to take comfort in Shaw. His logic amused and steadied her. Best of all, he was about to toss her a life-preserver in the form of a new play, written especially for her. When *Captain Brassbound's Conversion* was delivered to her, she devoured it at once and then sat down to write her reactions. Without warning, she dropped the bomb. ". . . it's not the sort of play for me in the least. . . . I believe it would never do for the stage . . . it comes as a great refreshment to the tired spirit, but it would not be so when it was acted!"

Shaw was torpedoed. He had counted on the play as much as she had, poured his convictions into it, not to mention his adoration for Ellen. He answered her only briefly at first, ending his note, "Silly Ellen." Two days later, still in shock, he opened fire. "Oh, you lie, Ellen, you lie: never was there a part so deeply written for a woman as this for you, silly, self-conscious, will o' the wisp be-glamoured child-actress as you still are."

His claim that "never was there a part so deeply writ-ten for a woman" was balderdash, excusable only on the grounds that no playwright who has struggled to deliver a play is rational right after the birth. His calling her a self-conscious child-actress contained a tiny grain of truth that made it inexcusable under any circumstances. He hit her where she was most vulnerable, where she felt so unsure of herself that she would accept the slur.

Changing his tone from snide to messianic, he pointed out that he had set her up as the hope of the world, a woman whose "heart-wisdom" could combat the cruelty and folly of European imperialists. "I try to show you," he harangued, "fearing nobody and managing them all as Daniel managed the lions, not by cunning . . . but by simple moral superiority."

Shaw made her feel that by rejecting his play she had betrayed the cause of morality and suggested that the play, once published, would become known as having been "re-pudiated by Miss Ellen Terry as unworthy of her profes-sional eminence," thus branding her forever as a woman without judgment or soul.

Ellen cried when she read Shaw's letter. She was so upset that she had to cancel her morning carriage ride. But after rereading the play, she decided that she liked it better and began to speculate with Shaw about when and where the play might someday be done. Her change of mind stemmed less from her wobbliness than from her honest feeling that she had underestimated the work.

People who have never seen *Captain Brassbound's Con-*

version—it is not one of Shaw's better-known, or better, plays—may wonder what all the ruckus was about. The essence of the play is the conflict between Lady Cicely, a humane Terry type, and a renegade English captain, festering for vengeance against his uncle, who had once wronged the captain's mother. It is Lady Cicely's hope to convert the captain from vengeance to forgiveness.

Shaw obviously enjoyed describing Ellen herself in the stage directions that introduce her into the play. "A woman of great vitality and humanity, who begins a casual acquaintance at the point usually attained by English people after thirty years' acquaintance when they are capable of reaching it at all."

The play is set in Morocco, where Lady Cicely comes with her brother-in-law, both tourists hoping to explore the wild hinterlands. They recruit the renegade captain as a guide, and by the long arm of coincidence, grown muscular in English melodrama, Cicely's brother-in-law turns out to be the very culprit whom the captain wants to do in. To gain his end indirectly, the captain leads them among hostile Moroccans who will enslave and slaughter them for being dirty Christians. This, of course, is where Ellen shines. For how can a Moroccan or anybody else be beastly to Ellen Terry? She mothers and soothes her startled enemies, washes their wounds, sews on their buttons, and tells them what nice faces they have. Eventually, she even drives vengeance from the heart of helpless Captain Brassbound.

Shaw boasted that the role fitted Ellen better than her own skin, and it did, almost to the point of caricature. But while Shaw was priding himself on his dramatic tailoring, he overlooked the play's fatal flaw. Lady Cicely, especially as played by Ellen Terry, was so invincible that never for one minute did she appear to be in danger; she could obviously charm her enemies to a pulp. As a result, robbed of its suspense, the play is static.

One can easily understand, and respect, Shaw's wanting to write the play for Ellen, for she exemplified the Christian spirit as Shaw liked to see it. With a not dissimilar heroine, Shaw was far more successful in *Saint Joan*, for the simple reason that the audience knew Joan was in terrible jeopardy, playing with fire.

As a token of her belated faith in *Brassbound*, Ellen gave a single "performance" of the play in Liverpool just before she and Henry set sail for America in October. This, according to English law at the time, permitted the play to be copyrighted and protected against future piracy, even though the performance was merely a public reading. Also, the play had to be advertised by a printed poster, at least one program had to be printed and one ticket sold—for a guinea.

After the Liverpool reading, Ellen wrote to Shaw that "everyone loved the play," but "they all loathe Lady Cicely, calling her a tremendous humbug . . . arch . . . detestable woman." As for herself, she felt she had read it wrong, though Edy said it was not Ellen's fault. Edy's opinion was, according to Ellen, that "Shaw had *thought* of Lady C. as one kind of a woman, and had written of her as another." Unsparingly, Ellen continued to quote Edy, who said that Lady C. on stage was not "either very clever, or humorous or vital, and certainly not of great humanity." Irving did not get around to the reading, but when he finally read the script he said it was "like a comic opera."

The Shaw period in Ellen's life came to a close. They remained friends, exchanged a few letters, and Ellen eventually made a fair success in *Captain Brassbound*. It was not as bad as she first thought it was—nor as good as Shaw first thought it was.

Chapter Eleven

THE EMERGENCE OF GORDON CRAIG

"New York is more marvelous than ever."

Arriving at the end of October 1899, Ellen wrote to Teddy from the Plaza Hotel at Central Park and Fifth Avenue. (On this same site the present Plaza Hotel was built in 1907.) "They are the wonderfulest people, the Americans— We were knee deep in flowers, letters, gifts of all sorts before we have been here six hours."

The day after her arrival she took samples of Teddy's cards, bookplates, and "other things" to Brentano's and Wanamaker's to see if they would carry them. We do not know what luck she had, but she sounded optimistic. "I shall get you several Book plates to do here—from 5 to 10 pounds" (possibly $50 to $100). Autumn in New York made Ellen euphoric. "All our seats are gone at most extraordinary prices for the whole three weeks we are here. It will be a tremendous tour. This is the place to make money!"

Ellen had with her a bookplate designed by Teddy with the initials J.D. It was meant for Jess Dorynne. But meeting her actor friend John Drew, she persuaded him that J.D. was for him and relieved him of forty dollars. To help Teddy, she was not missing a trick. She hunted a publisher for Teddy's *Book of Penny Toys*, visiting Scribner's, Harper's, and "Dodd and something." It reminded her of helping Godwin in the old days. "You are slaving. So am I," she wrote him. "But it is so fine we are both *capable people*." It pleased her too that Jess was being helpful, painting colors into the black and white woodcuts for the *Book of Penny Toys,* again, just as she used to for Godwin. She ended almost every letter to Teddy with "Love to Jess."

This tour, her sixth to America with Irving, made her feel important again. "Don't you say, my dear Ted," she wrote from Pittsburgh, "or rather imagine for one moment that Henry doesn't want me. *Never more so.* I really am not given to flattering myself (or as they say here, 'throwing Bowkays at myself'), but I know that for a fact." As proof, she said that on her days off "the house is half empty."

In America, Ellen and Irving felt closer to each other again. America was their joint territory, full of memories. The fact that Edy stayed back in London could make Ellen feel more carefree, and she was glad that young Laurence was along. Even though he spent his spare time working on a new play, both Irving and Ellen welcomed his presence which helped renew the tie between them.

Ellen was still thinking about *Captain Brassbound.* From Toledo, Ohio, she wrote to Shaw about Irving's hope of returning soon to America. "My plans are somewhat shattered for H. is wanting to arrange an autumn tour, and asks me to come too. A tour of six months beginning next October. This, if I agree to it, will probably see me through the rest of my working life." Then she apologized for philandering so long with *Brassbound.* "Must I give it up?" Speculating about some other actress doing Lady Cicely, she turned a bit coquettish, "I'm very fairly well, and look *very* well. My hair is getting nicely grey (lively for Lady C.) and is becoming!" After venting her disgust with the Boer War—"The only subject that excites me and makes me want to kill, Kill, KILL!"—she told Shaw he was often in her thoughts and added, "I hope your Charlotte is well and very happy." Shaw replied, "Very well, dear Ellen, we cry off *Brassbound.* . . . now I recognize that you and I can never be associated as author and player . . . and that you will remain Olivia. . . . I have pitched so many dreams out of the window that one more or less makes little difference." Shaw also was turning a bit coquettish.

Because the tour was profitable and theater business back in London was ailing because of the Boer War, Irving dropped his idea of returning to the United States in the autumn in favor of extending the current tour by six weeks. Ellen dreaded it. For much as she had enjoyed the beginning, enough was enough. Her usual homesickness had set in, she and Irving were both bedeviled by ill health—and she worried about Teddy.

In London, Teddy was approaching a turning point in his career: a staging of Purcell's opera *Dido and Aeneas* with his new and gifted musical friend Martin Shaw. For the first time Teddy had control of a large production, involving some seventy singers and dancers, and he could begin to experiment with his ideas—ideas that were to change the face of the modern theater. Most of the financing was provided by the two hundred members of the Purcell Operatic Society, a group of music-lovers and sponsors. But Teddy, out of habit, sent Ellen a cry for help. For once it fell on indifferent ears. Miss Terry was feeling wretched. She refused to send him a lump sum, but a weekly stipend of two pounds, ". . . for a chop . . . a boot, a bed." The very notion of joining Teddy in a business enterprise horrified her.

Writing from Cleveland, she warmed up to her refusal first by bawling him out for whimpering over money.

Really I rather suspect you must try harder to *give* happiness, than try to get it. Practice on Jess and me! We will serve for your experiments. Just try to appreciate what you *have,* and don't be hankering. If the great trouble comes from want of money, all I can say is that I believe the more you have, the more you would find trouble. I consider your bent towards cleverness does not lie in the management of money.

If I had seen before this that you had a turn for finance in small matters, I should have helped you to do bigger things—but during your self-management, since you were 21 years old you

237

have got rid, one way or another, of a very tidy little fortune. You change too much. You have spells of real good endeavor, but not nearly long enough to prove yourself to yourself, or to me. You should have *served,* my Dear Lad, all these years. Ich Dien—a splendid motto.

Now your idea, I know, is that you and I should work together. I fear it would be quite impossible. To work at all, under the very easiest circumstances, is, at times, a tremendous effort nowadays for me. I shall *probably* go on fairly much the same as now with H. as long as he wants me. *And he will want me as long as he is!* you can be quite sure of that. If I make any change, it might chance to be made at the end of the coming little Lyceum Season. For *I am dreadfully* in want of rest and some quiet comfort. Then *perhaps* I might tell H. it was an end of it all, as far as engaging with anybody was concerned, and after a good long rest, prepare to make a farewell engagement on my own, as Edy would call it, in which case, although I should be glad of certain help from you, I should not feel at all inclined to be entirely in the hands of my dear old rash and inexperienced-in-business-ways boy Edward. In other words, I fear we could not work together. I am not at the beginning of it all, and I would much rather furnish the wherewithal and turn you loose to run amock by yourself than topple down with you. For if I, as a money-making machine, should come to grief, there would be a pretty Kettle of Fish for more than you and your children and Edy and Boo.

. . . I have the blues pretty badly now and again. No use to give in though, not a bit of use. Best love from Mother.

By the time she was ready to sail home, her mood was less caustic and she was brimming again with love. She had bought more Walt Whitman books and manuscripts for Ted, and "a very nice Emerson volume for Stephen" (Coleridge), or for Ted if he wanted it. She felt in better health, "longed to see all my beloved brats." Henry was in better health, too, "but the poor dear doesn't long to see anybody or anything except a fine house." In Irving's parlance, "house" meant only audience. "He has seen 7 doctors in the last 7 weeks, and has taken new stuff from every one of them!! He lives!"

She was hurt that Ted, after her eight-month absence, did not greet her. "I wonder why you didn't stay *one* day longer in London to see me." But she was thrilled that in her absence his opera had won "tremendous praise," and she hurried to visit his children—four of them by now, and all "just delightful." She sent a gift to Jess. "Ask her to write me."

Ted had rebuffed her, probably by mail, for not being modern enough in her tastes and for not taking enough interest in "the things I wish to do." Incredulously, she repeated his words: " 'Not consider the things I wish to do,' sticks me, I confess. Don't give up!! Have patience. Teach me. I want to learn to the end, I assure you. But I am self-respecting and I don't like rude rough manners—and so, when you are rough, I just feel as if I curl up and tumble down from you, like those rum little insects which roll themselves into a ball. I believe in my soul you feel tenderly, but I have never seen you *behave* tenderly to any woman."

Teddy was spending part of the summer in a country cottage with Jess, who was pregnant. Now he was sure that women were conspiring—particularly Jess in cahoots with Ellen—to steal his freedom. Leaving Jess behind, he escaped to London, full of plans for rejoining Martin Shaw and reviving their *Dido and Aeneas*. They would add to it another Purcell work, which he retitled *The Masque of Love*, and thus make a full evening for a large London theater. To assure its success, they planned for Ellen to perform her short play *Nance Oldfield*. But Ellen's first duty, she was told, was to give the Purcell Operatic Society enough money to get the show going.

Ellen was dubious. "My dear. . . . You see it's a jump in the dark for me. I cannot think a great big sum such as 600 pounds should be spent upon a performance or two of *any* kind. And of course, as a matter of fact, the Purcell Society is nothing to me personally compared with many a Stage Play Society. The whole is in a nutshell when I say it for *your* benefit that I offer this £300. But will it benefit you to trot it out for another performance of *Dido,* and will all things come out straight and to your honor, or will the result go to make you *seem* to be 'bogus-ey'?''

While the answer pended, Ellen was on an autumn tour with Irving and his son Laurence. Between the last two bookings, Leeds and Brighton, she rushed to London to see a private Sunday night performance of *Captain Brassbound's Conversion* given by the Stage Society. Laurence played the title role, which was hectic for him because he had to manage London rehearsals with G.B.S. while he was on tour with Irving. Shaw's friend Janet Achurch was playing Lady Cicely. Ellen was immensely excited: after all, it was *her* play, she knew that someday she would play in it, and after five years of intimate correspondence she would meet Shaw face to face at the theater. It was almost too much.

As the performance date drew near, she wrote to Shaw again: "So many thanks for getting me the Box. . . . Poor old Laurence, I wish he could be let off. I'll find out whether it would be of any convenience to him to come straight to Barkston Gardens . . . after a night journey. I'm sure I would be as eager as *any* mother to welcome him by day or night and feed him and take care of him: he is a dear fellow. . . . I think he wishes I was acting Lady C. with him. (Not a word to Janet, please.) By the way, if you'd like it best I will sit 'way back in Dress Circle, Pit or Gallery. . . . Yours, E.T.''

The meeting between Ellen and Shaw took place backstage after the performance amid the gabble that always follows a premiere: Ellen with her daughter, Shaw with his wife, people watching the two "lovers," knowing it was their first meeting and wondering how it would go. Apparently, it hardly went at all. Ellen remarked later to Shaw, "They say you could not bear me, when we met, that one time, under the stage." Ellen was exaggerating. As for the *Brassbound* play, its future remained shadowy.

Meanwhile, Ellen decided to "jump in the dark" with the two Purcell works, giving Ted his debut as a designer-director in a real London theater. Through her influence, Ted and Martin Shaw were able to book the Coronet for a week in March.

During their long rehearsals, Ellen was on another provincial tour with Irving. But she mailed Teddy her advice about souvenir programs, seats for critics, lighting problems, carting scenery, and anything else that she hoped would be helpful. Directly after her last booking on tour (Birmingham), she planned to hurry to London to add *Nance Oldfield* to the opera bill, as promised. Irving had expected her to jump immediately into rehearsing her role as Volumnia in the Lyceum's big spring show *Coriolanus*. But she bilked him out of a week for Ted.

The Purcell-Terry package was a six-day success and Teddy's visual innovations were appreciated, at least by discerning eyes. William Butler Yeats wrote him: "Dear Mr. Craig: I thought your scenery to 'Aeneas and Dido' the only good scenery I ever saw. You have created a new art. . . ."

After it was over, the Purcell Operatic Society was richer by 400 pounds, although none of its sixty members who sang in the chorus received a penny, nor did Ellen Terry. Similarly, in the Stage Society's production of *Brassbound*, none of the actors were paid. It was already becoming apparent in the London theater that some stage enterprises were not commercial and had to depend on the generosity of actors, patrons, or, later, on government subsidy.

From Winchelsea, where Ellen had gone to collapse after her stint for Ted, she wrote to him, "Yes, I thought you'd be tired when it was all over. It's the same with me. *It was a lovely show.* Unfortunately, I've been in bed ever since with the 'Flu' and my temperature at 104. It's down now and I'm better, but I've not been able to go near the Lyceum, and as you may guess, it's pretty lively there."

241

One may also guess that Irving was irked at having Ellen absent from rehearsals after her allotted week off and feeling poorly when she did return. She asked him to let her off on the opening night. He refused, forgivably.

Coriolanus was the last new production that Irving and Ellen did together and their only Shakespearean fiasco. Six years before Irving had been determined to do it against Ellen's urging, and he had finally dropped the idea. Now the general verdict was that the two stars were badly miscast—which should have been evident at the start. Ellen at fifty-four played mother to Coriolanus, acted by Irving at sixty-three. When Ellen in act 5 called herself a "poor hen" who had "clucked" her arrogant son to the wars and accused him, "Thou has never in thy life show'd thy dear mother any courtesy," it must have struck her that, onstage or off, she certainly had her troubles with motherhood.

After thirty-four performances, *Coriolanus* expired. On its closing night Ellen observed that then "H.I. for the first time played Coriolanus *beautifully*. He discarded the disfiguring beard of the warrior he had worn through the 'run' of the show, and now that one could see his face, all was well. . . . even an actor of Irving's calibre hardly begins to play an immense part like Coriolanus for what it is worth until he has been doing it for fifty nights." Ellen may have exaggerated the length of time it takes to master a great part, but there is no denying that she and Irving suffered from the lack of previews and tryouts that today's actors think necessary.

Ellen restored herself by spending a few days in the country, her "cottage cure," with two of her grandchildren and then, because of the untimely *Coriolanus* demise, started working to fill in the schedule at the Lyceum. "We do several old plays at once, and rehearse and rehearse all the time: good heavens, it's awful! . . . What creatures we women are! If overtaxed above our physical capacity we go to pieces and are not ourselves."

Three days later Ellen wrote a furious letter to Ted. On the surface she was angry because he had accused her of being "amused" by his falling-out with Jess. She was also venting her deep dismay over Teddy's indifference and denial of love.

> 16 May, Thursday morning [1901]
>
> "*Amuse*" me? (You and J.). You Flat Iron—You Idiot. I can find no name to tell you what I think of your intelligence. You are doing your best to miss your salvation, your fortune that lies before you, your whole happiness (and by all this I mean J.) and with all it at your feet you are so blind with jealousy, vanity, discontent and obstinacy you don't see it. You refer, I supposed, when you speak of "amusing" me, to the evening when I laughed at your saying J. had no love for you? If you could only have known the weight you lifted from me, as you said that . . . (She "had no love for you"), that *all* was not yet lost—and that you did love her—and were not callous, as she thinks, but only jealous without knowing it.
>
> Now consider: she has done everything a woman can do for three years to prove her love for you, spite of your outrageous ungentleness and selfish inconsiderateness. She longs for you to be with her. I can't get a word from her upon any other subject but you—you—you. And no one but a really unintelligent person could fail to know her entire devotion and adoration of you. (I am blind sometimes but not so blind as not to see this laid out like a map before me.) You love her—you have said so and I believe you. . . . *Amuse* me—you! I could kill you almost for daring to say such a light word for all the heartbreak you have caused and are causing me.
>
> You have never appreciated any of the love you have had thickly thrown upon you. When I used to pour out just what I thought of you, with intent for your happiness solely before my eyes, you simply *fled*. That was your usual pretty unreasoning trick to avoid anyone's implorings or advice. Then, knowing how words of any kind but flattering words make you impatient (and I wouldn't give those), then I tried to be not so serious with you, avoided speaking of your affairs, and only just shouldered your difficulties time after time, you ungrateful son—hoping you might take the chances of love, and fortune that have presented

themselves before you, and which you have only blindly kicked aside. After all, and the last few months' intenser suffering than I have ever experienced for myself, you think you "Amuse" me!!

If you could see my ragged old heart.

Do you know *nothing?* Have you no perception? I keep from advising J. by one word about you (from fear of causing a wider breach) but in spite of the cowardly way in which you put the fault upon her shoulders, *I know you love her,* and I entreat you not to lose her. Heavens—she's not granite. You will wear all the beauty of her character by your constant unreasonableness. You could wear my love out because you are your Father's child and because of the blood being the same, yours and mine. Blind one, can't you see the dilemma I am in now about you? (This is another subject) I should think you could see . . . Great Heavens— how can one make you see the very nose upon your face.

This is my dilemma. You are in a tight corner again in regard to money. Now what am I to do? The same I have done before, again and again? Is that for your best good? I'd do it if I knew it would be the best. But as J. is doing now, I feel I ought to change my method with you, which has failed and failed and failed, and try some other way. Don't you see that we are two devoted women who long to befriend, and show our friendship to you, and that nothing we do seems to have the slightest effect upon you—or to be of any benefit whatever for your happiness.

Ellen's identification with Jess is self-evident: "We are two devoted women. . . . nothing we do seems to have the slightest effect. . . ." Ellen continued:

I've tried not to speak, for well I know how every word may mar instead of mend. But here am I at my age finding all my love not understood by you in the least, that you think I am *"amused"* by the case of Edward and the Rebellious J., and all the while you are both doing your best way to kill me. . . . I will change my plan, and try another way with you about your business affairs— unless you will be plain with me and tell me what to do for you— point out the way *you can see* for me to help you—in business— with regard to J.—with regard to anything on Earth for you and your better having.

I'm getting very doddery. So I'll end. One thing: don't dare to say or even think that I say or think lightly for one moment about you or Edy—or J.—or your children. You are all heart of my heart, breath of my body, Mother.

Later in the summer, Ted turned his back on family entanglements and went to France with a young musician who had helped him at Uxbridge, the Baroness Overbeck, known to her friends as "Jimmy"; she dressed as a boy, just for "adventure—no lovemaking—sheer FUN." And in the same summer Henry Irving was showing his new friend Mrs. Aria the landmarks of Stratford-on-Avon.

Ellen evidently retained some hope that Teddy and Jess would stick together; when Jess got a job acting with Charles Wyndham's company, Ellen cautioned Ted to be considerate of her, reminding him that after her preliminary rehearsals Jess could go back to "coloring." But Ellen was skeptical: "For myself, I think it takes more *reasonable* people than you two young ones, for one to be 'on the stage,' and the other off it. . . . Now don't you be a pair of young idiots and mess your lives, and make a hash of it. . . ." Then she shifted to a sunnier subject and called his latest issue of *The Page* "first class . . . splendid . . . the whole thing couldn't be better." It was the last number of *The Page* ever published.

Upon arriving back at the Plaza Hotel for her seventh and last American tour with Irving, Ellen felt the same old exhilaration. "Splendid journey . . . lovely day . . . New York wondrously improved! . . . Heavens they are a marvelous people. Flowers . . . letters . . . books. Everything waiting for me here. . . ." She hoped that now dear old Ted was "less harrassed by business worries . . . and Jess may be less busy and help you again." But a few days later she was consumed with anxiety: "Oh, my dear, my dear, you are in my mind from morning til night, and unfortunately all night long. . . . It is now 4 o'clock in the morning, and I cannot rest. While you are taking time to think, I fancy it will be of use to you to have that room at Edy's place of business to at least put your books and work in for

245

the present. So I will take the room from Edy, and you must not call it yours though! It *shall* be yours for all intents and purposes, but if it is called mine, no one will touch anything in it whilst you are looking around and getting out of debt. Though I fear you are 'getting into debt' instead of out of it. Too bad, too bad. However, I know there is no vice in all this, only immaturity of perception of what is 'fair play' to those you have attached to you, and to yourself. . . . I do hope you don't owe poor old M. Shaw anything. That would be insufferable to you, I should hope. *Tell me.* . . . If you only knew how I am always thinking of you."

In Philadelphia, Ellen, at Ted's request, sent him two hundred pounds to help subsidize a new Purcell Operatic Society production of Handel's *Acis and Galatea,* combined with a repeat showing of *The Masque of Love.* Ellen knew there was not a ghost of a chance of its making a profit, yet by now she was convinced of Ted's exceptional talent and knew that he needed a showcase.

In "marvelous" Chicago where it was "snowing madly," Ellen was still scurrying about on Teddy's behalf. After reminding him how he once went sledding years ago along the lake front, she got down to serious business. "I saw a set of your *Page* at Brentano's, 2 volumes in a *wonderful* leather cover, handmade. Thought I'd like to bring it back to you. Asked price. 85 Dollars! Heavens!! Had to give it up. It appears, however, a set of the same price, bound in same way, was sold to a lady who wanted her young daughter to 'have something most artistic.' (The eternal use of that phrase in Chicago is maddening.) You had better make a Memorandum of the lady's name and address, I asked for it. It is—Mrs. J. M. Longyear, Marquette, Michigan. I should send her notices, and ask if she would like you to make her a bookplate."

While Ellen was in America, Teddy met enchanting little Elena Meo, a violin prodigy, whose father, Gaetano Meo, was a painter and a friend of Burne-Jones and Ros-

setti. Before *Acis and Galatea* had finished its one unsuc-
cessful week, Teddy had persuaded his love-struck Elena to
flee with him into the country for a pastoral interlude, duly
followed by Elena's pregnancy. They were never married,
but they remained close to each other for many years, and
Elena became Ellen's favorite "daughter-in-law." At what
point Ellen became aware of Elena's importance to Teddy is
uncertain. Shortly after she returned to England, Ellen was
offering Smallhythe to Jess and Ted, as if she assumed they
would use it together.

Ellen was relieved in 1902 when Irving opened the
final Lyceum season with *Faust* that she was not playing
Margaret. She had begun to feel too old for it and was glad
to see her friend Cissie Loftus taking over. At the same
time, Herbert Beerbohm Tree was preparing a gala production of *The Merry Wives of Windsor* to celebrate the coronation of Edward VII and invited Ellen to play Mistress Page.
Irving consented to relinquish his star if she would play
two matinees a week with him at the Lyceum in *The Merchant of Venice* and *Charles I.* All parties consented, and at
the opening of *Merry Wives,* Irving wired Ellen, "Heaven
give you many many merry days and nights."

In view of the coronation, Irving obtained permission
from the Lord Chamberlain for a gala showing of *The Bells,*
to be followed by a bang-up reception at the Lyceum for
the visiting princes and potentates. Forty minutes after the
play was over, the Lyceum was stripped; stalls were ripped
out, the interior was carpeted and draped in scarlet, and tables were set up for food and drink. For Irving it was a
grandly moving occasion, both a welcome to the new ruler
and a farewell to himself.

Ellen was present, naturally, though troubled by the
absence of Teddy, who always claimed to be Irving's devout admirer. The next day she wrote him, "Hope you are
not ill? Why were you not at the Lyceum gathering last
night? Write Henry a line, I think, or it is an affront from
your age to his. I had hoped to see you there. My *remains*

were present. To be in 'The World,' I suppose, is pleasant—but—Lord, the compensations to those *out* of it!"
Teddy's indifference was fabulous.

Two weeks later Ellen and Irving took their last Lyceum curtian call after *The Merchant of Venice* on a Saturday
matinee. As they stood, hand in hand, their eyes filled
with real tears, and, for once, they held them back. The audience was unaware of witnessing a historic moment, and
the old partners were not quite sure of it either. But Ellen
whispered to Irving, "I shall never be in this theater again.
I feel it—I know it."

Ellen and Irving never really parted. Being practical
workers in the theater, they would come together easily
and with good humor whenever expediency demanded.
Sticking to old habits like migratory birds, they planned a
twelve-week tour in the provinces in October. To rest up
for it, Ellen went to Paris where she met old friends and
called on "Sally B." "Sarah's house is just like her," she
wrote to Teddy, "always full of people—and other animals.
Three lovely pumas amongst them, one going about all
over the house with Sarah." Then, back in harness with
Irving, she wrote from Leeds about his forthcoming new
spectacle *Dante*, which Victorien Sardou had helped con-
coct and which Laurence Irving was translating into English.

Irving had offered Ellen twelve thousand pounds to
tour America in *Dante*, but she refused because her part
was negligible, and she hated to accept so much for doing
so little. Thinking of Teddy's skill with scenery, she informed Irving that her son was "the only one nowadays
who could do his *Dante* play." Irving replied cautiously,
"Ah, well that might be very good—we'll see about it."

"I did not add at the time," Ellen told Teddy, "that
probably he and I will be busy together in the
spring. . . ."

The next spring, as Ellen foresaw, mother and son
were presenting, for the first time in English, Ibsen's early

tragedy *The Vikings.* Ellen knew she was badly miscast as the warrior wife, Hjordia, who finally murders her weakling husband with an arrow, then drowns herself. She feared it would be like trying to act "three lady Macbeths." But although she realized she was "too old now to experiment *handicapped*," still she felt "like getting up and *trying.*"

For her first stab at independent production, Ellen leased the luxurious but poorly located Imperial Theatre, built for her friend Lillie Langtry, and hired a finicky business manager to count pennies, collect receipts, and write contracts. Teddy was outraged. This idiot skimped on publicity and made him sign a contract with his own mother!

Nonetheless, Teddy came off handsomely. He gutted the Imperial stage of its grids, ropes, and tormentors, confiscated footlights and border lights, and sent down shafts of radiance from big spotlights concealed overhead or high at the sides. Using the techniques of Hubert Herkomer, a pioneer in stage lighting and simplified scenery, he created Norwegian skies that were deep and luminous. His crags loomed ominously, and the furniture he designed for the warriors' mess hall was superbly neo-Walkyrian.

Ellen decided that, in the event of failure, Teddy should get ready an inexpensive production (partly from old sets and dresses) of *Much Ado about Nothing,* which, as she put it, they could "pop in" to the Imperial to help recoup their losses. When *The Vikings,* as she feared, bit the dust after three weeks, she popped in *Much Ado.* Later, she toured it with the addition of a stark new play, *The Good Hope,* translated from the Dutch by Edy's cherished new friend Christabel Marshall, who changed her name to Christopher St. John. Ellen played an old fisherwoman and thoroughly enjoyed being "out of character."

With a theater man's facility for finding alibis, Teddy blamed the Imperial fiasco entirely on his mother's misjudgments. Ellen was certainly not blameless. She fussed too much at Teddy and hired some wrong people. But the chief difficulty was Ibsen's play, which Teddy had selected. For all its barbaric power, *The Vikings* was never a crowd-winner outside of Scandinavia. When it was over, Teddy announced firmly, "My mother and I parted company in our work," which was a double-barreled blessing.

When Irving embarked for America, the first time without Ellen, he wrote to a friend there: "It will be strange and somewhat sad without Ellen. . . . Poor dear, she had been absolutely under the influence and spell of her two children—who have launched her on a sea of troubles. . . ."

Irving's comment was true, but he overlooked another, far greater, launching that escaped general notice. Ellen had launched her son as a pioneer in the history of theater arts. She gave birth to him, as it were, a second time. Now Teddy was no longer Teddy, but Gordon Craig. Thanks to her coddling as well as her cash, Craig's genius was being recognized, not as yet by ordinary playgoers, but by people in the arts who could spread his gospel and further his career.

One was Count Harry Kessler, a distinguished German diplomat and art patron from Weimar, who had been struck with Craig's work in London, especially *The Vikings,* and suggested he work in Berlin at the Lessing Theater under the direction of Dr. Otto Brahm. It took a year before the negotiations were completed. Meanwhile, Craig seriously considered starting a theater school in England and was able to give more time to his devoted Elena Meo. Their first child had died shortly after birth, but they were to have two more. By the time Craig reached Berlin in 1904, he left six small children behind in England, all of them more or less dependent on Ellen Terry for support and love. "How queer you are!" Ellen once wrote to him. "You are fonder of folks when *away* from them. I'm much fonder of 'em when I'm *with them*—and especially *quietly* with them. A custom, a habit, of people, to me is perfect rest."

Craig's indifference to people, unless they were helping him work or make love, is reflected in his stage settings. They are beautiful, regal, hauntingly aloof; people seem to have little place in them, except to be grouped and moved around as elements of a design. Craig seemed to be repelled by the humanness of living actors. If his sets had to be inhabited, he suggested that they be peopled with godlike puppets, or *über-Marionettes*. "I believe in the time when we shall be able to create works of Art in the theater without the use of written plays and without the use of actors." Some years later, Craig repudiated this statement, saying he only meant to take conceited actors down a peg, as if to say to them, "Go to the Devil . . . get a little of his fire and come back cured."

But there is no denying that in Craig's vision the stage tended to be depersonalized and that he often saw it as an animated abstraction, a fluid composition of moving screens, pylons, and phantom ramparts. Even the floor and ceiling were divided into units which might throb upward or downward. Movement was all, produced either by mechanical devices or simulated by his skillful use of lights. Craig's stage had to be meticulously controlled, allowing no room for accidents or variations. One can hardly help believing that intensely personal and uneven performers like Ellen Terry and Henry Irving would have to be excluded from Craig's stage world. Perhaps Craig was declaring his independence of them.

Craig was as important for what he abolished as for what he created. He destroyed the childish toy-theater scenery, the facsimiles of reality, which audiences adored. Craig ordained that stage art need no longer kowtow to reality; it must be a separate art, an expression of the artist's boundless vision. His great contribution was that he made the modern stage safe for the artist's imagination.

Ellen Terry's contribution to Craig's development did not go altogether unappreciated at the time. Young Will Rothenstein wrote to her after seeing *The Vikings:* "You have been so brave and good to Teddie. I am so delighted he has been able to show you how wise you have been: I am sure that in a very short time he will have won that foremost place in the modern theater he has already shown his right to."

Another note of endorsement was sent by Laurence Irving, when Ellen played the fisherwoman in *The Good Hope*. Commending her for doing a play that dealt with "lives as they are really lived," he called it proof that "you are not going to let the times leave you behind them."

It could hardly be said that Ellen was straining to be modern. She simply walked into modern times and made herself at home where she could. Her catholicity produced a fantastic contrast when within two years she acted the arrow-shooting wife in *The Vikings* and the fluttery British wife in *Alice Sit-by-the-Fire*, which James Barrie wrote especially for her. Barrie made the same mistake that Shaw made in *Brassbound*: failing to provide any strong dramatic conflict, Barrie let his comedy coast along on Ellen's charm, and the results were tepid.

No longer associated with the Lyceum, Ellen and Irving, on July 14, 1903, acted together for the last time for a benefit matinee of *The Merchant of Venice* at Drury Lane, where Irving was doing *Dante*. Their careers necessitated no further meeting until 1905 when Irving was taken seriously ill during a tour and was confined to a hotel in Wolverhampton. Ellen set forth to visit him and just before reaching his bedside talked to his doctor. "His heart is dangerously weak," he said.

"Have you told him?" she asked.

"I had to, because the heart being in that condition he must be careful."

Ellen found the sick man sitting up in bed, drinking coffee and looking, she said later, "like some beautiful grey tree that I have seen in Savannah. . . ."

"I'm glad you've come," he said. "Two queens have been kind to me this morning. Queen Alexandra telegraphed to say how sorry she was I was ill, and now you—"

They chatted a bit about work. He hoped she had a good manager now. She said she did: the American Charles Frohman.

Then she said, "What a wonderful life you've had, haven't you?"

It was an odd question to ask a very sick man, for it assumed that life was over and there was nothing ahead but death.

But between two veteran actors it had a different ring. They were used to standing apart from their roles and talking objectively about their own performances. It made them feel closer.

Irving answered, "Oh, yes, a wonderful life of work."

"And there's nothing better after all, is there?"

"Nothing."

"What have you got out of it all . . . ? You and I are 'getting on' as they say. Do you ever think, as I do sometimes, what you have got out of life?"

"What have I got out of it?" said Henry, stroking his chin and smiling slightly, "Let me see. . . . Well, a good cigar, a good glass of wine—good friends."

"Here he kissed my hand with courtesy," Ellen recalled. "Always he was so courteous; always his actions, like this little one of kissing my hand, were so beautifully timed. They came just before the spoken words, and gave them special value. . . ."

The scene continued. Ellen picked up her cue from his "good glass of wine—good friends."

"That's not a bad summing up of it all," she said. "And the End. . . . How would you like it to come?"

"How would I like it to come?"

Ellen remembered vividly his actions. "He repeated my question lightly, yet meditatively too. Then he was silent for some thirty seconds before he snapped his fingers—the action again before the words."

"Like that!"

They were silent for a long time, visualizing how the death scene would work. For an instant, Ellen imagined

253

Irving in costume "like some splendid Doge of Venice . . . sitting up in bed, his beautiful mobile hand stroking his chin."

Before she left Wolverhampton, Ellen talked once more to the local doctor, who warned that Irving must never again play Mathias in *The Bells*. The strain of gasping for breath, shaking in terror, turning cold and pale (as he always did), and rolling his eyes upward into his skull might be fatal to his weakened heart.

Ellen's "beautiful grey tree," however, proved to have more life in his limbs than anyone dared hope. Irving got better. His new friend Mrs. Aria came to see him and, with the doctor's approval, took Irving to recuperate in the country. He played a six-week season at Drury Lane and hit the road again. At Bradford he performed *The Bells*. But this time, after his customary death throes, Irving was so exhausted that Bram Stoker easily persuaded him to drop the play from his repertory and send the scenery back to London. On the next night, Friday, October 13, 1905, Irving played *Becket*. Its death scene, not so strenuous, closes gently with Becket's dying words, "Into Thy hands, Oh Lord, into Thy hands." They were the last lines spoken by Henry Irving on a stage.

After being driven back to the Midland Hotel, Irving began to lose balance in the lobby. He was helped to a chair, then he slumped to the floor. His dresser, Walter Collinson, kneeled beside him and cried. Irving died in his arms—"like that."

Ellen heard about Irving's death from a maid who brought breakfast to her room in Birmingham while she was touring in *Alice Sit-by-the-Fire*. That night she was composed during her performance until the last minutes of the last act. When she heard herself saying the lines, "It's summer done, autumn begun. . . . I had a beautiful husband once . . . black as raven was his hair . . . ," she broke into sobs. The consequence of feeling entirely at home on the stage was that she behaved there as if she *were* at home. The curtain was lowered, and the respectful audience left the theater in silence.

Ellen returned to London for Irving's funeral. She once asked him if he wanted to be buried in Westminster Abbey, and he had replied, discreetly, that he knew his friends would do their duty by him. His faith was justified. Through the influence of important friends, the Dean of Westminster finally agreed to his burial in the Poet's Corner of the Abbey. As his funeral day approached, flags were lowered to half-mast throughout London, crepe was hung on the six Lyceum pillars, and every London cabbie tied a black bow on his whip.

England was not only mourning one great actor. It was mourning his disguises: a dozen kings, princes, counts, a czar, an archbishop, Napoleon, the devil. Irving was loved for his humanity and kindness. But he was also highly valued on the stage as a figure of authority. He symbolized the power and style of the ruling class better than many of its members, and he often sent people home from the theater feeling, if only subliminally, safer in their houses.

His body lay in state in the home of his old friend the Baroness Burdett-Coutts. His new friend Mrs. Aria had hired a squad of seamstresses to sew hundreds of fresh laurel leaves on a pall, a blanket of deep green draped over his coffin. Ellen had sent a simple wreath of primroses and carnations, which was placed on a small table near Irving. On the day before the funeral, the body was cremated, and the coffin, containing the ashes, was set at the base of Shakespeare's statue.

Thinking how she took comfort from Irving's face at Tennyson's funeral in the Abbey, she wrote: "How terribly I missed that face at Henry's own funeral! I kept on expecting to see it, for indeed it seemed to me that he was directing the whole most moving and impressive ceremony. I could almost hear him saying, 'Get on! Get on!' in the parts of the service that dragged." And when the sun's rays slanted across the hazy gray of the Abbey exactly when the coffin was carried up the choir, Ellen felt that Henry had planned the effect with the light man, and it made her happy.

This was not the first time Ellen called up theatrical images in moments of stress. Years before, one remembers, at Wardell's deathbed, she had imagined herself at Romeo's bier. After Irving's funeral, friends who rode with her in a compartment back to Manchester reported that she was "wildly elated" and "like a cat on hot bricks," as if reacting violently against a direct expression of emotion. She had her own ways of adjusting to shock and grief.

Ellen would have been grateful if her son had seen fit to join her at the obsequies. During his Berlin visit, which ended with quarrels and nothing accomplished at the Lessing Theater, Craig became the lover of the great American dancer Isadora Duncan and gradually assumed the position of her business manager on tour. At the time of Irving's death, they were in Holland. Craig might have journeyed to London for a day or so, if not to fortify his mother, at least to honor the man whom he proclaimed his master and who gave him so much attention.

At one time Ellen and Irving had talked about a joint celebration of their fifty years in the theater, both having made their stage debuts in 1856. Since Irving's death, Ellen's friends decided to hold the celebration for her—it would also serve as a benefit—and took over the Drury Lane Theatre for a mammoth matinee on June 12, 1906. The biggest theatrical shindig London had ever seen, its general sponsoring committee included leaders from every sphere of public life, and numbered—just as a sampler—a half-dozen dukes, a dozen earls, and a hero of letters, Rudyard Kipling. Among the participants on stage were many stars no longer remembered today, but enough are still known to indicate the power of the attractions. Caruso sang. Mrs. Patrick Campbell recited. Sir Arthur Sullivan presented *Trial by Jury* and Sir Arthur Conan Doyle was a juryman. Eleanora Duse came especially from Florence, and

Réjane and Coquelin came from Paris. Lillie Langtry posed in a *tableau vivant* as Cleopatra. In act one of *Much Ado about Nothing*, Ellen herself played Beatrice with Beerbohm Tree as her Benedick. *Much Ado* was a wonderful catchall, serving as a family reunion for twenty-two members of the Terry clan. Ellen's sister Kate was a Gentlewoman; Kate's married daughter, Kate Terry Gielgud, was Third Torchbearer; her son (now Sir John Gielgud) was two years old and stayed home. Gordon Craig had designed the setting (left over from Ellen's recent tour of *Much Ado*), and three of his children by May were pages. Ellen's brother, Fred Terry, played Don Pedro. Both of Henry Irving's sons were in the act, and among the masked dancers were Gerald du Maurier and James Carew, a young American from Indiana, whom Ellen found immensely attractive.

Toward the end of the five-hour jubilee, a troupe of "Leading Comedians of London" put on a minstrel show with such songs as *Razors in the Air, Tapioca, Mary Had a Little Lamb,* and then kicked up a rousing finale with *Dem Golden Slippers.*

After the show, Ellen rushed off to her evening performance at the Royal Court in Sloane Square, where she was acting, at last, in Shaw's *Captain Brassbound's Conversion* with her new admirer, James Carew, in the small but prominent role of the American naval officer, Captain Kearney. That night, when the take from the jubilee was counted, Ellen was richer by six thousand pounds. In view of her heavy family expenses, it was a godsend.

Five days after the jubilee, Ellen was guest of honor at a festival dinner given at the Hotel Cecil with Winston Churchill as chairman and speechmaker. The menu included Consommé Sarah Bernhardt, Suprème of Sole Ellen Terry, and, after the meat course, Bombe Ophelia. At the table her sister Kate sat on Churchill's left, Ellen at his right.

At the time of the jubilee, Gordon Craig was still in Europe. Part of his time he spent with Isadora Duncan, who was about six months pregnant with his child. That he did not join his family in London at Ellen's celebration may have caused him guilt, for, writing about it forty years later, he presented his excuse: "Somehow this Jubilee thoroughly upset me—because my father, E.W.G., was forgot—like the Hobby Horse!

"My father, my master and I, all loved the same woman—and we all left her for the same reason—a commonplace one: our work called to us and we went. But we did love her. Strange, it was she who could not follow us. My father died in 1886, my master in 1905, and I still live on—older now than they were when they died. Both died tired out. Of us three, my master was the greatest man. Both he and my father did more for her than ever I did: yet I believe she loved me most: how strange. . . . I was the least of the three, the weakest and the smallest: is that why she loved me most? Yes and no: for in loving me so much, she loved my father at the same time."

Craig's attempt at self-justification raises questions. Was he truly upset at the time of Ellen's Jubilee because "my father was forgot?" Or forty years later was he ashamed of his absence from his mother's great anniversary and trying to build up a case for himself? Is there an implied rebuke to his mother when he said it was "strange" she could not follow the three men who loved her, when their work called them and they went? If so, was he pinning the blame on his mother for "abandoning" her men, thus unloading on her the secret guilt he felt for abandoning his "wives"?

Despite her jubilee welcome, Ellen felt jilted. Irving had left her for Mrs. Aria, and then forever. Her son had decamped to Europe, Shaw had curtailed his life-giving letters. Ellen missed men in her life.

Her first meeting with James Carew was witnessed by Shaw when Ellen turned up for *Brassbound* rehearsals at the Royal Court. "Who is that?" she asked when Carew walked in. And almost before Shaw introduced him, Ellen had him spotted as her prey and shot him through the heart. Shaw was stunned by her marksmanship. "So swift a decision by a huntress who, far from being promiscuous in her attachments, was highly fastidious, made me marvel and say to myself, 'There but for the grace of God goes Bernard Shaw.' "

Carew's forebears were German-Jewish, his real name was Usselman, and he was said to have a touch of Indian blood. He was handsome, kindly, and full of life. As a boy, he had once seen Ellen and Irving perform in Chicago, and that sealed his fate. He decided to be an actor. He played with the American actress Maxine Elliott in London, then acted in Shaw's *Man and Superman,* and then met Ellen Terry.

To Ellen he represented the kind of masculine vigor that she found attractive in Wardell. He was in his thirties, she in her late fifties. Yet she was a dazzling celebrity, and Carew was immensely flattered and bewitched. He attended her in London, visited her at Smallhythe. To Edy and her coterie of well-intentioned women friends, Ellen Terry's Hoosier Romeo was commonplace and, well, unsuitable. They were shocked. But when Ellen made her eighth tour to America in 1907, Carew went with her and *Brassbound* was the main attraction. Carew was promoted to the title role.

They were married in Pittsburgh but kept it secret, even from Edy, until they reached England. Carew was said to have opposed the marriage, while Ellen insisted on it in order to quash gossip about her private life. There was no doubt that for a while they loved each other. After Ellen's death Carew confided to his close actor friend Malcolm Keene that Ellen was a tender companion and enjoyed their connubial pleasures.

Brassbound became their career. During their second English tour, Shaw saw it in Fulham and wrote to Ellen, "I was quite appalled on Saturday by the consequence of my writing *Brassbound* for you. At the Court, you were always merely trying to remember your part. But now you have realized you are Lady Cicely. Her history has become your history; and instead of trying to remember somebody else's words, you simply say what is right to say in the situation (which, by the way, is mostly much better than my dialogue) and there you have the whole thing alive and perfect. It is really a very wonderful performance now; and the others are not half good enough for you."

Shaw went on to say, half in jest, that Ellen would be stuck with Cicely forever, which would be terrible for her and worse for young Jim Carew as Brassbound. "Jim's brain is visibly half gone: he holds on to the part as if nothing but the grimmest determination could save him from going mad on the spot."

As a parting shot, Shaw challenged her. "Suppose one wanted Jim for anything at the Savoy or elsewhere, would you let him loose to do it, or is he tied to your apron strings for the rest of his life? This habit of getting married is the ruin of theatrical art. . . . Why could you not have been content with my adoration?"

Ellen untied the apron strings about two and a half years after the marriage, when she and Carew had an unofficial separation and stopped living under the same roof. As such things go, it was an amicable parting. Despite the separation, in 1910 she was writing to Shaw: "Remember James Carew is a very good actor of some parts, and give him one if you can. It would do me a good turn." Shaw sent them tickets for his new play, *Misalliance*. They went together and "enjoyed every minute of it."

Chapter Twelve

KISSING THE WORLD GOOD-BYE

When the actress Lynn Fontanne was in her early teens and determined to go on the stage, her mother arranged, through mutual friends, for her to meet Ellen Terry and receive the advice of an expert. Miss Terry was resting in bed at noon when she welcomed young Lynn and suggested right off that she recite something. Lynn dove into Portia's "quality of mercy" speech, which was Miss Terry's celebrated *spécialité*. It was like a student fiddler daring to play *The Devil's Trill* for Paganini. Miss Terry liked it, and said so, and took Lynn under her wing. In her diary she wrote: "Must get Lynn more money. It's wicked. She is so intelligent."

Knowing that Lynn's family was not well off, Ellen invited her several times to Smallhythe, paying her for helping around the house and coaching her between times in diction and stage deportment. She taught her to walk properly by pinning a sheet to her front, another to her back, and obliging her to navigate through the draperies. Ellen herself was always a sorceress with scarves and robes, swirling them with a dancer's grace, and Lynn was a brilliant pupil. When she moved to New York to become one of the major enchantments of the American stage, Lynn Fontanne stood out for her elegance, for the Terry grace she gave to her Valentina gowns. Lynn profited too by the Terry diction, especially by its lilt and its effect of spontaneity. "*Think* of the *meaning* of what you are saying," Ellen

261

told her at Smallhythe, "and let the words pour out of your mouth."

Perhaps Lynn's sharpest memory from Smallhythe was seeing Ellen Terry one morning by accident through the half-open door of her bedroom, standing in her underwear. Ellen was startled to see Lynn pass by. But she tossed her a smile, did a perky little backward kick like a Gaiety Girl, and danced out of sight. It was the kind of exit that American vaudevillians used to call an "off-to-Buffalo," a way of capering off stage with style. To the young girl it was unforgettable because it implied that Ellen took Lynn into the profession, accepting her, despite the half-century difference in their ages, as a sister conspirator.

In one way or another, Ellen's last two decades were a prolonged off-to-Buffalo, keeping up her spirits, kissing the world good-bye.

Ellen had a card up her sleeve: lectures. For eleven years, from 1910 to 1921, she hit the podium trail around the world, beginning in New York, on November 3, 1910, at the Hudson Theater. Her subject was Shakespearean heroines that she had played. Doing a one-woman show was strenuous, but it had its advantages. She did not have to adhere strictly to a script but could ad-lib or interpolate as her mood or memory dictated. Her scripts, prepared with the help of Edy's friend Christopher St. John, were marked up, line by line, with her stage directions to herself. "Take time." "Dark, fierce, violent." "With humor, rather reckless!" "Whisper." If she happened to make a funny remark to the audience—a gag she called it—and it went over well, she made a note to try it again. In other words, she continually tinkered with her talks, embellishing them to fit the occasion. She took pains to dress dramatically in scarlet or white robes, to keep flowers on the stage, and to have herself properly spot-lighted. By December 8, she had reached Seattle and Portland, where she had played with Irving seventeen years earlier, and was greeted with poems, flattering sentiments painted on white satin, and sold-out houses. To outdo herself, she also played Vancouver, where she was given sprigs of English oak and Canadian maple and hailed in the *British Columbia Saturday Sunset*, "Ellen Terry is not coming to Vancouver to act; she is coming to talk, chat, gossip (thank heaven! not to 'lecture')."

When news of her success reached home, Ellen extensively booked in England. In 1914 she carried her "discourses" to Australia, stayed a while with her great prima donna friend Nellie Melba, and at the outbreak of World War I, teamed up with Melba in charity shows for the Aussie troops. She sailed from Australia to New York, where she underwent a painful eye operation. Ellen was already booked to sail home on the American ship *New York* when her erstwhile manager, Frohman, offered to give her swifter and more luxurious passage, free of charge, on the English liner *Lusitania*. Edy had warned her against English ships which the Germans might torpedo, so Ellen stuck to the neutral *New York*. As she neared Liverpool, she learned that the *Lusitania* had been sunk. (Ellen was shocked by Frohman's death, but a deeper shock was the drowning of Laurence Irving in 1913 in a ship collision in the Gulf of St. Lawrence.)

Between bookings and war benefits, Ellen was busy. She played a short act at the famous music hall, the Coliseum, and brought down the house, seemingly on cue, for as she spoke Portia's line about mercy "droppeth as the gentle rain from Heaven," the German bombs began dropping. The laughter drowned out the air raid sirens. She toured provincial music halls with her *Shakespeare Heroines* and had a splendid time barnstorming with young Edith Evans in a scene from *The Merry Wives of Windsor*. It almost seemed as if life had come full circle and she was a country trouper once again with her family.

Ellen had become such a personage that she had trouble fitting into a normal theatrical production. When she acted the nurse in *Romeo and Juliet* with beautiful Doris Keane as Juliet, she nearly ruined the production because her portrayal of the bawdy old servant outshone everybody else on the stage. Playing the role of Paris was a young English actor, Reginald Denham, who became a noted director. Denham today recalls that Ellen never missed a performance during the three-month run and never spoke her lines precisely the same. But it didn't matter. She knew exactly what the nurse was feeling, first as she gaily tried to waken Juliet on her wedding morning, and then as she realized with a scream of horror that her beloved charge was dead. The words served her only as the vessels for her emotions, and the effect on the audience was overpowering.

A few years later, Shaw met Ellen near a film studio, and as he reports it, she asked if he could give her some work in the theater. "I do not expect leading parts. . . . I am too old. . . . I should like to play a charwoman." Shaw told her that he feared for the fate of the play, "Imagine a scene in which the part of a canal barge was played by a battleship." Shaw pointed out that she would steal attention away from hero and heroine and the audience would "think of nothing but the wonderful things the charwoman was going to say and do." It was a sad situation that made them both want to cry. He noted: "She was astonishingly beautiful. She had passed through the middle phase, so trying to handsome women, of matronly amplitude, and was again tall and slender, with a new delicacy and intensity in her saddened expression."

Shaw was always her best witness. Wasting no words on her charm, except to admit he was "fascinated," he saw beyond the actress and measured the human being. "She was not the sort of actress who is a genius on the stage and nobody off it. She could do without the stage both as artist and woman." For all her charities and handouts, "she lived and died within her means. . . . she would have run through her money too generously if she had not given it to businesslike friends to keep it for her; but she died solvent, an honest woman with no vices." She was said to have the eyes of a trained painter. She described to Shaw the joy of seeing the sun come through the half-opened door of her bedroom, the slanting shadows on an old kitchen chair, rush-bottomed, sturdy-legged, and wavy-backed. "Thank the Lord for my eyes. I think they have got ill from over-enjoying themselves." She was partial to the moon and admitted that she used to go outdoors in the middle of the night and kneel to it. In Monte Carlo, she was so delighted by the pine trees that she threw her arms around a tree trunk and kissed it.

Ellen carried motherhood to perilous extremes. But she did not always wish to be the engulfing maternal presence. She also craved to be engulfed. At the age of fifty, she cried out to Shaw: "Oh I wish I had a Mammy. I'm so dreadfully comfortless." She daydreamed about a big Frenchwoman who was once her servant: "When I'm ill she takes me up in her arms . . . and puts me to bed, and washes me all over, and mothers me well again."

She loved her many grandchildren, though Craig never got around to letting her see them all; their number has been estimated roughly at fifteen. She never saw Craig's gifted son David Lees, a distinguished photographer whose English mother, Dorothy Neville Lees, was Craig's indispensable editorial assistant for years on his magazine *Mask*. And Ellen never saw Isadora's beautiful little daughter, Deirdre, who at eight was drowned in Paris when riding in a chauffeur-driven limousine that plunged out of control into the Seine. Killed in the same tragic accident was Isadora's younger son, Patrick, whose father was her devoted patron, Paris Singer. After the childrens' funeral, which Craig did not attend, Isadora visited London and met Ellen Terry. Though they had not met before, Isadora had built up a long-distance devotion to Craig's mother. Writing to him of their encounter, she said, "I am half mad with grief and pain and I wanted to feel your Mother's arms about me—as I used to dream they were before Deirdre was born—and to feel that dear pity and love that *she* gives that no one else has known how to give me since their death." Apparently, in Isadora's meeting with Ellen her dream came alive, for she wrote, "In your Mother's arms I found what I was hungry for and which I think has saved my reason in this dreadful time when it seems giving way. . . . ''

Ellen, though, found great delight in Craig's two children by Elena Meo. In a notebook, presumably from the year 1914, she wrote: "For the last four years Elena and her two wonderful children, my most beloved grandchildren, have lived with me and I am most happy, and not alone. Ted comes and goes from his work in Italy and this must soon fix them all up there. Meanwhile, they are my joys."

Elena's youngest, child, Teddy, born while his father was in Germany, still carries vivid recollections of his grandmother. He first met her when he was about five and came with his parents and his elder sister, Nellie, on a family visit to London. After leaving their luggage at a hotel, the little group proceeded to His Majesty's Theatre, where Ellen was playing again under the management of Beerbohm Tree in a brief revival of *The Merry Wives of Windsor*. She wanted to send them tickets but didn't know where they would be staying. Soon after their arrival, they had queued up for the front row of the pit. Before the show started, while Teddy was gazing at the stage curtain and wondering what his grandmother could be doing back there, a peculiar thing happened. The curtain bulged a little near the bottom as if somebody was bumping it. Then under the curtain a hand reached out holding a picture postcard that Teddy recognized. It was of a dachshund with a tail made of coiled wire, a card that the family had sent Ellen from Paris a few days before. The hand shook the card so the tail wagged in a very friendly fashion.

Teddy had not yet set eyes on his grandmother. But he

knew now that she liked jokes, and he knew that he was going to love her.

After her performance, they all went back to Granny's dressing room, and other actors crowded in to see Ellen's family. Teddy was most excited by Pistol, who had a red nose and shouted, "Have you got that boy who laughed at me in all the right places?" And Teddy was proud because he *was* that boy. Then, after Ellen went behind a screen to finish dressing, the family piled into a carriage and were driven to Ellen's house at 215 King's Road. When they were inside, Ellen said, "Now I can kiss you, my pickles," by which she meant a long, proper hug. Teddy recalls that a real Spanish sword hung on the wall, and his new grandmother let him hold it.

Later, when Elena Meo and her children made another visit to London just before the war, they lived in a flat on John Street, but when war broke out they moved in with Ellen on King's Road. Once in a while, Gordon Craig came to London, sweeping home like a glamorous Ulysses in his big hat and flowing cape, making a holiday time with his jokes and tales and laughter.

Ellen became a stabilizing force among this contingent of Craig's scattered family. She even effected a reconciliation between Elena and her father, Gaetano Meo, who had long been dismayed by his daughter's devotion to Craig.

As the war drew on, Elena and her children spent more time with Ellen in her cottage at Smallhythe. Nights when she was wakeful, Ellen would sometimes tiptoe into Teddy's room, holding a candle. If he was awake or showed signs of restlessness, she sat cross-legged at the foot of his bed and did scenes from *Hamlet* or *Romeo and Juliet, The Merchant* or *Macbeth*. She knew most of the roles by heart—had known them, in fact, since she was Teddy's age. At his bedside theater, Teddy saw Ellen Terry in more Shakespearean roles than anybody else had seen her perform. And not only female roles. She loved being King Lear on the heath, or both gravediggers in *Hamlet,* or Polonius, or Hamlet himself talking to his father's ghost. She took pains not to let Teddy get scared. "You mustn't be terrified," she reassured him as if she were an official ambassador between the living and the dead. "All ghosts are nice. They are lonely. They need friends." Then for comic relief she would do a bit of Lancelot Gobbo, the clown, arguing with the Fiend.

A midnight wayfarer passing the cottage at Smallhythe might see a dim light in an upstairs window and hear a woman's deep, melodious voice mingling with a little boy's laughter as Teddy rolled with mirth in his blankets. These nocturnal sessions were stopped by Edy, who scolded Ellen for stealing sleep from a growing boy. But when they had to go back to the house on King's Road, Ellen and Teddy were sometimes reunited at night when they repaired to the ground floor during a zeppelin raid and both slept back to back on the dining room table.

Joined together by their common love for Craig, Elena Meo and Ellen Terry became close companions. At heart, Elena knew that she held a unique place in Craig's affections; he had told her over and over that she was his first real love. But it is doubtful that their alliance would have lasted so many years if Ellen, from comparable experience, had not given Elena so much comfort and understanding. Both women knew what it was to be an unmarried mother of two, and both of them, where Craig was concerned, shared a singular capacity for forgiveness.

Ellen was perceptively wary of her own forgiving nature and cautioned herself not to feel smug about it. "Call it forgiveness, if you will, but I prefer not to. Forgiveness seems to imply that *we* are in the right, and as often as not, we are the stumbling blocks, only we don't know it."

The same friendship that Ellen gave to all of Craig's housemates, at least the ones whom she had a chance to know, she bestowed on Edy's housemate, Christopher St.

John. As a team, Edy and Miss St. John were often accused of ruling Ellen too firmly in her old age and keeping her apart from some of her old friends. This probably was so, but it has to be weighed against the problem of protecting Ellen, who in her last years had spells of vagueness about the identity of her friends and herself. When her third husband, James Carew, paid his occasional visits, she did not always remember that they had been married.

Christopher St. John was immensely helpful to Ellen in preparing her writings for publication, but was not a ghost-writer in the usual sense. At spare moments, Ellen dictated her *Memoirs* to Miss St. John, or wrote out some passages herself, and turned over her diaries and many of her letters. By comparing these *Memoirs*, which were published in 1908, with Ellen's unedited letters, it is clear that Ellen was the author and no one else. Her brisk, conversational way with words, her startling but apt sketches of people, which Max Beerbohm called "her harlequin leaps," bear unmistakably the Terry trademark. When it was first published, *The Story of My Life* was among the best theater autobiographies in English; it still stands as an exceptional performance. After Ellen's death, it was republished as *Ellen Terry's Memoirs*, with extra notes and an account of Ellen's last twenty years by Edith Craig and Christopher St. John.

Ellen made five films between 1916 and 1922, acting mostly small parts and doing rather badly. She was entering her seventies at the time and knew little about film acting except the work of Charlie Chaplin, whom she adored but could hardly emulate. Ellen thrived on live audiences. How could she love a cold camera? Her last appearance on the stage was in 1925 in a fantasy for children, *Crossings*, by Walter de la Mare. Fragile and thin, she stood very erect under her halo of luxuriant white hair. The young spectators at the dress rehearsal were too impressed to applaud her entrance. Their only sound was a long "Oh!" They knew they beheld a wonder.

In her last few years, Ellen sold her house in King's Road and took a flat in St. Martin's Lane, among a thicket of West End theaters. Getting into a theater was a kind of homecoming; she loved being recognized by audiences and conveying her congratulations to the actors. Her centrally located flat made it easy for friends to visit her, so easy in fact that Ellen's protectors often had to shoo them away. One of Ellen's old friends, Dame Sybil Thorndike, recalled that sometimes Ellen was "naughty and escaped from her flat," staying away so long that her servants or Edy (who lived nearby) had to go out and look for her. When Dame Sybil was asked what possessed her friend to do such a thing, she answered: "Oh, it was very simple. Ellen liked to be *among* people."

Dame Sybil packed a world of meaning in the word *among* that set Ellen Terry apart from most other actors. Whereas they craved to be *in front of* people, Ellen opted for *among*. Even on the stage she felt *among* audiences and made them share her "amongness."

A major event for Ellen was the honor accorded to Gordon Craig, whose work was conspicuously displayed in the 1922 International Exhibit of Theater Art and Craft at the Victoria and Albert Museum. Craig was on hand for the occasion, looking very much the grand old man of the stage, although he was only fifty, with flowing messianic white hair and a cloak that rivaled a robe of state. At the opening reception, Ellen was aglow beneath a large hat that represented a discreet marriage between ostrich feathers and black lace.

As witnessed by Marguerite Steen, who lent her the hat: "She was triumphant in the honor which was paid to her son—at last. Not only the English art world, but that of France, Italy, and Germany was there to acclaim Gordon Craig as the prophet of theatrical art." On exhibit were his illuminated stage models, masks, puppets, and costume designs, most of them for plays that were never produced. But Craig's vision was so potent, his innovations so striking, that his influence was soon to permeate the Western theater. For love of Godwin, and for love of his son, Ellen had coddled Gordon Craig to excess, supported him beyond reason, and scolded him until she made herself sick. Now the world was the richer for it.

Honors for herself seemed to be loitering. Meanwhile, an American actress, Genevieve Ward, who made her home in London, had acted briefly with Irving and Ellen, and had gone on to win considerable renown, was given an honor that many people felt in all justice belonged to Ellen Terry. In 1921, Miss Ward was the first actress ever to be dubbed Dame Grand Cross of the Most Excellent Order of the British Empire. There was gossip of "wire-pulling" and understandable dismay that such an award should go to an American-born actress. It was conjectured that the Godwin episode in Ellen's past had stood in her way. In any case, four years later Ellen was notified that she too was to become "Dame" and rode off to Buckingham Palace with Edy. It was customary for the investiture ceremony to be held in the throne room, but to spare Ellen as much fatigue as possible—she was seventy-eight—she was wheeled down the long corridor, with Edy at her side, to a chamber where King George V awaited her. Ellen stepped from her chair and according to her daughter "made a most wonderful curtsey on entering—slow, stately, and very impressive." But just as she was walking out the door, she remembered that she had flubbed her stage business and cried out, "Oh, dear, I quite forgot to walk out backwards." The king laughed and then told Ellen that the queen wanted a chat with her. Ellen was wheeled around to Queen Mary's quarters. They had met several times before, beginning with the time when Mary, on her twentieth birthday, was taken to the Lyceum and later had supper in the Beefsteak Room. Altogether, the queen had seen fourteen different productions at the Lyceum, most of them with Ellen Terry. At the end of their talk the queen tucked Ellen's cloak in her wheelchair lest it catch in the wheels.

Later that day in her diary, Ellen wrote: "Lovely time. Gracious people."

Ellen's last months were spent amid much squabbling between her lady "protectors" as to whether she should be sent to a "home" or sanitarium and as to whom she could be allowed to see. But Ellen stayed at her beloved Smallhythe, sometimes escaping at night into the garden to smell the flowers or stealing off alone to pore over her collection of keepsakes—old photographs, trinkets, bits of costumes that she had worn or that friends had given her. Between Smallhythe and her London flat, she was exactly where she wanted to be, watching the world around her.

Being born into the theater and always taking it for granted, Ellen Terry was never stagestruck. But, from this different vantage point, she found a similar excitement. As an habituée of the world of artifice, she gazed afresh at the enthralling world of reality, of animals, people, trees, sunsets, flowers—all the scenery and cast of creation—and instead of being stagestruck, she was lifestruck.

She had given instructions that her funeral be held in the village church at Smallhythe and asked that the church bells not be tolled at her death but joyously rung. She preferred to be cremated. She did not say where her ashes were to be housed, but she would have liked their home-to-be, the little St. Paul's Church in Covent Garden, London.

After a stroke that brought Ellen close to death, Edy telephoned Gordon Craig, who by chance happened to be in London. Early in the day of July 21, 1928, he arrived at Smallhythe to see his mother just before she died.

A NOTE ON BOOKS AND BENEFACTORS

So many people have helped with this book that I am convinced Ellen Terry's spirit has been sailing overhead, infusing them all with her generosity. My chief benefactor has been her grandson, Edward Craig, who has welcomed me under his roof and into his memorabilia. Having lived with her in his early boyhood, he conveys, as no other living person can, her sweet, wise playfulness, and being thoroughly practiced in theater and film himself, he sees her in the context of her profession. He has imposed no strictures on the use of the material he has shown me, so what I have said and surmised is on my own responsibility.

I have also benefited from the cooperation of George Nash and the staff of the Enthoven Collection at the Victoria and Albert Museum in London; and from the help of Miss Elizabeth Aslin, also at the V. and A. I am grateful to Miss Jennifer Aylmer, acting curator of the British Theatre Museum Archives and Library; to Mrs. Molly Thomas, curator of the Ellen Terry Museum under the National Trust at Smallhythe in Kent; and to Jack Reading, an Honorary Secretary of the Society for Theatre Research. He gave me the two letters from Mrs. Tom Taylor to her husband.

All my thanks to the British Museum for letting me consult the Shaw-Terry letters, and to the Garrick Club for the use of its library. I profited by illuminating conversations with Dame Sybil Thorndike, Wendy Hiller, and Lynn Fontanne, and by the many kindnesses of Sir John Gielgud, who, above and beyond words, made me sense the magnetism of his great-aunt Ellen when she came to family dinners with coral combs in her hair and commanded him to keep working at his Shakespeare. In New York I was given valuable insights into Gordon Craig by Donald Oenslager, Jo Mielziner, and the leading American authority on Craig, Professor Arnold Rood. One day in the elevator of my New York apartment house, I discovered that my neighbor, Reginald Denham, had, in his youth, acted with Ellen Terry. So I thank him

273

for being both informative and handy. The Library of Performing Arts at Lincoln Center in New York City has served me well, and I am also grateful for the many courtesies of Professor F. W. Roberts and his staff at the Humanities Research Library at the University of Texas at Austin, where I examined, and was given permission to include in this book, many unpublished letters from Ellen Terry to her son, Gordon Craig.

Before the vocabulary of gratitude runs dry, I must give thanks to Vivian Campbell Stoll for her superior research help, and to my virtuoso typist, Janet Hubbard. Valuable nuggets of research were supplied by Laura Ludwig, Lucy Vulgaris, Hope Malik, by Dorothy Bacon in London, and by Mr. and Mrs. Thomas Blom of the University of British Columbia in Vancouver.

My indebtedness to books is immense. Topping the list is Ellen Terry's *The Story of My Life,* first published in 1908. The same text was republished twenty-five years later in a more useful book called *Ellen Terry's Memoirs: with Preface, Notes, and Additional Biographical Chapters* by Edith Craig and Christopher St. John (London, 1933). It still possesses the "freshness and life" that Max Beerbohm called "adorable."

Another major standby, rich in facts and notes, is *Ellen Terry* by Roger Manvell (New York, 1968). A good companion volume, concerning the whole Terry tribe, is Marguerite Steen's *A Pride of Terrys* (London, 1962). Being a skilled novelist, Miss Steen has been accused, perhaps justly, of giving a fictional slant to her book. Still, as a friend of the family, she had a lot to tell, all of it interesting. Edward Craig's excellent biography of his father, *Gordon Craig* (New York, 1968), deals only secondarily with Ellen. Yet it is eloquent about her devotion to her son, and therefore is essential to an understanding of her character. Edward Craig gave me permission to quote four items from his book: a telegram from Ellen's father, Ben Terry; Ellen's letter to "a Mr. Wilson"; Ellen's note to Stephen Coleridge about her son's misbehavior; a letter to Ellen from Coleridge's wife, Geraldine. Gordon Craig comes to life, indirectly, in *Your Isadora* (New York, 1974), a collection of hitherto unpublished letters of Isadora Duncan to her lover, Gordon Craig, edited, with an astute connecting text, by Francis Steegmuller. Gordon Craig's early splash as a stage designer and director is chronicled in *Up to Now* by Martin Shaw

274

(London, 1929). A first-rate musician, Shaw was associated with Ellen Terry and Craig in several projects.

Ellen shines off and on in Gordon Craig's unfinished autobiography, *Index to the Story of My Days* (New York, 1957), and dominates his *Ellen Terry and Her Secret Self* (London, 1931). Craig's tribute to his mother has many beautiful passages, but it is marred by his irrational scorn of her close friends, Charles Reade, Stephen Coleridge, and George Bernard Shaw, and, worse, by a faintly patronizing tone toward his subject.

Out of the abundance of writing on the Victorian theater, I have referred most often to *British Drama: An Historical Survey . . .* by Allardyce Nicoll (New York, 1963); *History of the London Stage* by H. Barton Baker; and *London's Lost Theaters of the Nineteenth Century* by Erroll Sherson. These last two volumes were reissued in New York in 1969.

For background on the Lyceum, I soaked up atmosphere by prowling around the old playhouse, talking to its manager, A. A. Hutchins, and reading A. E. Wilson's book, *The Lyceum* (London, 1952). Another source of theater lore is Clement Scott's *The Drama of Yesterday and Today* (London, 1899), a two-volume collection of his reviews and essays for various London periodicals. Clement Scott is worth reading more for his enthusiasm than for his perceptiveness. For brilliance one must turn, of course, to *The Scenic Art* by Henry James (New Brunswick, N.J., 1948); to the three volumes of Max Beerbohm's reviews: *Around Theatres, More Theaters,* and *Last Theaters* (New York, 1954, 1969, and 1970); to G. B. Shaw's *Dramatic Opinions and Essays* (London: Constable, 1913).

Ellen's first important benefactors, Mr. and Mrs. Charles Kean, are portrayed in *The Life and Theatrical Times of Charles Kean,* by John W. Cole (London, 1859); her first husband, George Frederick Watts, is the subject of *The Laurel and the Thorn* by Ronald Chapman (London, 1943); and the architect Edward Godwin, father of her two children, is portrayed in *The Conscious Stone* by Dudley Harbron (London, 1949). Her prodigiously active friend, Charles Reade, overflows two extensive biographies, *Charles L. Reade: A Memoir* by the Reverend Compton Reade (London, 1887), and *Charles Reade* by Malcolm Elwin (London, 1931). Although Tennyson figured only fitfully in her life, his grandson, Charles Tennyson, takes note of their friendship in his standard biography, *Alfred Tennyson* (New York, 1949). Glimpses of Ellen's social life at the time she married Watts and shortly afterwards are given in Leonée Ormond's entrancing biography, *George Du Maurier* (London, 1969).

Memorable flashes of Ellen illumine a number of books by her close friends: *Reminiscences* by Alice Comyns Carr (London, n.d.); *Time Was* by Graham Robertson (London, 1931); Sir Johnston Forbes-Robertson, *A Player under Three Reigns* (New York, 1971). Aunt Ellen is regarded rather condescendingly in *Kate Terry Gielgud: An Autobiography* (London, 1953), but this account of late Victorian family life by the daughter of Ellen's sister Kate (and the mother of Sir John Gielgud) is good reading. Ellen comes off better in Margaret Webster's *The Same Only Different* (New York, 1969). The author's mother, Dame May Whitty, toured America with Irving and Terry in 1895, and told some very funny stories about Ellen.

I am grateful to the publishers of *The Diaries of Lewis Carroll* (London, 1953) for permission to quote several entries from this record of his busy life. Carroll kept track of Ellen—devotedly and warily—for forty-one years.

When Ellen joined forces with Henry Irving in 1878, she began to appear in most of his biographies. His grandson Laurence (he was the son of Irving's son "Harry" Irving) produced a masterly work, *Henry Irving* (New York, 1952), which ranks high among English biographies of recent years. Ellen, to be sure, plays a subordinate role in this work, but the book does her a service because it makes clear why she found Irving so worthy of devotion.

Irving's stalwart manager, Bram Stoker, provided in his *Personal Reminiscences of Henry Irving* (London, 1906) two volumes of nonstop idolatry—some of it also for Ellen. Unless one is allergic to elegies, this year-by-year account of Irving's tours and triumphs is irresistible. Gordon Craig's similarly worshipful book, *Henry Irving* (London, 1930), represents Craig at his best, sounding passionately disputatious even when there is nothing to dispute. I am fond of a grab bag called *We Saw Him Act: A Symposium on the Art of Sir Henry Irving*, edited by H. S. Saintsbury and Cecil Palmer (London, 1939). It seems as if everybody in England put in his tuppence worth of opinion, and it includes some seventy references to Ellen Terry.

George Bernard Shaw's involvement with Ellen Terry is documented in *Ellen Terry and Bernard Shaw: A Correspondence* (New York, 1949). I am grateful for permission to quote from this collection, which I believe is probably the purest distillation of their personalities that either of them ever produced.

In closing I wish to tell Jacques Barzun, who is a consulting editor at Scribners, how highly I valued his aid and encouragement. His editorial advice, moreover, was often so humorously put that it gave me as much pleasure as profit. Finally, I send thanks to another one of Ellen Terry's grandsons, my old friend David Lees of Rome. He and his grandmother never had the good fortune to meet. But his support of my efforts was one more example of the Terry generosity.

INDEX